Christoph P. Mayer

Hybrid Routing in Delay Tolerant Networks

Hybrid Routing in Delay Tolerant Networks

von
Christoph P. Mayer

 Scientific Publishing

Dissertation, Karlsruher Institut für Technologie,
Fakultät für Informatik
Tag der mündlichen Prüfung: 21. Oktober 2011
Referenten: Prof. Dr. Martina Zitterbart, Prof. Dr. Jörg Ott

Impressum

Karlsruher Institut für Technologie (KIT)
KIT Scientific Publishing
Straße am Forum 2
D-76131 Karlsruhe
www.ksp.kit.edu

KIT – Universität des Landes Baden-Württemberg und nationales
Forschungszentrum in der Helmholtz-Gemeinschaft

KIT Scientific Publishing 2012
Print on Demand

ISBN 978-3-86644-807-0

FÜR MEINE ELTERN
HELMA UND HANS-PETER

Vorwort

DIE vorliegende Arbeit entstand in den letzten vier Jahren während meiner Tätigkeit als wissenschaftlicher Mitarbeiter am Institut für Telematik des Karlsruher Institut für Technologie (KIT). An erster Stelle gilt mein Dank Frau Prof. Dr. Martina Zitterbart, die mir durch die Anstellung an ihrem Institut die Promotion ermöglichte und mich während der gesamten Zeit mit hilfreichen Diskussionen und Ratschlägen begleitete. Ebenso bedanken möchte ich mich bei Herrn Prof. Dr. Jörg Ott, der sich trotz zahlreicher Verpflichtungen in Forschung und Lehre sofort bereit erklärte, das Korreferat für meine Promotion zu übernehmen.

Allen Kolleginnen und Kollegen des Instituts für Telematik möchte ich herzlich für die letzten vier Jahre danken. Mein besonderer Dank gilt Dr. Thomas Gamer für die Betreuung meiner Studien- und Diplomarbeit und die Heranführung an die wissenschaftliche Arbeit. Weiter danke ich Christian Hübsch für die Freundschaft und die vielen spannenden und anregenden Diskussionen. Allen voran möchte ich Dr. Oliver P. Waldhorst danken, der mich stets an seinem wissenschaftlichen Scharfsinn teilhaben ließ, was meine Promotionszeit zu der bis jetzt lehrreichsten Zeit machte.

Während meiner gesamten Promotionszeit haben mich all meine Freunde unterstützt und begleitet, insbesondere meine aktuellen und ehemaligen Mitbewohner. Mein besonderer Dank gilt Christoph Schmid für eine unvergleichbare Freundschaft. Mein größter Dank gilt meiner Familie und meinen Eltern, die mir die Möglichkeit zum Studium und zur Promotion gaben und ohne die diese Arbeit nicht zustande gekommen wäre. Ihnen ist diese Arbeit gewidmet. Schließlich gilt mein allergrößter Dank meiner Freundin, die immer für mich da war und mich immer unterstützt und ermutigt hat.

Karlsruhe, im Januar 2012

Zusammenfassung

Mobile Geräte wie Smartphones gewinnen sowohl im privaten als auch im geschäftlichen Sektor zunehmend an Bedeutung. Das von diesen Geräten erzeugte Verkehrsaufkommen weist exponentielles Wachstum auf und führt zu einer starken Belastung der heutigen rein *Infrastruktur-basierten* Netze. Die große Anzahl mobiler Geräte birgt jedoch auch Möglichkeiten zum Betrieb neuartiger *Infrastruktur-loser* Netze, sogenannter *Delay Tolerant Networks*, welche durch opportunistische ad-hoc Kommunikation Nachrichten Ende-zu-Ende zustellen. Ziel dieser Dissertation ist die Integration von Infrastruktur-basierten und Infrastruktur-losen Netzen. Hierdurch kann zum einen Ende-zu-Ende Kommunikation ermöglicht werden, wenn Infrastruktur nur in geringem Umfang vorhanden ist, wie beispielsweise in Entwicklungsländern. Zum anderen kann im Fall von umfangreich vorhandener Infrastruktur Verkehr in Infrastruktur-lose Netze ausgelagert und somit eine Entlastung der Infrastruktur erreicht werden.

Die Mobilität von Geräten ist für die Funktion von Delay Tolerant Networks eine notwendige Voraussetzung, da diese auf dem *store-carry-forward* Prinzip basieren. Hierbei werden Nachrichten über einen längeren Zeitraum auf Geräten gespeichert, durch Mobilität von Geräten physikalisch in Richtung Zielgerät transportiert und bei Kontakt mit anderen Geräten weitergereicht oder repliziert. Der erste Teil dieser Dissertation untersucht den Einfluss von durch Graphen modellierter Beschränkungen auf diese Mobilität und im Speziellen auf die aus Mobilität resultierenden Kontakte zwischen Geräten. Graphen werden in dieser Arbeit verwendet um Straßennetze zu modellieren. Die in dieser Dissertation entwickelte Methodik kann jedoch auch zur Modellierung anderer Beschränkungen der Mobilität verwendet werden. Zuerst wird der Einfluss unterschiedlicher Graphen auf die in der Literatur als wichtig angesehene Metrik der Zwischenkontaktzeit mit Hilfe von Simulationen aufgezeigt. Hierbei werden zum einen Graphen realer Städtekarten verwendet und zum anderen Gitter-basierte Graphen mit unterschiedlicher Gitterdichte. Der Einfluss dieser Graphen auf die Verteilung von Zwischenkontaktzeiten bei zufälligem sowie sozialem Mobilitätsmodell wird analysiert und durch Annäherung an Modelle numerisch charakterisiert. Hiermit wird ein numerischer Vergleich des Einflusses von Graphen auf die Zwischenkontaktzeit etabliert. Hierauf basierend wird ein analytischer Zusammenhang von Eigenschaften des Graphen sowie deren Einfluss auf Parameter der Verteilung von Zwischenkontaktzeiten erarbeitet. Dieser Zusammenhang ist auf Spektraleigenschaften des Graphen sowie auf Random Walk Prozessen begründet. Die gewonnenen Ergebnisse unterstützen das Verständnis, die Konfiguration sowie die Ausbringung von Delay Tolerant Networks.

Im zweiten Teil dieser Dissertation wird ein dezentrales System entwickelt, welches das Routing über Infrastruktur-basierte und Infrastruktur-lose Netze – sogenannte *hybride Netze* – hinweg ermöglicht. Für beide Netztypen existieren heute getrennte Routingverfahren, welche nicht direkt miteinander integriert oder gekoppelt werden können, da sie auf unterschiedlichen Paradigmen beruhen. Beim Routing in Infrastruktur-basierten Netzen werden Ende-zu-Ende Pfade aufgebaut und gewartet. Dieser Ansatz ist für Infrastrukturlose Netze nicht einsetzbar, da die dortigen Pfade instabil sind und meist zu keinem Zeitpunkt durchgängig Ende-zu-Ende existieren. Routing in Infrastruktur-losen Netzen basiert daher auf probabilistischen Entscheidungen die bei opportunistischen Kommunikationsmöglichkeiten autonom von Geräten getroffen werden. In dieser Dissertation wird eine Integration der beiden Paradigmen durch ein neues Routingsystem realisiert, welches in beiden Netztypen das jeweils bewährte Routingverfahren betreibt und eine Verbindung der Routingverfahren durch Austausch von Information zwischen den Netzen schafft. Hinsichtlich Infrastruktur-loser Netze kann durch eine neue Kategorisierung eine Vielzahl existierender Protokolle im Bereich Delay Tolerant Networks eingesetzt werden. Im Hinblick auf Infrastruktur-basierte Netze kommen strukturierte Overlaynetze zum Einsatz, welche durch ihre flache Adressierung, Skalierbarkeit und Identifizierer-basiertes Routing eine gute Grundlage zur Integration bereitstellen. Mit dem in dieser Dissertation entwickelten dezentralen System für Kommunikation über hybride Netze werden zwei beispielhafte Anwendungsfälle implementiert und simulativ evaluiert: Falls ein nur geringer Anteil Infrastruktur vorhanden ist, erbringt das hybride Routingsystem trotz heterogener Infrastruktur-Fähigkeiten Ende-zu-Ende Kommunikation zwischen Teilnehmern. Beispielhaft erhöht sich der Anteil erfolgreich zugestellter Nachrichten um den Faktor 3, sobald nur 20% der mobilen Geräte Infrastruktur-fähig sind. Falls ein hoher Anteil an Infrastruktur vorhanden ist, kann das hybride Routingsystem verwendet werden um Verkehr in das Infrastruktur-lose Netz auszulagern und somit die Infrastruktur zu entlasten. Bei einer akzeptierten Zustellverzögerung von maximal 5 Stunden kann somit beispielsweise über 35% des Verkehrsaufkommens aus der Infrastruktur ausgelagert werden.

Die Implementierung und Ausbringung des entwickelten hybriden Routingsystems gestaltet sich auf Grund der heute zunehmend komplexer werdenden Netze schwierig. Im dritten Teil dieser Dissertation wird eine Netzabstraktion entwickelt, welche einerseits die einfache Implementierung und Ausbringung des hybriden Routingsystems ermöglicht und andererseits allgemeine Anwendbarkeit als Rahmenwerk zur einfachen Implementierung und Ausbringung von Diensten zur Verfügung stellt. Das mit Kollegen entwickelte Rahmenwerk basiert auf Overlaynetzen und ermöglicht eine Abstraktion von unterliegenden Netzen. Mit Hilfe des Rahmenwerks können Dienste einfach entwickelt sowie skalierbar, sicher und kostengünstig betrieben werden.

Contents

List of Figures

List of Tables

List of Algorithms

List of Symbols

d_i	mobile device
id_i	identifier of device d_i
$\mathcal{D}$	set of mobile devices
n	number of mobile devices, $n = |\mathcal{D}|$
$\bar{k}$	overlay instance
N	number of nodes in overlay
b	number of infrastructure access points
q_i	message queue of device d_i
r	wireless communication range in meter
$r(n)$	wireless communication range as function of n
m_{ij}	message with sender d_i, destination d_j
m_j	message with destination d_j
c	allowed message replications
t_i	i'th step in discrete time
A	network area size
$\mathcal{D}_p/\mathcal{D}_t/\mathcal{D}_n$	infrastructure-capability classes
$P(x)$	probability of x
$\mathcal{C}_i$	infrastructure capability classes of encountered devices
$\mathcal{T}_i$	destination-awareness table of device d_i
$p_i(d_j)$	awareness of device d_i for device d_j, $p_i(d_j) \in [0,1]$
$p'_i(d_j)$	normalized awareness
Δ	time duration
$d_\mathcal{I}$	virtual device for infrastructure access
$id_\mathcal{I}$	identifier for virtual infrastructure access
α	static mixed metric parametrization
$\alpha(m_{ij})$	$\alpha(\cdot)$ function based on message m_{ij}
$\mathcal{D}_{\text{ignore}}$	ignored list of devices
$\mathcal{V}_i$	virtual set, subset of devices in $\mathcal{T}_i$
$vmax$	maximal number of device in virtual set, $|\mathcal{V}_i| \leq vmax$
p_{join}	awareness threshold for virtual set

id_j^i	virtual identifier of d_i for representing d_j
$t_i(m)$	initial TTL of message m
$t_e(m)$	elapsed lifetime of message m
γ	fraction of infrastructure enabled devices, $\gamma \in [0,1]$
δ	fraction of ad hoc enabled devices, $\delta \in [0,1]$
$s_i \in S$	state s_i, set of states S
$P = (p_{ij})$	probability transition matrix
$G = (V, E)$	graph G with vertices $v_i \in V$ and edges $e_i \in E$
$\deg(v_i)$	degree of vertex v_i
π	steady-state distribution vector
ω	power-law slope
$x_{\min}$	power-law lower bound
λ_k	k-th eigenvalue
χ	challenge value, e. g. random number
$h(x)$	one-way hash function
$priv_i / pub_i$	asymmetric private and public key of d_i

1. Introduction

Mobile devices like smartphones gain increasing importance, both in private and professional sectors. 7.1 billion mobile-connected devices are estimated to exist by 2015, equaling the world's population[1] [47]. Traffic volume generated by these devices shows exponential growth with an expected 26-fold increase between 2010 and 2015, reaching over 6 Exabyte per month in 2015 [47]. Already today, such traffic volumes put heavy load on wireless networks, resulting in high cost [10, 11], and network unavailability [2, 140, 180, 249]. This trend is expected to continue, especially as the fraction of users accessing Internet resources solely through mobile devices grows steadily, reaching an estimated 788 million by 2015—a 25-fold increase compared to 2010 [47]. In strong contrast to ubiquitous Internet access in the developed world, only 21% of the population in developing countries have access to Internet resources [127]. Out of those, 48 million mobile phone users—138 million estimated by 2015—have no electricity in their homes [47]; underlining the importance and people's desire for information access. Still, technical availability of Internet infrastructure does not guarantee free access to information: Repressing regimes censor, shut down, and destroy infrastructure-based networks [52, 75], with countermeasures being taken, e. g., through deployment of infrastructure-less ad hoc networks [85].

Such overload and unavailability issues in today's networks result from their infrastructure-based nature: Communication between end-system devices *requires* infrastructure. While today's networks are infrastructure-based by design, the large number of mobile devices can be used to deploy *infrastructure-*

---

[1][34] gives a per-country overview of mobile phone usage and average number of mobile phones per capita.

less networks, based upon opportunistic communication. So-called *Delay Tolerant Networks* (DTN) [51, 259] forward messages opportunistically and cooperatively on occurrence of physical device contacts that arise when mobile devices come into mutual communication range. Delay Tolerant Networks employ a *store-carry-forward* routing strategy where messages are *stored* for longer duration, *carried* through mobility devices are exposed to, and *forwarded* if the destination device or a better suited device is encountered. Due to their infrastructure-less nature, Delay Tolerant Networks can be deployed when infrastructure access is not available or possible, or to offload traffic from congested infrastructure networks.

1.1   Problem Statement

While Delay Tolerant Networks have shown to provide promising additions to infrastructure-based networks [91, 153, 188], they introduce new complexity, e. g. due to stochastic mobility. Routing protocols exploit mobility-induced device contacts for message forwarding or replication; i. e. mobility is the main "driver" of Delay Tolerant Networks. This mobility is subject to constraints that limit possible movement paths. One such constraint in urban city scenarios is the street graph of a city that prevents arbitrary movement. Impact of such graph-based constraints on mobility is important to understand Delay Tolerant Network performance in different environments, however, such impact is insufficiently understood.

Both approaches of infrastructure-based networks and Delay Tolerant Networks represent extremes: While infrastructure-based networks offer good performance at high cost, Delay Tolerant Networks have low cost but comparably poor performance due to mobility. Depending on existence and coverage of infrastructure—as well as communication requirements by the application—both approaches of infrastructure-based as well as infrastructure-less networks can be applicable. Studies [120, 123, 156] have empirically shown that the combination of infrastructure-based networks and infrastructure-less Delay Tolerant Networks is promising. Those studies analyzed the communication benefits under an idealized model by assuming a routing scheme with perfect global knowledge that performs optimal forwarding decisions. On the one hand, such *hybrid networks* offer the possibility of outsourcing traffic from congested infrastructure networks into cheap Delay Tolerant Networks [98, 203, 253], and on the other hand enable shortcuts for Delay Tolerant Network routing through the infrastructure network; e. g. by enabling communication between geographically distant Delay Tolerant Networks [92]. However, no system for hybrid routing integrates the routing paradigms used in infrastructure-based and infrastructure-less networks seamlessly and transparently without employing dedicated systems.

For implementation of hybrid routing, distributed systems are preferred, as they allow for scalability, cost-efficiency, and manageability. For deployment of new routing schemes upon today's networks, overlay networks have proven beneficial as they do not require changes to the underlying network—the so-called *underlay*—and can be set up flexibly. From a developer's perspective, however, development and deployment of distributed overlay networks is more complex in contrast to centralized server-based systems. New challenges arise such as management of mobility, handling of middleboxes like Network Address Translation, heterogeneous network access and protocols, and multihoming [100]. Solutions for each challenge exist, their integration, deployment, and developer usage are, however, complex. While decentralized systems are cheap, can be deployed spontaneously, and provide manageability through mechanisms of self-organization, they are more complex from the protocol and algorithmic perspective compared to centralized server-based systems. For development and deployment of a decentralized system for hybrid routing, a framework is required that abstracts from the complexity of the underlying network, as well as the complexity of distributed systems.

1.2 Objectives and Contributions

First objective of this thesis is to enhance the understanding of mobility that devices in Delay Tolerant Networks are exposed to. While mobility in scenarios of human-carried devices is determined by social intention, movement paths are restricted by underlying graphs, e. g. streets, that can be modeled as graphs. Understanding of the impact that such underlying graphs have on mobility is important for development, deployment, and configuration of Delay Tolerant Networks. Especially the mobility metric of inter-contact times has shown of importance for performance of Delay Tolerant Networks and has to be analyzed.

Second objective of this thesis is the integration of infrastructure-based networks, and infrastructure-less Delay Tolerant Networks into hybrid networks. Distributed overlay networks have in the past proven beneficial for developing and deploying novel routing schemes and are to be explored in this thesis for hybrid networks. While development of new routing protocols for Delay Tolerant Networks is no objective of this thesis, focus is on generic applicability for integration of existing routing protocols. Two important use cases are focus in this thesis and are to be supported by the developed system: Providing communication if infrastructure access is sparse, and offloading traffic from infrastructure networks if infrastructure access is widely available.

Third objective of this thesis is development of an underlay abstraction that allows seamless development and deployment of the routing system for hybrid networks. While focus is on supporting aforementioned communication over infrastructure-based, and infrastructure-less networks, generic applicability as general abstraction framework is desired. Overlay networks have proven beneficial for developing network abstractions and are to be explored. Security mechanisms can be integrated directly into such a frame-

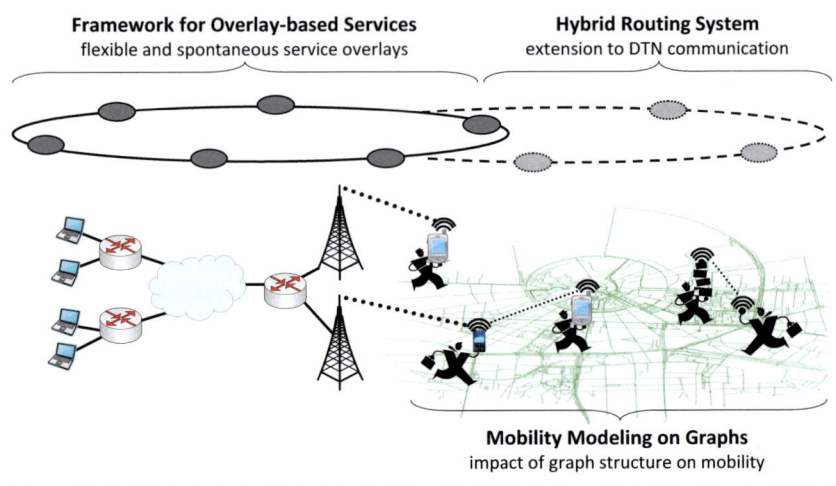

Figure 1.1 Overview of contributions in this thesis.

work to transparently provide cryptographic goals like, e. g., confidentiality. The integration of security mechanisms into the abstraction framework provides benefits for services and applications and is to be explored.

Figure 1.1 shows an overview of contributions in this thesis:

- **Mobility Modeling on Graphs** is performed through simulative and analytical analysis of the impact of graph structure on mobility, with focus on urban city graphs, and synthetic grid-based graphs.

- A **Hybrid Routing System** that integrates infrastructure-based, and infrastructure-less networks with the help of overlay-based systems. A novel categorization is the basis for integration of existing Delay Tolerant Network routing protocols. Two overlay schemes are presented that are applicable for different time scales of device contact stability.

- A **Framework for Overlay-based Services** that allows seamless development and deployment of distributed services over heterogeneous and dynamic networks. The framework is used as enabling platform for the Hybrid Routing System.

Mobility Modeling on Graphs

Analysis of real-world mobility traces provides insight into human and social behavior [43, 86, 136]. Especially the inter-contact time distribution between pairs of devices has shown to allow conclusions on performance of Delay Tolerant Networks. While the destination of a movement path is dictated by social intention, the actual path towards this destination is restricted by an underlying city street graph. While most simulations and models use a plain network area where devices can move freely on shortest line of sight towards their destination, it is not realistic. This thesis contributes to the understanding of mobility processes through analysis how mobility is impacted through underlying graphs that restrict movement. Using simulation, social and random mobility models are analyzed upon real-world city graphs, and synthetic grid-based graphs. Model fitting of simulation data is used to compare inter-contact time distributions. An analytical model is developed based on spectral graph theory. A graph's spectral gap is found to give insight into mobility behavior and a correlation is derived with inter-contact time. Analytical and simulative results are then combined. The underlying graph has strong impact on the slope of the inter-contact times distribution. This variation in slope describes the change in probability of inter-contact time duration and is important for routing protocols. Over grid-based graphs under social mobility a variation in power-law slope of 0.25 between 0.76 to 1.01 is observed. City street graphs are not so different to another and only show variation of 0.1 between 0.89 and 0.99.

Hybrid Routing System

The Hybrid Routing System developed in this thesis provides seamless and transparent routing over infrastructure-based, and infrastructure-less networks. Its design is based on a novel probabilistic extension of distributed overlay networks into Delay Tolerant Networks. Mobile devices act as opportunistic gateways to provide routing towards infrastructure, and register at a distributed announcement system according to their applicability for routing in the Delay Tolerant Network towards other mobile devices. Two overlay-based designs are presented that implement this announcement system, each applicable for different time-scales of device contact stability. Addressing is based on flat identifiers alone, without requiring knowledge of geographic locations or current network attachment of devices. Using a novel categorization, existing Delay Tolerant Network routing protocols can be integrated into the Hybrid Routing System. This categorization is built upon how routing information is structured, and used. The framework for overlay-based services is used as enabling platform for the announcement system that is built up in the infrastructure-based part of the hybrid network. General steps for the integration of existing Delay Tolerant Network routing protocols are explained, and three exemplary protocols integrated. Two use cases are implemented using the Hybrid Routing System: Providing communication in face of few infrastructure-capable devices, and offloading infrastructure-based networks in case of a large number of infrastructure-capable devices. Extensive simulations provide insight into performance and cost metrics. For example, equipping 40% of mobile devices in a Delay Tolerant Network with infrastructure access boosts the message delivery probability $6\times$ compared to a pure Delay

Tolerant Network, even when only routing a single copy of a message and re-signing from replication. For infrastructure offloading, over 30% of traffic can be relieved from infrastructure by accepting a maximal delay of 5 h, and over 50% by accepting maximal delay of 10 h. Compared to the state of the art, the Hybrid Routing Systems does not require dedicated systems, does not require information about geographic location or current network access of devices, and can integrate existing Delay Tolerant Network routing protocols.

Framework for Overlay-based Services

The framework for overlay-based services provides an underlay abstraction to ease development and deployment of distributed services. It is used as enabling platform for the Hybrid Routing System. The framework builds up one distributed overlay per service instance to provide a separation of services. The two main components of the framework are the *BaseCommunication*, and the *BaseOverlay*: The *BaseCommunication* provides end-to-end connectivity between devices and provides the abstraction of *virtual links*. Such *virtual links* are end-to-end contexts that are established through one or multiple connections, and—if required—through the help of other devices from the same service instance, so-called *relays*. Upon the *BaseCommunication*, the *BaseOverlay* implements a distributed control structure that provides logarithmic scaling with growing number of nodes. It implements an identifier/locator split that is the enabler for mobility and multihoming support. A developer interface allows to implement novel services, and a legacy interface enables to transparently run existing services upon the framework. Underlay challenges such as middleboxes, mobility, multihoming, heterogeneous protocols, complexity of distributed systems, and complexity of network security are abstracted internally through the framework. Novel services can benefit from this underlay abstraction and focus on their actual service functionality. The framework has been developed with colleagues in the *Spontaneous Virtual Networks* (SpoVNet) [28] project, and is implemented in the Open Source software library *Ariba* [110–112].

1.3   Structure

Background and related work is introduced in Chapter 2. First, as alternative for costly infrastructure-based communication, Delay Tolerant Networks are reviewed. Such networks can work in disconnected environments when continuous end-to-end paths are not available. As Delay Tolerant Networks are driven by mobility of devices, background and state of the art in mobility modeling is given. Related work in hybrid network routing and background on overlay networks completes this chapter.

Delay Tolerant Networks are powered by mobility that devices are exposed to. While prior mobility modeling focused on social intentions that describe movement destinations, underlying street graphs constrain mobility paths towards those destinations. Chapter 3 analyzes the impact of different graph structures—real-world city graphs and synthetic grid-based graphs—on mobility of devices with focus on inter-contact times.

Infrastructure-based networks and Delay Tolerant Networks both represent extremes. Chapter 4 develops the Hybrid Routing System that integrates infrastructure-based networks, and infrastructure-less Delay Tolerant Networks. This allows communication in mixed infrastructure-based and infrastructure-less networks and can be used to provide communication when infrastructure is sparse, or to offload infrastructure networks through Delay Tolerant Networks.

Chapter 5 presents a framework for overlay-based services that enables flexible and spontaneous development and deployment of distributed services. The framework provides an important abstraction of complex heterogeneous and dynamic underlay networks. It is used as example for an enabling platform for the Hybrid Routing System but has general applicability for distributed overlay-based services.

Finally, Chapter 6 concludes, provides a summary of this thesis, and discusses future work.

2. Background and State of the Art

In this chapter background and state of the art required for the understanding of this thesis is presented. First, Section 2.1 introduces Delay Tolerant Networks that build up disconnected ad hoc networks and perform probabilistic routing through store-carry-forward. Different aspects for evaluation of Delay Tolerant Networks are discussed in Section 2.2. As Delay Tolerant Networks build upon contacts of devices that are generated through device mobility, Section 2.3 introduces mobility modeling. Pure Delay Tolerant Networks have limited applicability as mobility becomes a limiting factor to overcome distance. Related work for the integration of Delay Tolerant Networks with infrastructure-based networks is given in Section 2.4. The system presented in this thesis for routing in hybrid networks is based on overlay networks, which are introduced in Section 2.5. Section 2.6 reviews the presented state of the art and discusses how the remainder of this thesis enhances it.

2.1 Delay Tolerant Networks

Delay Tolerant Networks (DTN) [51, 259] are store-carry-forward networks that exploit mobility that devices are exposed to for routing in intermittently connected networks. Opportunistic communication possibilities are exploited that occur when mobile devices come into mutual communication range of their wireless transceivers. While infrastructure-based mobile networks are costly [10, 11] and increasingly overloaded [2, 140, 180], DTNs are cheap as they do not require any infrastructure components. Especially in face of exponential increase in traffic volumes in infrastructure-based mobile network [47]—growing from 0.6 Exabyte in 2011 up to 6.3 Exabyte in 2015—DTNs become an interesting way to offload data that is not delay-critical. On

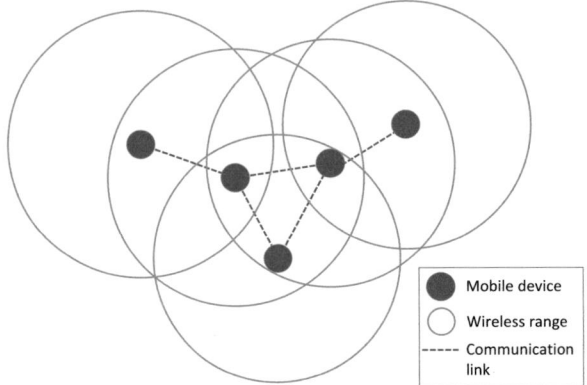

Figure 2.1 Mobile ad hoc network with multi-hop communication.

the other hand, in case of non-existent infrastructure access—the case for 79% of the population in developing countries [127] and in rural areas [153, 188]—DTNs can be used to provide communication.

2.1.1 Mobile Ad hoc Networks

In comparison to infrastructure-based wireless networks, *Mobile Ad hoc Networks* (MANET) are wireless networks made up solely of mobile devices. Routing in MANETs is challenging as the network is highly dynamic in structure and subject to link failure due to device mobility. This results in constant restructuring of the network graph and adaptation of routes. Still, routing in mobile ad hoc networks assumes availability of end-to-end paths, either in the form of direct, or relayed connectivity. Routing is based on the assumption that a continuous end-to-end paths exists between a sender and a destination. To implement routing functionality, routes in MANETs are maintained in a *proactive* or *reactive* manner: Proactive protocols signal end-to-end paths for all source-destination pairs in advance of actual communication and repair routes on failure. In contrast, reactive protocols only build up end-to-end paths on demand. Figure 2.1 shows a MANET: Circular areas indicate wireless transmission range of devices and straight lines indicate wireless links. For communication between two devices, a path must be built up based upon intermediate devices in mutual wireless communication range.

The history of MANETs originated from research on wireless communication in the 1970's in the *Packet Radio Network* (PRNET) [135] project, and during the 1980's in the *Survivable Adaptive Radio Networks* (SURAN) [202] project. Both projects were military-driven with the goal of deploying infrastructure-less communication in the battlefield. During the 1990's the emergence of portable computers in the form of laptops resulted in interest in ad hoc communication for the civil sector. The seminal papers by Perkins and Bhagwat [191], and by Johnson [132] presented routing protocols to form infrastructure-less networks of mobile devices. The term *ad hoc network* was, according to Perkins [191], coined by the IEEE 802.11 subcommittee in an early description of wireless medium access control in 1993. There, Diepstraten and Ennis [63] define the term ad hoc network as follows:

- [63, Sec. 1.1]: *"[An] Ad Hoc Wireless LAN, [. . .] is a [. . .] network of stations, normally all within range of each other station's wireless transceivers."*

- [63, Sec. 2.2]: *"A special case is a single ESA that does not have an Infrastructure. This is called an Ad-Hoc Network, which can be formed by a number of stations (such as in a meeting room, for instance). This network should be able to be set up fast, and would perhaps only last for the duration of the meeting, without the need for any infrastructure provisions. It would further allow communication between stations without the need to be registered to an available infrastructure, and is independent of any installed infrastructure."*

MANET routing protocols can be broadly categorized into *reactive* and *proactive* protocols. Reactive protocols like *Dynamic Source Routing* (DSR) [132], or *Ad-hoc On-Demand Distance Vector Routing* (AODV) [190] build up routes upon request and therefore have low maintenance overhead but longer route setup-duration. This is in contrary to proactive routing protocols like *Destination-Sequenced Distance Vector routing* (DSDV) [191], or *Virtual Ring Routing* (VRR) [37] that detect and compute routes ahead of time, and perform maintenance to repair route failures. This proactive behavior results in higher protocol overhead compared to reactive protocols, especially if the actual communication is relatively infrequent in comparison to route maintenance.

2.1.2 From Mobile Ad hoc to Delay Tolerant Networks

A special class of intermittently connected MANETs—called *Delay Tolerant Networks*, or *Disruption Tolerant Networks* (DTN)—does not obey the condition that a continuous link over a connected graph must exist between sender and destination device at one point in time. DTNs support varying degrees of strong partitioning as they to not require continuous end-to-end paths. Such partitioning is inherent to these networks and does not represent exceptional network conditions that only occur rarely. Figure 2.2 shows an exemplary DTN scenario where a message is carried through mobility of a device towards the destination device: At time t_1 device 5 forwards a message with destination device 7 to device 3, as device 3 is more applicable for carrying the message towards device 7. At time t_2 device 3 and destination device 7 are in mutual communication range and the message can be delivered to the final destination device 7. Note, that the communication path where the message is delivered does not exist in a continuous way at any given point

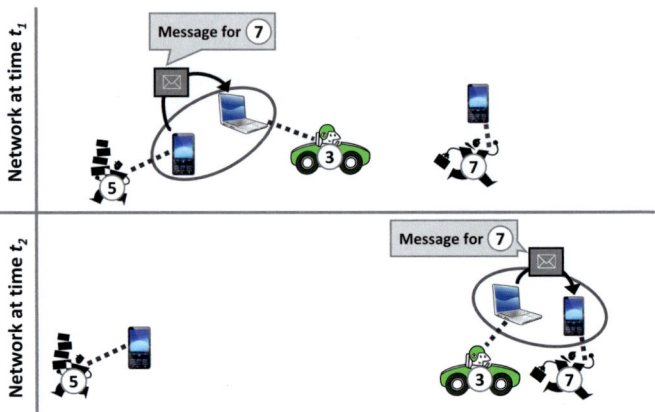

Figure 2.2 Message delivery in a Delay Tolerant Network.

in time. Rather, the path only exists in parts over time. While a MANET can be modeled as graph, a DTN can be modeled as time-varying graph where on-off processes are attached to its edges [130].

While in MANETs mobility of devices is a challenge that protocols have to cope with, mobility is seen as beneficial and an enabler for routing in DTNs, as the low device density in DTNs *requires* mobility of devices for carrying messages towards their destinations. To achieve end-to-end routing, mobility of devices is exploited using store-carry-forward schemes: Devices store messages—or groups of messages called *bundles*—and carry them through mobility closer towards the destination. A special kind of DTNs—sometimes called *Pocket Switched Networks*—are built around human-carried devices [42]. Such DTNs base their routing decisions on the non-randomness of human behavior by exploiting knowledge about social relations and human habits for efficient routing decisions [55, 121, 155, 176].

To give an overview on the broad topic of DTN routing protocols the classification from Zhang [259] is used. The main differentiation is *deterministic routing* and *stochastic routing*. Deterministic approaches are based on the fact that device movement—and therewith future ad hoc communication opportunities—are completely known. Such protocols are described later in Section 2.1.5. When device movement is not known, random, or follows a probability distribution, stochastic routing mechanisms are employed which are described later in Section 2.1.6.

2.1.3   Applicability of MANET Protocols for DTN

MANETs are based on the assumption that a connected graph of devices exists, i. e., each device can communicate with any other device through a connected path of relay devices. When the network area where mobile devices move is large compared to the number of devices—i.e. device density is low—and no connected graph can be established, DTNs arise. In contrast to MANETs, DTNs relax the assumption on connectivity, but on the other hand can often only provide probabilistic delivery guarantees.

Routing protocols employed in MANETs are not applicable in DTNs, mainly due to long delays, and unstable topology. In case of reactive protocols the following problems arise [230]:

- Route requests can not reach the destination due to long delay.
- Topology changes result in breaking of paths during build-up, or right after a path has been established.
- Flooding of the network to discover routes is not possible in DTNs due to long delays.

Proactive protocols, on the other hand, have the following problems when employed in DTNs [230]:

- They fail to converge due to the highly dynamic topology.
- Topology updates fail due to long delays.
- Flooding on topology changes is not possible due to long delays.

2.1.4 History of Delay Tolerant Networks

While DTNs can be seen as a special type of MANET, their origin is different. Delay Tolerant Networks evolved from work in *Interplanetary Internetworking* [107, 165]. As spacecrafts are often out of sight for direct communication with earth stations and contemporaneous end-to-end paths are rare, protocols were required that are able to cope with long delays and frequent disruptions. Research on delay and disruption tolerance emerged as a key factor for communication in the interplanetary environment and was mainly discussed in the Internet Society's *Interplanetary Internet Special Interest Group* (IPNSIG) which resulted in the IRTF's *Interplanetary Internet Research Group* (IPNRG). Recognizing the potential of the delay tolerant communication paradigm for the broader networking area marked the beginning of the IRTF's *Delay Tolerant Networking Research Group* (DTNRG) that is developing the DTN Reference Architecture [41] and corresponding protocols [152, 201, 219].

With the emergence of small portable mobile devices like smartphones the applicability of DTNs for infrastructure-less communication between such devices was realized, sometimes called *Pocket Switched Networks* (PSN) [117]. This spawned a new research area for protocols [130, 155], architectures [218], and analysis of mobility [43, 136]. A good overview of current research areas in Delay Tolerant Networks is given by Conti and Kumar [51].

2.1.5 Overview of DTN Approaches

While the remainder of this thesis focuses around human-centric networks made up of mobile devices such as smartphones, this section gives a broader

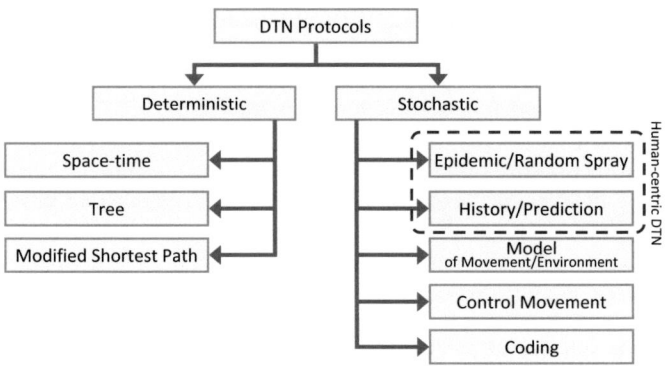

Figure 2.3 Categorization of DTN protocols, based on [259].

overview of DTNs. Goal of this section is to introduce a wide range of possible DTN routing mechanisms and give insight into their internal working.

Figure 2.3 shows an overview of DTN protocol categories, based on the categorization by Zhang [259]. A first differentiation is made based on *deterministic* approaches, and *stochastic* approaches. Deterministic approaches make use of exact and known mobility patterns to perform scheduling of messages over time-varying links. Stochastic approaches work based on probabilities that e. g. describe contacts of devices, or recurrence of devices to specific geographic areas. Protocols in subcategories Epidemic/Random Spray, and History/Prediction are applicable for DTNs built upon human-carried devices.

Deterministic Approaches

An example of deterministic DTNs are inter-planetary satellite communication networks where the exact times of communication opportunities between devices can be calculated due to known device movement. The network dynamics are deterministic in such networks and routing can be pre-computed.

Space-time: Space-time routing presented in [167] predicts characteristic device movement profiles over time using space-time graphs. Such graphs are then used as input for shortest path and dynamic programming algorithms to compute routing paths.

Tree: In [102] protocols for deterministic routing are proposed that build up trees based on the time variance of device contacts. In the simplest case global knowledge about device movement is available to all devices in the network. Each device can build up a tree that reflects the most time-efficient path to route a message to its destination device.

Modified Shortest Path: Jain et al. [130] present a set of protocols based on available global information oracles for device contacts, device queuing, and traffic demands. Depending on which oracles are available, the authors present algorithms based on linear programming and Dijkstra variants to calculate shortest paths over time-varying graphs. Such time-varying graphs represent device contacts through on-off processes that are attached to its edges.

Stochastic Approaches

When device movement can not be described with exact contact times but only through stochastic models, deterministic approaches are not applicable as they require exact information. Stochastic routing mechanisms are used in this case, e.g. based on probabilities of device contacts [154], or the use of social structure [55, 121, 176].

Epidemic/Random Spray: The simplest DTN protocol is *Direct-delivery* where the source device waits until it directly encounters the destination device [230]. This scheme has smallest overhead but highest message delay. On the other side of extremes lies the *Epidemic* [244] protocol where messages are flooded through the network. Under infinite bandwidth and storage models, Epidemic exhibits lowest bound in delay and upper bound in overhead. In between those two extreme protocols of Direct-delivery and Epidemic are protocols that perform limited flooding [15, 35, 241], or control the number of replications per message [179, 228, 229].

History/Prediction: Several protocols learn contact patterns of devices over time and use this information to perform routing. Lindgren et al. propose *Prophet* [154] where devices collect probabilities of encounter with other devices. Collected contact probabilities are exchanged transitively through a damping factor. A message is replicated to another device if its probability of encountering the destination device is higher. *MobySpace* by Leguay et al. [149, 150] builds up a high-dimensional space, based upon device mobility patterns, with dimensions reflecting geographic locations. The space describes the probability of a device for being found in the respective location. Routing in MobySpace is based on the assumption that a device is a good forwarder if its MobySpace is similar to that of the destination device.

Model of Movement/Environment: If more information about device movement is known through externally given models, better routing decisions can be performed. *Model Based Routing* (MBR) [25] uses external information such as road maps or building charts, as well as user profiles to perform routing.

Control Movement: Prior approaches assumed that devices are autonomous in their movement. If the protocol can control some devices in their movement, new possibilities arise. *Message ferries* [260], or *data mules* [223] build upon control of devices to collect and deliver messages. The general goal of such approaches is to introduce non-randomness into the device movement and therewith achieve better performance. Depending on the specific variant, devices are aware of the controlled devices and can adjust their own behavior. Data mules [223] allow collection of data from static devices though a mobile data mule device. Those data mule devices have large storage and strong power resources to collect data and carry it, e. g., towards a WiFi access point that provides Internet connectivity and allows to send out the collected data.

Coding: Erasure coding and network coding techniques can be used to make up for the missing reliability due to message loss, or link failure. Through replication redundant messages are created that are sent over different links to achieve higher resilience in the message transfer. The application of such replication-based schemes to DTNs has been presented in [129]. Widmer and Boudec [254], e. g., showed how to use network coding for stateless routing in DTNs, based on flooding.

2.1.6 Protocols for Human-centric DTN

Using DTN for communication with human-carried devices, mobility patterns of humans are of interest as mobile devices are directly exposed to the mobility patterns of their human carrier. As human mobility is not deterministic, only stochastic protocols are applicable. While an overview of DTN approaches was given in the prior section, now specific DTN protocols are described to give insight into their internal mechanisms. Presented protocols that can be deployed for human-centric DTNs are from the subcategories Epidemic/Random Spray, and History/Prediction, shown in Figure 2.3.

Prophet: The *Prophet* [152, 154, 155] protocol proposed by Lindgren et al. was one of the first protocols to perform limited flooding based on the forwarding quality of devices. Each device locally gathers meeting probabilities with other devices when in mutual communication range. Meeting probabilities are updated when devices are in contact, are propagated transitively through a damping factor, and age over time. Replication of a message between two devices in transmission range is performed if the device currently not storing the message has a higher meeting probability for the message's destination device than the device currently storing the message. Several extensions have been proposed, e. g. automatic parameter adaptation depending on mobility of devices [137]. Prophet is an experimental Internet draft [152] within the DTN Research Group[1].

FRESH: Dubois-Ferriere et al. [69] exploit the time-distance correlation in mobile ad hoc networks. This states that a device A currently close to device B will be still in the nearer neighborhood after a short time, and with high probability nearer to B than to another device C that it was close a longer time ago. This so-called "distance-effect" holds true under the assumption of homogeneous mobility processes, i. e. device velocities are similar. Based on time-distance correlation the authors present the *FResher Encounter SearcH* (FRESH) [69] protocol that iteratively moves messages closer to the destination by forwarding it to devices that were in contact with the destination more recently.

---

[1]http://www.dtnrg.org

EASE: Grossglauser and Vetterli present *Exponential Age SEarch* (EASE) [90]. EASE routes messages based on timestamps and geographic location of last device encounters. Messages are routed greedy towards the destination device, exploiting the distance effect—similar to FRESH—while taking the geographic location into account. EASE is based on the following three observations: (1) The last location where a device was encountered is still a relatively good estimate for a device's current location, (2) the elapsed time since last encounter is an estimate for the quality of this last location, and (3) the locality in the mobility process leads to the distance-effect in that better estimates for the destination device become available as the message travels closer towards its destination.

Spray&Wait: To prevent uncontrolled flooding of the network, Spyropoulos et al. [228] present the quota-based protocol *Spray&Wait*. Given an initial number of allowed replicas per message c, the protocol *sprays* the message to the first encountered devices, keeping $\lceil c/2 \rceil$ replicas and forwarding $\lfloor c/2 \rfloor$ replicas. This process is continued recursively until $c = 1$. Then the protocol switches into the *wait* phase where the devices wait to encounter the message's destination device directly, i. e. Direct-delivery.

Spray&Focus: Spray&Wait [228] does not work well if mobility results in geographical clusters, e. g., due to social behavior. To cope with such clustering, Spyropoulos et al. present an extension of Spray&Wait called *Spray&Focus* [229]. Spray&Focus performs the spraying phase identical to Spray&Wait but differs in the second phase. Whereas in Spray&Wait devices wait to encounter the destination directly, Spray&Focus adapts the approach of FRESH [69] based on encounter ages. Every device stores local tables that store timestamps of last device encounters. The elapsed time since last encounter is used to perform a single-copy forwarding scheme in the focus phase. Furthermore, devices exchange encounter tables to calculate transitivity.

Mobility Pattern Space: *Mobility Pattern Space* (MobySpace) by Leguay et al. [149, 150] is a high-dimensional space that is based upon mobility patterns of devices. The dimension of the space reflects the number of locations where a device potentially resides. Values on those axis for each dimension indicate the probability to find the device in the respective location. Routing in MobySpace is based on the assumption that a device is a good forwarder if it has a MobySpace similar to the MobySpace of the destination device. Maintaining the local MobySpace requires a way to track locations for a device to realize that it resides in a specific location. To be able to forward the message to a device who's MobySpace is similar to the destination's MobySpace, the destination's MobySpace must be known. The authors propose flooding of the MobySpaces through the DTN to distribute the MobySpaces of individual devices. Different distance metrics for comparing of MobySpaces are presented, as well as reduction of the high-dimensional MobySpaces to lower dimensions.

SimBet: One of the first protocols to exploit social structure in ad hoc networks was proposed by Daly and Haahr, called *SimBet* [55]. SimBet performs distributed detection of device similarity, and betweenness centrality; both social graph metrics. Betweenness centrality is used to identify bridge devices in the network, while similarity is used for identifying clusters. The SimBet utility value is a weighted combination of normalized similarity and centrality measures. Messages are routed based on comparison of SimBet utility values. Taking the strength of social ties additionally into account, the same authors present *SimBetTS* [56] as extension of SimBet. Further extensions in form of time-variant aging links have been presented by Link et al. to account for temporal changes in the network [7].

Label: Hui and Crowcroft [118, 119] first used the concept of communities for forwarding in human-centric DTNs. They present the *Label* protocol that uses affiliation labels assigned to pre-defined simple static communities. Label is based on the observation that devices within the same community meet more often than devices from different communities. The protocol requires knowledge about the destination device's community. Routing is based on forwarding of messages to devices that are within the same community as the destination device, i. e. have the same label.

Bubble: In [120, 121] Hui et al. present the Bubble protocol for forwarding in social-based DTNs by taking advantage of the inter-human social structures. Bubble performs community detection and selects highly central devices and community members as relays. Using a global ranking that defines the global centrality of a device, and a local ranking that defines the centrality of a device within its local community, the Bubble protocols works as follows: A message is first passed up the hierarchical ranking tree by using the global ranking of devices. This forwarding is performed until the message reaches a device that is member of the same community as the destination device. Then, the local ranking is used to further forward the message up the local hierarchy until the destination device is reached. Therefore, the message "bubbles" up, first through the global and then through the local community. Bubble requires community information, either detected through the distributed version of community detection *DiBuBB* [124], or given through external information.

PeopleRank: Mtibaa et al. showed that online social contacts and real-world contacts can be mapped well [175]. Using this idea the authors present *PeopleRank* [176], a DTN routing protocol that builds upon social contact information for routing, based upon physical device encounters. The metric used by PeopleRank defines how *important* a device is in the social network, inspired by PageRank calculation based on social graph structure. Routing is based by forwarding messages towards devices with higher PeopleRank value. The authors present a distributed algorithm for calculating PeopleRank values, based on knowledge about the local view of the social contact graph.

Encounter-based Routing: Nelson et al. present *Encounter-based Routing* (EBR) [179], a DTN protocol that builds upon the frequency of device encounters. EBR is built upon the idea that in scenarios such as disaster recovery certain devices have a special function and are more mobile, e.g. ambulance or police. Detecting the encounter rate allows prediction of the future rate of encounters, which is used for DTN routing. EBR routes messages towards devices with higher encounter values, based on the idea that these devices encounter the destination device, too, with higher probability. The number of messages exchanged between two devices is relative to the difference in their encounter values.

MaxProp: Burgess et al. focus on DTNs where duration of wireless links between devices is short. They present *MaxProp* [35] that decides on the order of messages to replicate. This order is based on delivery likelihoods of devices, based on historical data of device encounters. Probabilities reflect link weights in a time-space variant graph. Link weights are computed on device contact and distributed to obtain a more complete view of the contact graph. This way, the local view of the graph is enhanced with each device contact.

RAPID: The RAPID protocol presented by Balasubramanian et al. [14, 15] takes a generic approach on DTN routing with different pluggable metrics. Their approach is based on the resource allocation problem, by taking into account the utility of a message replication. A message is replicated if the utility generated by the replication is higher than the utility by not replicating the message. The authors present three different metrics for calculating the utility of replication: minimizing average delay, minimizing missed deadlines, and minimizing maximum delay. At every message transfer the marginal utility of performing this transfer is calculated to decide whether the replication justifies the increase in resource consumption. For calculating the marginal utility based on the three metrics, RAPID uses additional metadata that is distributed in the network, including past replications of messages, available bandwidth, and expected meeting times with other devices.

2.2 Evaluation Methodologies for Delay Tolerant Networks

The analysis of DTN behavior can be roughly divided into *Delay/Capacity Scaling*, and *DTN Performance*, which will be presented in Section 2.2.1 and Section 2.2.2, respectively. While Delay/Capacity scaling analyzes the interplay between wireless interference and device density in models of asymptotically large networks, DTN performance analyzes the forwarding and replication strategy of DTN protocols.

2.2.1 Delay/Capacity Scaling

Increasing the number of devices in a wireless network results in increased interference on the wireless channel. By reducing transmission range, interference can be reduced but delivery of messages becomes complicated and subject to delay as multi-hop communication is required. The methodology of analyzing the performance of wireless networks under variation of device density, transmission range, and mobility is called *delay/capacity scaling*. Before background in delay/capacity scaling is presented, required definitions are given:

- *Throughput capacity* of a single/multi-hop source-destination pair of devices is the average number of bits delivered from source device to destination device per second. Summing up over all source-destination pairs, the throughput capacity of the complete network results.

- *Transport capacity* is the number of bits that are transported by the complete network towards destination devices. The unit of transport capacity is $bit \cdot \frac{m}{s}$, i.e. the number of bits transported per second over distance in meters.

- *Delay* is the duration from sending a message from the original message sender, to delivery of the message at the message's destination device.

The network is made up of n devices, each with transmission range r, placed on an area A. If the transmission range is scaled and a function of the number of overall devices n, it is written as $r(n)$. For simplicity of analysis, devices are placed on a circle disc of unit size $A = 1\,m^2$, i.e. the diameter of the area is $2 \cdot \sqrt{A/\pi} \approx 1.13\,m$. The analysis of delay/capacity scaling is concerned with the performance under asymptotically large networks, i.e. $n \rightarrow \infty$ under fixed area A. If no variation in wireless transmission is performed, this results in increasing density of devices on the network area. Figure 2.4 gives an overview of the most important results from delay/capacity scaling that will be described in the following. The static, one-hop and multi-hop results are due to [94], the mobile multi-hop result are due to [89].

Static, one-hop: In a static network of n devices the transmission range can be scaled up so that every device can directly reach any other device without any intermediate hops. This way messages are delivered directly with constant delay of $\Theta(1)$. However, interference is increased as a single sending device prevents all other $n - 1$ devices from sending and reduces the throughput capacity of a device as $\Theta(1/n)$.

Static, multi-hop: In 2000 Gupta and Kumar published their seminal article *"The Capacity of Wireless Networks"* [94] that describes the interplay between achievable throughput and wireless interference. Gupta and Kumar focus on a network of stationary devices that are placed uniformly at random on a circle disc of unit size, allowing scaling of transmission range and multi-hop delivery of messages. They show that the throughput capacity of each device is $\Theta(1/\sqrt{n \log n})$ and therewith falls quickly as the network size increases.

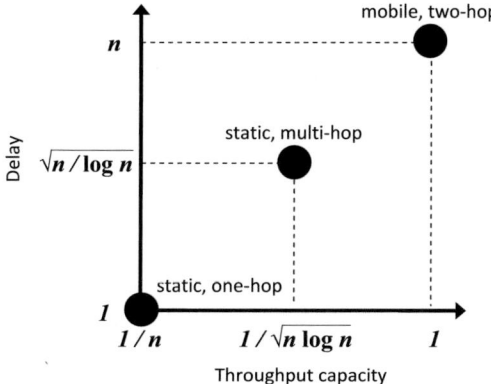

Figure 2.4 Overview of delay/capacity scaling results, based on [83].

The resulting average delay per message is $\Theta\left(\sqrt{n/\log n}\right)$ [83]. Even under optimal scheduling strategy, optimal placement of devices, and optimal transmission range, the throughput capacity can only be raised up to $\Theta(1/\sqrt{n})$. The transport capacity of the complete network is in the order of $\Theta(\sqrt{n})$ bit-meters per second. This led Gupta and Kumar to the conclusion that *"Perhaps efforts should be targeted at designing networks with small numbers of nodes"* [94], as an increase of network size results in strong decrease of performance.

Mobile, two-hop: Grossglauser and Tse showed that using devices which are mobile, a per-device throughput of $\Theta(1)$ can be achieved [89], i.e. the throughput scales constantly with the number of devices, at the cost of delay in the order of $\Theta(n)$. Their scheme uses intermediate mobile devices to store and carry messages, i.e. *store-carry-forward* routing. Their results show that large networks are feasible, by exploiting the mobility of devices and multi-hop communication.

Variation in transmission range: Generally, an increase in wireless transmission range results in higher probability to reach another device directly, and therewith increase capacity. However, interference limits capacity on the other hand. Garetto et al. show that the capacity of a network can not be increased by scaling the transmission range beyond $\Theta(1/\sqrt{n})$ [84].

Critical connectivity threshold: Gupta and Kumar showed in [93] the condition for a network to be connected with high probability. Under asymptotically large networks of $n \to \infty$, the network is connected with high probability if $\pi r^2(n) = (\log n + \text{const}(n))/n$ for communication range $r(n)$ and constant $\text{const}(n) \to +\infty$. They further proved that the network is disconnected with high probability if $n\pi \cdot r^2(n) = \ln n + \text{const}(n)$ with $\limsup_n \text{const}(n) < +\infty$. For example following the argumentation in [21, p. 196] that uses a stronger result of Penrose [187], the network is connected with probability

Work	Trace mobility	Simulative mobility	Analytical
Prophet [154, 155]	no	yes	no
FRESH [69]	no	yes	yes
EASE [90]	no	yes	yes
Spray&Wait [228]	no	yes	yes
Spray&Focus [229]	no	yes	yes
MobySpace [149, 150]	no	yes	no
SimBet [55]	yes	no	no
Label [118, 119]	yes	no	no
Bubble [120, 121]	yes	no	no
PeopleRank [175]	yes	no	no
EBR [179]	no	yes	yes
MaxProp [35]	yes	no	no
RAPID [14, 15]	yes	yes	yes

Table 2.1 DTN evaluation methodology.

$e^{-1/n}$ if for the transmission range $r(n)$ holds $n\pi r^2(n) = 2\ln n$. Note, that the probability of connectivity holds as $n \to \infty$, but is smaller in case of low n [21, p. 196]. Lee et al. summarize the connectivity results by stating that the network becomes disconnected with high probability if the transmission range scales below $\Theta(\sqrt{\log n/n})$ [148].

Hybrid Networks While work presented so far analyzed pure ad hoc networks made up of end-user devices, the works presented in the following analyzed hybrid networks made up of ad hoc end-user devices, and infrastructure support in the form of base stations. Base stations are connected through a high-capacity backbone. In contrast to devices in ad hoc networks, base stations are neither message sources nor destinations, they rather relay data and allow to overcome long distance with short delay compared to device mobility. Liu et al. [157] show that if the number of base stations b grows faster than $\sqrt{n}$, the throughput capacity increases linearly with b. Otherwise, if b grows slower than n, the benefit of adding infrastructure is small. Agarwal and Kumar [6] show that through scaling of base station's power-levels, a throughput of $\Theta(1)$ can be achieved for a subset of devices $\Theta(n)$. Considering all devices n, a throughput of $\Theta(1/\log n)$ is possible. Kozat and Tassiulas [144] show that a per-source capacity of $\Theta(1/\log n)$ can be achieved by a hybrid network, compared to a static multi-hop ad hoc network which achieves $\Theta(1/\sqrt{n\log n})$. The results show that hybrid networks provide strong improvements in terms of delay/capacity scaling compared to pure ad hoc networks.

2.2.2 DTN Performance

Most works presenting a new DTN protocol include a performance analysis evaluation and comparison to other protocols. The methodology and scenarios used for these evaluations, however, differ strongly. Generally, a differentiation between trace-driven and simulative evaluation can be made. Table 2.1

Work	Mobility Model	Speed	Network area and network size
Prophet [154, 155]	community	$0\text{--}20\,\frac{m}{s}$	1500 m × 300 m, 50 devices
FRESH [69]	random	–	fixed area, 1 000–64 000
EASE [90]	random	0.3/step	fixed density, 1 000 devices
Spray&Wait [228]	random	–	500×500, 100 devices, range 10 m
Spray&Focus [229]	random, community	–	500×500, 100 devices
MobySpace [149, 150]	trace	trace	25 locations, 50 devices
SimBet [55]	trace	trace	100 devices
Label [118, 119]	trace	trace	80 devices
Bubble [120, 121]	trace	trace	37–97
PeopleRank [175]	trace	trace	27–414
EBR [179]	random, disaster	$2.7\text{--}13.9\,\frac{m}{s}$	5 000 m × 3 000 m, 25–250 devices
MaxProp [35]	trace	trace	30 buses
RAPID [14, 15]	power-law, trace	–, trace	20, 40

Table 2.2 DTN evaluation mobility details.

gives an overview of the DTN protocols presented in Section 2.1 and the evaluation methodology used by their authors. Most works either follow a trace-driven evaluation, or simulative evaluation using mobility models. About half of the works further include analytical observations. Section A.1 argues that traces should be used to develop new mobility models, however actual evaluation of DTN protocols should be performed based on mobility models and simulations. More information on mobility characteristics is given in Table 2.2. A broad scale of mobility models and parameters can be observed. Information in publications are sometimes incomplete which prevents reproducibility of results.

Table 2.3 gives an overview of performance and cost metrics that are used for evaluation and comparison with other protocols. Normally, delivery ratio and delivery delay are used as performance metric, and the number of transmissions and hop count as cost metric.

Work	Performance metrics	Cost metrics
Prophet [154, 155]	delivered messages, delay, no TTL	queue size, transmissions
FRESH [69]	route quality, delay	search cost, route length, overhead
EASE [90]	no TTL	transmission cost, hops
Spray&Wait [228]	TTL 4 000–6 000, delay	transmissions
Spray&Focus [229]	TTL 1 000–10 000, delay	transmissions
MobySpace [149, 150]	delay	hops
SimBet [55]	delivered, delay	hops, transmissions
Label [118, 119]	delivery, delay	hops, transmissions
Bubble [120, 121]	delivery	transmissions, hops
PeopleRank [175]	delay	number of replicas
EBR [179]	delivery, delay	goodput
MaxProp [35]	delivery, delay	hop count, buffer
RAPID [14, 15]	delivery, delay	channel utilization

Table 2.3 DTN evaluation metrics.

2.3 Mobility Modeling

This thesis focuses on DTNs in the context of human-carried mobile devices like smartphones [42, 117]. As mobility of DTN-participating devices has influence on routing performance, understanding human mobility is of interest for the design and evaluation of routing protocols. To understand the properties of human mobility, stochastic background is presented in Section 2.3.1 before state of the art in modeling of human mobility is presented in Section 2.3.2. Based on this modeling, several mobility models have been proposed. They are presented in Section 2.3.3 and can, e. g., be used for simulation. For analytical modeling Random walks are introduced in Section 2.3.4.

2.3.1 Stochastic Background

In this section an overview of power-law, exponential, and mixed distributions is given that are required to understand modeling of human mobility and parameter estimation used in this thesis. As reference the reader is referred to the overview article by Newman [181].

Power-law Distribution

A power-law describes a mathematical relationship between two quantities, one being the frequency of an event and one being the occurrence of the event. The law states that small events are very common and occur with high frequency, whereas large events are extremely rare and occur with very low frequency. Technically, a power-law is a polynomial relationship that exhibits scale invariance. This relationship between the two quantities is commonly expressed as[2]

$$f(x) = Cx^{-\omega} \tag{2.1}$$

with $C = \exp(c)$ being a function of a constant c, and ω being the exponent of the power-law. Of interest is the exponent ω, C is implicitly given by requiring that the sum over the distribution is 1. Functions that follow a power-law exhibit the property of *scale invariance*, expressed as

$$f(gx) \propto f(x) \tag{2.2}$$

with g being a constant. Scale invariance results in a linear relationship of the two quantities on double logarithmic scales—short *log-log scale*[3]—that can be written based on Equation 2.1 as

$$\log(f(x)) = c - \log(x^{\omega}). \tag{2.3}$$

---

[2]Normally α is used as power-law slope. In this thesis α has a different meaning, to prevent confusion the power-law slope is depicted ω.

[3]Logarithmic x and y-axis are called *log-log*, linear x and logarithmic y axis called *lin-log*, logarithmic x and linear y axis called *log-lin*, and linear x and y axis called *lin-lin*.

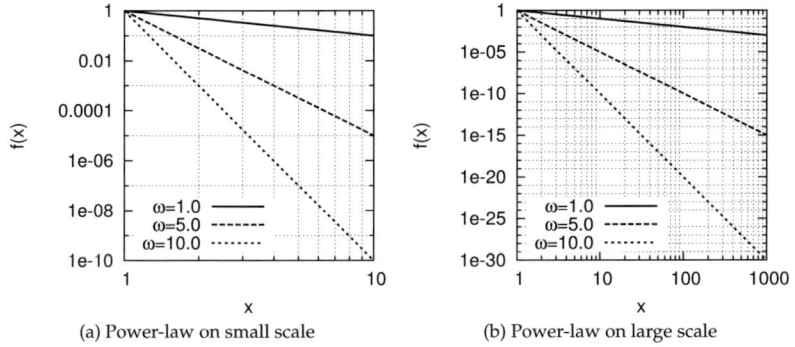

(a) Power-law on small scale   (b) Power-law on large scale

Figure 2.5 Scale invariance of power-laws.

Figure 2.5 shows the scale-invariance property of power-laws: Both figures show the same functions but on different scales of x and y-axis The visual characteristic and relations of the function does not chance under scale. Due to this relationship, a power-law function appears as linear line on a log-log plot. A *distribution* that follows a power-law has the following basic form

$$f(x) = \frac{\omega - 1}{x_{\min}} \left(\frac{x}{x_{\min}} \right)^{-\omega}, x \in [x_{\min}, +\infty]. \tag{2.4}$$

Parameter $x_{\min}$ defines the point where the distribution turns into power-law, i. e. the point where the data set becomes *heavy tailed*. Using e. g. a timescale of $[1, +\infty]$ and $x_{\min} = 1$, it results

$$f(x) = (\omega - 1)x^{-\omega} \tag{2.5}$$

and after normalizing the y-axis to $y \in [0, 1]$ this can be simplified to

$$f(x) = \frac{1}{\omega - 1} \left((\omega - 1)x^{-\omega} \right). \tag{2.6}$$

In a last step Equation 2.6 can be simplified to the most basic form of a power-law distribution

$$f(x) = x^{-\omega}. \tag{2.7}$$

Figure 2.6 shows the impact of the ω parameter on the shape of the function as well as different scales of x and y-axis on the appearance of the power-law.

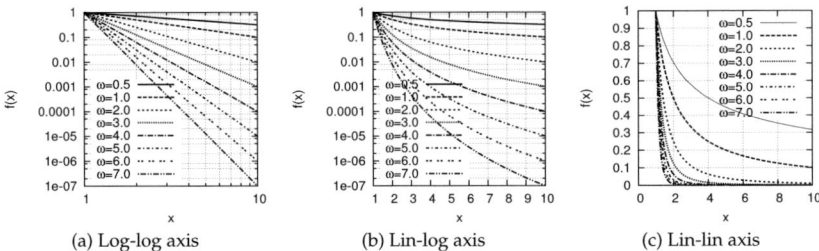

(a) Log-log axis   (b) Lin-log axis   (c) Lin-lin axis

Figure 2.6 Power-law distribution with different ω and different scaling of x and y-axis.

Instead of the *Probability Density Function* (PDF) the *Cumulative Distribution Function* (CDF), or the *Complementary Cumulative Distribution Function* (CCDF) are often used as they are continuous. The functions are defined as

- *Probability Density Function* (PDF): $P(X = x)$,
- *Cumulative Distribution Function* (CDF): $P(X \leq x)$, and
- *Complementary Cumulative Distribution Function* (CCDF) = $P(X > x)$ = $1 - P(X \leq x)$.

The CCDF of a power-law can be described in its general form as

$$P(X > x) = \left(\frac{x}{x_{\min}}\right)^{-\omega+1} \tag{2.8}$$

and by using $x_{\min} = 1$ as example it follows

$$P(X > x) = x^{-\omega+1}. \tag{2.9}$$

Comparing with Equation 2.7 the CCDF of a power-law is again a power-law function, however with shallower slope by adding $+1$ to the exponent.

Exponential Distribution

Besides power-law distributions *exponential* distributions are required background for this thesis. A *Poisson process* generates independent events at a rate λ. The time between such successive events can be described by an exponential distribution

$$f(x; \lambda) = \begin{cases} \lambda e^{-\lambda x}, & x \geq 0, \\ 0, & x < 0. \end{cases} \tag{2.10}$$

$f(x; \lambda)$ describes the probability of occurrence of the duration x between two successive events in a Poisson process with rate λ. Figure 2.7 shows exponential distributions with different λ values and different scaling of x and

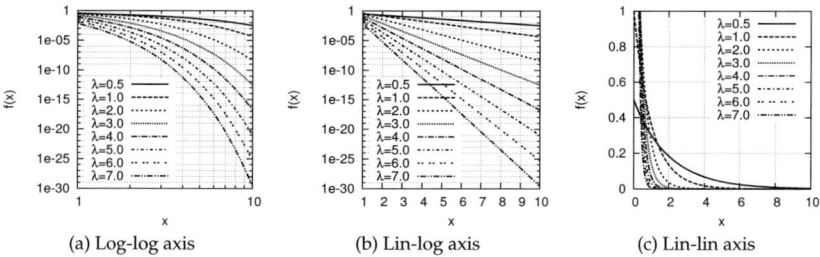

Figure 2.7 Exponential distribution with different rate λ and different scaling of x and y-axis.

y-axis. It can be observed that an exponential distribution falls faster than a power-law distribution, i.e. the occurrence of rare events falls fast, while in a power-law these events make up for the heavy tail. While a power-law distribution appears as straight line on a log-log plot, an exponential distribution appears as straight line on a lin-log plot.

Power-law with Exponential Cutoff

Important for the analysis in this thesis is a special combination of exponential and power-law, called *power-law with exponential cutoff*. By multiplying a power-law with an exponential distribution, the initial behavior of the power-law maintains up to a point on the x-axis where the exponential distribution becomes stronger and drags the power-law down. Based on Equation 2.7 and Equation 2.10 this combined distribution can be defined for $x \geq 1$ as

$$f(x; \omega, \lambda) = x^{-\omega} \cdot \lambda e^{-\lambda x}. \tag{2.11}$$

Figure 2.8 shows such mixed distributions with exemplary parameters.

Power-law Estimation

Several methods for estimation of power-law parameter ω are used in literature. A stable method for estimation of ω is the maximum likelihood method, which is discussed in the work of Clauset, Shalizi, and Newman [50]. Given n data samples[4] $x = (x_1, \ldots, x_n)$ the ω parameter can be estimated according to Clauset et al. as [50, Sec. 3.1]

$$\hat{\omega} = 1 + n \left[\sum_{i=1}^{n} \ln \frac{x_i}{x_{\min}} \right]^{-1}. \tag{2.12}$$

---

[4]Data samples are the samples from the real data, not from the PDF or CDF/CCDF.

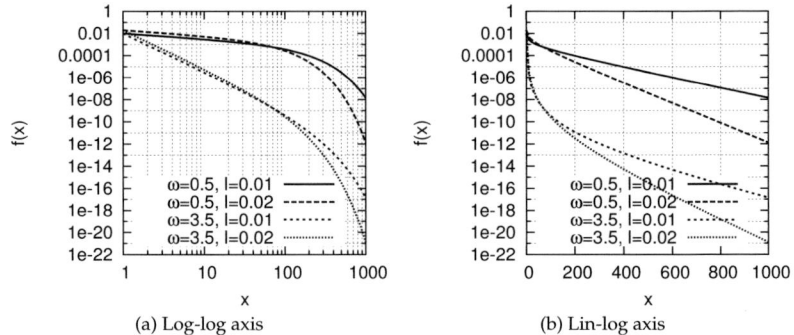

Figure 2.8 Power-law with exponential cutoff on log-log and lin-log axis.

Equation 2.12 is based on the so-called Hill estimator which is known to converge for large number of samples n, i.e. $\lim_{n \to \infty} \hat{\omega} = \omega$. While estimation of ω is comparably easy, estimating the point x_{min} where the power-law begins is more difficult. Clauset et al. describe in [50, Sec. 3.3] an iterative method based on the Kolmogorov-Smirnov test. Using

$$D = \max_{x \geq x_{min}} |S(x) - P(x)| \tag{2.13}$$

with $S(x)$ being defined as $P(X \leq x)$ of the real data (i.e. its CDF), and $P(x)$ defined as CDF of the power-law model that can fit the data best in the region $x \geq x_{min}$. The final estimate for x_{min} minimizes D. I.e. x_{min} defines the region where the power-law fits best.

2.3.2 Properties of Human Mobility

DTNs directly rely on the mobility of devices to perform the *carrying* part of store-carry-forward routing. Insight into mobility processes is therefore essential to understand the behavior of DTNs. In this section state of the art on modeling of mobility in the context of human behavior is presented.

Inter-Contact Time

Several works have analyzed mobility metrics, and found that the *inter-contact time* between pairs of devices has strong impact on DTN performance. Chaintreau et al. define inter-contact time as [43]: *"The time elapsed between two successive contact periods for a given pair of devices"*. Figure 2.9 gives a visual representation of inter-contact time between two devices. The inter-contact time is the timespan between the end of one contact phase and the beginning of the

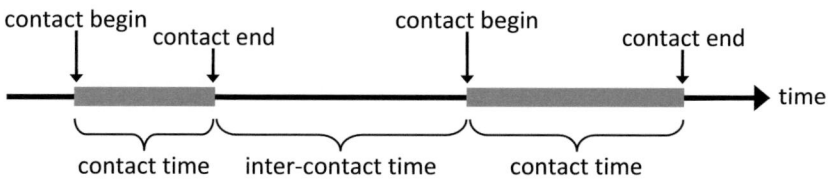

Figure 2.9 Visual representation of contact time, and inter-contact time.

next contact phase. More formally, given a pair of mobile devices (d, d') and a slotted time $t = 0, 1, \ldots$ the contact process $U_t^{(d,d')}$ can be defined [43] as

$$\left(U_t^{(d,d')} \right)_{t \geq 0} = \begin{cases} 1 & \text{if } d \text{ and } d' \text{ in contact at } t, \\ 0 & \text{else.} \end{cases} \tag{2.14}$$

Based on the times t where (d, d') are in contact, a sequence of time slots can be defined where $U_t^{(d,d')} = 1$:

$$T_0^{(d,d')} < \ldots < T_k^{(d,d')}. \tag{2.15}$$

The *inter-contact time* is defined [43] as the time between two successive contact phases $T_k^{(d,d')}$ and $T_{k+1}^{(d,d')}$ for the device pair (d, d') as

$$\tau_k^{(d,d')} = T_{k+1}^{(d,d')} - T_k^{(d,d')}. \tag{2.16}$$

The distribution $P(X = t)$ of inter-contact times is made up of all inter-contact time samples over all pairs $d \times d'$.

Power-law of Inter-Contact Times

The distribution made up of all pairwise inter-contact times has a special form that is characteristic for human mobility [43, 86, 136]: a power-law distribution. Chaintreau et al. [43] first discovered that the distribution of inter-contact times between humans follows an approximate power-law with parameter $\omega < 1$. This observation questions the validity of several mobility-models that have been used in research. E. g. the *Random Waypoint* model (see e. g. [26]) produces an exponential inter-contact times distribution [3, 88] that can e. g. be modeled through a Poisson processes [18].

The power-law in human inter-contact times can be best observed in the CCDF of inter-contact time distribution where it exhibits as straight line on log-log scale (cf. Section 2.3.1). Figure 2.10 shows such a representation of inter-contact time and contact time CCDF of four real-world experiments that

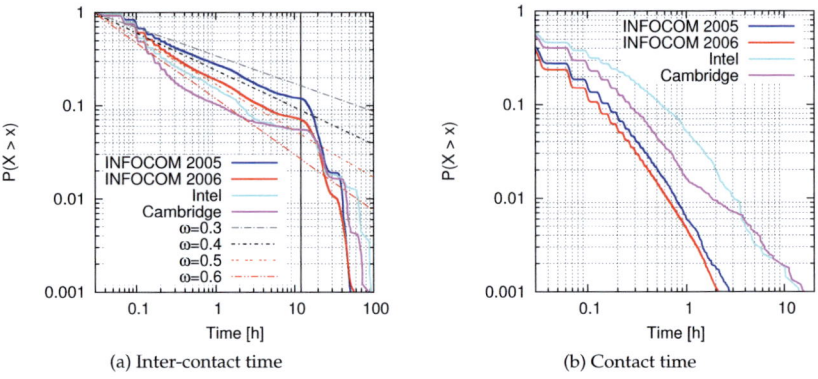

(a) Inter-contact time   (b) Contact time

Figure 2.10 Inter-contact time and contact time CCDF for real-world experiments [214–217]. The legend shows the name of the dataset.

have been carried out within the scope of the Haggle[5] project. Two of the experiments have been carried out in conference environments (datasets called INFOCOM 2005 [215], INFOCOM 2006 [217]), and two in daily work environments (datasets called Intel [216], Cambridge [214]). Participants have been given small Bluetooth devices that log contacts with other devices when in mutual wireless communication range. During the experiments—that lasted multiple days—the participants carried the devices so that contacts between the devices represent potential communication opportunities as well as human contacts in the sense that participants are, aware or unaware, geographically close within distance of a few meters.

Chaintreau et al. provide an analytical analysis of the performance of DTNs under different power-law slopes ω [43, Theorem 2]:

1. For $\omega > 2$ a simple algorithm—operating without knowledge about device movements, nor device contacts—achieves a delivery delay with finite mean using only one copy of a message.

2. For $1 < \omega < 2$ the 2-hop relaying algorithm [89] is not stable but can achieve a delay with finite mean by using $m > \frac{1}{\omega-1}$ relays that the message is replicated to, given a network with $\geq 2m = \frac{2}{\omega-1}$ devices.

3. For $\omega < 1$ not even flooding can achieve a delay with finite expectation.

In most real-world traces a slope of $\omega < 1$ has been observed, e. g. between $\omega \approx 0.3$ and $\omega \approx 0.6$ in the datasets shown in Figure 2.10a. This indicates that simple DTN protocols fail in these scenarios and protocols are required that

---

[5]http://www.cl.cam.ac.uk/research/srg/netos/haggle/

perform strategic forwarding/replication, e.g. using probabilities of device encounters based on historic observations. Only probabilistic delivery guarantees can be given under such scenarios, as the mean expectation of delivery delay is infinite.

Power-law and Exponential Decay of Inter-Contact Times

Shortly after Chaintreau et al. [43] published their findings on the power-law nature of inter-contact times in human traces, Karagiannis et al. found that inter-contact time follows a *combination* of power-law and exponential distribution [136]. They confirm the power-law nature of inter-contact times but further argue that this only holds true up to a timescale of about half a day. The remaining distribution of inter-contact times larger than half a day follows an exponential model. While the exponential drop is visually obvious, e.g. the vertical line at $x = 12\,h$ in Figure 2.10a, such a behavior can result from the finite time duration of the experiment so that probability of longer inter-contact time samples is artificially decreased. Karagiannis et al. showed, however, that the exponential drop is not an artifact of the experiment duration, but rather an inherent characteristic. This indicates that the analysis of forwarding algorithms in [43] may be overly pessimistic. To explain the effect of a combined distribution the authors argue that devices have specific locations to which they return regularly, e.g. their home or work location. Through analysis of traces the authors show that the *return time*—the probability of a device to return to a location—exhibits the same dichotomy of power-law with exponential decay found in inter-contact times. Further, the authors show that device contacts are mostly performed in a small number of geographic sites. Those two properties—return time of power-law with exponential decay, and regular device contacts at few geographic sites—are the basic properties that result in the inter-contact times being power-law with exponential cutoff. The analysis of return time is further interesting as it is generated by a single device and presents a more elementary property of human behavior than inter-contact time that is generated by pairs of devices.

In [43] it was shown that power-law inter-contact times result in infinite delivery delay in case $\omega < 1$. The analysis that the distribution turns exponential after a characteristic time eliminates this infinite delivery delay. Forwarding schemes that are based on the assumption of finite mean inter-contact time— e.g. throwboxes that are stationary devices acting as message exchange relays [261]—do not work under the model of [43] but work under the model of Karagiannis et al. [136].

Cai and Eun presented in [38, 39] further analysis of the anatomy of inter-contact time distributions. They e.g. found that the position of the drop between power-law and exponential decay results from the finite network area in which devices move, due to their finite movement speed.

2.3.3   Mobility Models for Human Behavior

Several mobility models have been proposed with the goal of reproducing human behavior. In the following, four popular mobility models are presented.

Random Waypoint with Hotspots: Abdulla and Simon showed analytically that the inter-contact time in Random Waypoint and Random Direction mobility models can be approximated using an exponential distribution [3]. Simulative validation is given in [4], where additionally a modified Random Waypoint mobility model is described that exhibits power-law and exponential decay inter-contact times. Devices have common pre-defined hotspots where they move with higher probability. Additionally, waiting times inside a hotspot are higher than outside.

Working Day Movement Model: Ekman et al. present in [73] a mobility model based upon a typical human working day. Each device initially selects a home location, and working places which are shared between devices. Based upon mobility sub-models—like home-activity model, office-activity model, evening-activity model, and transport model—the model provides intuitive human behavior and generates characteristic power-law and exponential decay inter-contact times.

SLAW: The *Self-similar Least-Action Walk* (SLAW) mobility model presented by Lee et al. [146] combines four features of human mobility found in real-world traces: truncated power-law flights and pause-times, heterogeneously bounded mobility areas, truncated power-law inter-contact times, and fractal waypoints. The authors show that those features are related to each other—e. g. that fractal waypoints induce power-law flights—and provide a mobility model that exhibits all four features. SLAW models social context among devices through common gathering places, and further expresses regular and spontaneous path patterns that have been observed in human mobility. SLAW first generates fractal waypoints and then power-law flights on top of them. Each device is given an individual walker model based on a subset of fractal waypoint clusters.

SWIM: Social behavior exhibits geographical clustering of devices [43]. *Small World in Motion* (SWIM) [142, 166] generates such small world behavior. SWIM segments the network area into square cells, with the diagonal of a cell being equal to the wireless transmission range. Two devices within the same cell are therewith sure to be able to communicate. Every device has an independent weighting for all cells, based on the distance from its randomly selected home location, and the number of devices that have been encountered within the respective cell. The next destination is chosen by random selection of a cell according to cell weights. One parameter $\alpha_{swim} \in [0, 1]$ allows to trade off the weighting of cells according to distance from home location, and number of devices that have been met in the cell. SWIM needs a longer warmup phase, as the cell weights need to stabilize over time into steady state, resulting in social clusters.

2.3.4 Markov Chains and Random Walks

Chapter 3 will use Random walk theory to analyze mobility on graphs, basic background is given in this section. The definitions for Markov chains and Random walks summarized in the following can be found in [158, 256].

A *Markov chain* is defined as set of states $S = \{s_1, \ldots, s_r\}$ and a probability matrix $P = (p_{ij})$. The chain initially starts in state s_i and moves to state s_j with transition probability p_{ij}. A probability distribution defined on S specifies the initial distribution probabilities of states $s_i \in S$. The next state s_{t+1} only depends on the current state s_t at time t, and not on prior states $s_{t-1}, s_{t-2}, \ldots$.

Using the vertices of a graph as states S, the Random walk on a graph can be defined as follows: Let $G = (V, E)$ be a graph with vertices V and edges E. A *Random walk* on G starts at vertex v_0 and moves to neighboring vertices in each step t. Being currently at vertex v_t at time t, the next vertex v_{t+1} is selected from the set of neighbors $n(v_t) = \{v_i \in V | (v_t, v_i) \in E\}$ with probability $\frac{1}{\deg(v_t)}$ uniformly at random. The function $\deg(v_t)$ gives the degree of v_t, i.e. the number of edges connected to v_t. The probability to move a vertex depends only on the number of neighboring vertices, and not on how the Random walk has reached v_t, i.e. the Random walk is *memory-less*. The sequence of vertices, or *states*, $(v_t : t = 0, 1, \ldots)$ is a Markov chain.

Let $P_t(i)$ be the probability of the Random walk residing on v_i at the t'th step, and A_G the $|V| \times |V|$ adjacency matrix that represents the graph G in binary $0/1$ form. The diagonal matrix $D = (d_{ii})$ with $d_{ii} = \frac{1}{\deg(v_i)}$ defines a matrix over all degrees of all vertices $v_i \in V$. The rule of the Random walk is defined as follows: Let $M = D \cdot A_G = (p_{ij})_{i,j \in V}$ be the transition probability matrix of the Random walk. The rule of the Random walk, i.e. moving from step t to step $t + 1$ is defined as $P_{t+1} = M^T P_t$, or $P_{t+1} = (M^T)^{t+1} P_0$. The vector P_0 describes the initial probability distribution over all vertices, and P_t describes the probability distribution over all vertices at time t. Note, that the sum of elements over P_t is always 1, i.e. the Random walk is defined to "exist" and sure to reside on one of the vertices V. Most importantly, if $P_t = P_{t-1}$ the Random walk has converged and the vector $\pi = P_t$ is called the *steady state distribution* of the Random walk. The steady state distribution assigns each vertex a probability that describes the relative frequency the Random walk will be on this vertex in the long run, based on the *Law of Large Numbers*. There can be none, one, or multiple steady-state distributions depending on the type of Random walk. If a steady state distribution is sure to exist—which is the case for Random walks in this thesis—one such distribution (although not necessarily unique) is, according to [158], always defined through $\pi_i = \frac{\deg(v_i)}{2|E|}$. Note, that the graphs in this thesis are defined to be symmetric, i. e. an edge introduces two degree points, one to each vertex it is attached to. Therewith, the overall sum of degrees over G is $2|E|$. The steady state distribution $\pi_i = \frac{\deg(v_i)}{2|E|}$ is therewith defined as the fraction of degrees $\deg(v_i)$ of vertex v_i, in relation to the overall $2|E|$ degrees of the graph.

2.4   Routing in Hybrid Networks

A hybrid network is a combination of an ad hoc network, and an infrastructure-based network. The infrastructure-based network is made up of wireless access, e. g. WiFi or cellular networks, that are interconnected through a backbone, e. g. the Internet. The ad-hoc network is made up of the mobile devices and ad-hoc communication links that are time-variant. Section 2.2.1 described delay/capacity scaling and the beneficial effect of hybrid networks in terms of interference and hop-count. In this section, protocols, architectures, and systems are described that support communication over hybrid networks. A comparison to the system developed in this thesis is given in Section 4.10.

2.4.1   Hybrid Routing Approaches

Seth et al. present in [91, 220, 221] the KioskNet architecture for Internet access in rural areas. Kiosks are stationary systems that provide delay tolerant Internet access through mechanical backhaul, e. g. a motorbike that commutes between the kiosks and the next city that provides an Internet uplink. The association of mobile devices to kiosks is reflected in a hierarchical addressing scheme, i. e. addressing of a device includes its stationary kiosk. If the responsible kiosk is unknown, messages are replicated to all kiosks. Kiosks store received messages until they are picked up by the destination device when it is in geographic proximity to the kiosk.

The MeDeHa framework [198–200] allows for communication over heterogeneous networks made up of different protocols, and integrates networks that are connected and disconnected. At the core MeDeHa uses a notification protocol. Neighborhood information is exchanged through this protocol to disseminate gateway information and build up routes to support communication with disconnected devices. For identifier-based addressing and support of mobility MeDeHa runs a location and lookup service, called HeNNA, inside the infrastructure part of the network.

Pitkänen et al. show in [192] how the strict association between a device and a WiFi access point can be relaxed to support communication if the association is short due to device mobility, or a device can not access an access point itself. With focus on web access, the authors relax the assumption that a HTTP request and response must be routed through the same path. DTN communication is used behind access points to provide connectivity for otherwise unconnected devices, either due to coverage, or non-authorization. Access points additionally support DTN routing and caching functionality. Different strategies are presented for routing HTTP replies back to the mobile device which might have moved, and is no longer associated with the access point the query was routed through. This reply routing is e. g. based on disseminating the reply to several access points within a geographic region.

2.4.2 Infrastructure Elements

Mobility of devices in DTNs results in temporal mismatch of contacts, i. e. devices miss a communication opportunity as they are in the same geographic place at different times. To increase contact opportunities, Zhao et al. [17, 19, 261] propose the deployment of stationary devices, called *throwboxes*, that act as message relays, and can be placed strategically. Compared to DTN devices that perform store-carry-forward, a throwbox performs only store and forward steps as it is stationary. For placing a limited number of throwboxes into an existing DTN the authors present optimization algorithms for calculating optimal placement. As example the authors show that by placing a single throwbox into a vehicular DTN [35] the network capacity can be increased, and delivery delay decreased heavily.

The work of Banerjee et al. provides a framework for comparison of elements for infrastructure enrichment [18]. Three infrastructure enrichments are presented: (1) Base stations that are all fully connected through an Internet infrastructure, (2) mesh nodes that are not connected to the Internet but connected to each other using a mesh topology and perform store-and-forward, and (3) static relays like throwboxes that make up for timely missed contacts, act as store-and-forward devices, but are not connected with each other. The authors show that when end-to-end delay can be reduced by a factor of 2 through addition of x base stations, the same reduction requires $2 \cdot x$ mesh nodes, or $5 \cdot x$ throwboxes.

2.4.3 Empirical Evaluation

Several works analyzed the impact of enriching DTNs with partial opportunistic infrastructure. Lindgren et al. [156] empirically studied how the integration of infrastructure changes the characteristics of the inter-contact time distribution. The authors show that, first, integration of infrastructure does not remove the power-law characteristic of the inter-contact time distribution, and second, infrastructure increases communication opportunities–and therewith DTN routing—significantly.

Hui et al. [122, 123] analyzed mobility traces by artificially introducing wireless access points that are connected through a backbone. They find a phase transition, i. e. the utility of additional access points decreases after a certain density. Evaluations show that pure DTN-based forwarding, and infrastructure-supported forwarding complement each other. To achieve the same performance with an infrastructure-based scenario alone, the amount of access points needs to be increased heavily, i. e. high coverage. In case of short-delay requirements a combination of DTN and infrastructure-supported network is required. In case long delay is acceptable, both pure DTN networks, and pure infrastructure-based networks can be deployed.

2.4.4 Infrastructure Offloading

DTNs can be used to offload infrastructure by routing messages over opportunistic mobile device contacts. Han et al. [98, 99] investigate the *target-set selection* problem for content dissemination. They present *MADNet*, a system for infrastructure offloading. Content is distributed from the infrastructure not to all devices, but only a subset, called the *target-set*. Devices in the target-set further disseminate the content to devices outside the target-set through opportunistic DTN communication. Compared to today's usage of sending content to all devices over cellular networks—i. e. all devices are in the target-set—cellular load decreases as the size of the target-set decreases. Different strategies for target-set selection are evaluation through simulations. The authors show that a greedy strategy, where the additional utility of adding a device to the target-set is evaluated, performs best.

Whitbeck et al. [253] follow a similar idea with *Push-and-Track*. Push-and-Track determines how many copies of a message should be disseminated from a central server to a subset of mobile devices, which devices to send the copies to, and when to send the copies. Devices receiving the content opportunistically disseminate it further through epidemic spreading in the DTN. Based on the elapsed TTL of a message, an objective function is used that determines replication strength. The authors find that strong replication of young messages is beneficial—similar to the finding of Burgess et al. [35]. Devices acknowledge the receipt of messages to the central server, which can then send the messages to devices that did not receive it through the DTN.

In contrast to cellular networks, WiFi provides cheaper communication in terms of operational cost, and energy cost for the mobile device. As WiFi coverage in urban cities is not yet comprehensive, delaying of data transfer requests until WiFi is available can offload cellular networks. Lee et al. study [147] how much traffic can be offloaded to WiFi networks under acceptance of different delay-tolerance. They find that already 65% of mobile data traffic is routed over WiFi networks today, as smartphones automatically switch to WiFi if available. By additionally accepting delay of several minutes or hours to wait for WiFi access, load in the cellular network can be further decreased. A similar study has been presented by Balasubramanian et al. [16] using vehicular DTNs. Additionally, the authors present mechanisms to quickly switch between 3G and WiFi, and vice versa.

2.4.5 DTN and MANET Integration

Several works proposed the integration of MANETs with DTNs. Chen et al. consider in [46] a hybrid scenario of connected MANET clusters, where communication between clusters is performed through delay tolerant message ferries. A single message ferry operates on a fixed route between clusters. Each cluster has a well-defined gateway device that performs communication with the ferry. When no MANET communication path inside a cluster can be established for a destination, this destination is assumed to be in a different cluster. In this case the message is sent to the cluster-specific gateway and stored until it is offloaded to the ferry. Every time the ferry comes into contact with a cluster gateway, messages with destination addresses inside this cluster are transferred to the gateway and sent over the cluster-specific MANET routing protocol.

Hybrid DTN and MANET Routing (HYMAD) [252] performs routing between disconnected clusters of devices. Within clusters MANET routing is employed, while DTN routing is used to connect clusters. HYMAD periodically broadcasts hop-distances, lists of messages, and information on whether a device is a border device that can connect to another cluster inside a cluster. This way, all devices in the same cluster are aware of all messages stored on any device of their cluster. A message with destination outside its cluster is routed through the DTN. The authors use Spray&Wait [228] (cf. Section 2.1.6) to distribute messages with one copy being given to each cluster that is encountered. Once the message counter in Spray&Wait reaches $c = 1$, the protocol waits until the correct destination cluster is encountered.

Ott, Kutscher, and Dwertmann present an integration of DTN with AODV MANET routing [186]. Based on the (non-)existence of an end-to-end path—determined with AODV—applications can decide whether to use DTN routing or not. Sending a message from a MANET to a DTN-reachable device is performed in two steps: First, AODV is used to perform an expanding ring search for the destination device. If the destination device is not found, each device in the MANET returns its applicability for DTN routing, and a quality metric that describes their applicability for routing the message towards its destination in the DTN. If the destination device is reachable through MANET routing, the sender device can directly employ the MANET for final delivery. If the destination device is not reachable, the message is routed to the MANET device with best applicability for routing in the DTN, and is then routed through the DTN towards the destination device.

2.5 Overlay Networks

End-systems exchange data over a network of communication links, routers, and gateways—commonly referred to as the *underlay*. Generally, such underlays perform routing based on the *Internet Protocol* (IP) [195]. IP has been designed as *overlay* for end-to-end communication upon heterogeneous layer 2 protocols. Upon the network layer, transport layer protocols are operated e. g. *Transmission Control Protocol* (TCP) [196], *User Datagram Protocol* [194], or *Stream Control Transmission Protocol* (SCTP) [235]. Such protocols allow for

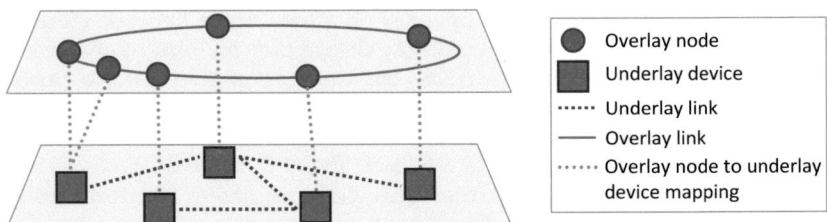

Figure 2.11 Underlay network and exemplary overlay network.

communication between two devices if a stable, and continuous end-to-end communication path exists in the underlay's routing layer.

Often, services require communication between a—static or dynamic—group of devices. Examples for such applications are instant messaging, file sharing, games, or video conferencing. Such groups of devices are often heterogeneous in their energy resources, communication links, protocols, and capabilities. To overcome heterogeneity in both underlay and device capabilities, *Overlay Networks* [159]—commonly referred to as *Overlays*—have been used to implement new functionality, and provide network abstractions. A broad range of services, functional, and non-functional properties can be implemented using overlays, ranging from routing, to data storage, over quality of service, and data distribution. Overlays can overcome protocol heterogeneity, and allow for scalability, robustness, and self-organization. Overlays build up *logical links* between participating devices using *structured*, or *unstructured* forms.

Figure 2.11 shows an exemplary underlay and overlay network. One or multiple *overlay nodes* can be deployed upon an underlay device. The structure of the overlay network and respective links are independent of the structure of the underlay. Therefore, overlay links are considered *logical*.

2.5.1   History of Overlay Networks

While the general idea of overlay networks has, e. g., been used in the IP protocol to overcome heterogeneous layer 2 protocols, overlay networks have been used as experimental tool for researching new protocols and mechanisms upon existing networks. Back in 1997 the DARPA-funded X-Bone project [243] was one of the first to propose the use of *virtual networks* that allowed to run different networks as overlays in parallel on top of a common IP underlay. X-Bone was designed as experimental facility for research on virtual networks and overlays. Individual overlay topologies allowed deployment of new and experimental mechanisms upon a shared common underlay through a level of abstraction, and to adapt to new topologies and requirements of services.

Other networks for flexible experiments based on virtual networks are e. g. the multicast network M-Bone [212], or the IPv6 testbed 6-Bone [1].

An important design principle of virtual networks—as defined in the X-Bone project [243]—is *recursion*. Recursion describes the fact that virtual networks can be run on top of other virtual networks without modifications, and without being aware of their virtual underlay. Furthermore, the principle of *concurrency* must allow to run multiple virtual networks in parallel upon the same underlay, and even allow devices to take part in multiple virtual networks in parallel, called *revisitation*. Finally, *security* of the virtual network can be decoupled from security of the underlay.

Overlay networks were originally never meant to be used as productive systems [53]. They were developed as experimental facility to research novel mechanisms that—once mature—would be built into the underlay directly. However, the complexity of integrating new mechanisms into widely deployed underlays and the flexibility provided by overlay networks resulted in strong growth of overlay-based systems.

2.5.2   Peer-to-Peer Networks

A special class of overlay networks are *Peer-to-Peer Networks* (P2P) [159]. Such networks are deployed purely upon end-systems—called *peers*—and provide services without costly infrastructure. Notably, peers contribute resources to the overall system, in contrast to client-server systems. The server-less architecture of P2P networks requires mechanisms for self-organization, as well as algorithms that allow them to work in a decentralized setting. P2P systems therefore pose several challenges in contrast to client-server systems [233]:

- Peers exhibit heterogeneous hardware, processing power, and network connectivity, amongst others.
- As peers are generally employed by end-users, they are subject to sudden leave and unexpected behavior, resulting in *churn*.
- As all peers have equal impact and responsibility, malicious or malfunctioning peers pose critical threats to the system.

End-systems participating in the P2P system are denoted peers, the virtual instances participating in the overlay structure and running the overlay protocol are called *nodes*. Every node owns a unique *Node IDentifier* (NodeID) that describes its identity. A peer can join the overlay with one or multiple nodes. Depending on whether the overlay protocol uses the NodeIDs to arrange nodes using a distance metric, or not, the resulting network is either called *unstructured overlay network*, or *structured overlay network* [233]. Figure 2.12 shows two overlay networks, one being structured using NodeIDs to build up a tree, and the other being unstructured. The following Sections 2.5.3 and 2.5.4 will describe protocols for structured, and unstructured overlays in more detail.

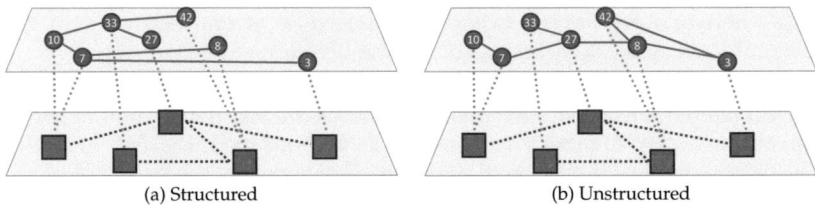

(a) Structured   (b) Unstructured

Figure 2.12 Structured overlay networks (left) build up a structure of nodes
based on their NodeID. In contrast, unstructured overlay networks (right) do not exhibit structure that resides on NodeIDs.

The concept of peers and nodes does not yet give information on the centralized or decentralized implementation of an overlay. Early P2P systems like
Napster [103] employed a central server for administrative tasks, as well as
search. Later systems showed a complete decentralized P2P design without
any central servers, e. g. Freenet [49], or KAD [232]. The KAD network is
one of most famous real-world deployments of structured overlay networks,
based upon the Kademlia [164] protocol. Furthermore, hybrid schemes such
as Gnutella2 [103] don't rely on central servers but rather select strong peers
that take over special administrative tasks, so called *super peers*.

2.5.3   Unstructured Overlay Networks

In unstructured overlay networks node identifiers are not used for structur-
ing of the topology. This, however, does not imply that unstructured overlay
networks don't exhibit a structure. E. g. the NICE [20] overlay protocol for
Application Layer Multicast (ALM) builds up a hierarchical clustering topology, but does not base the structure upon node identifiers. Rather, a metric
that takes latency measurements between nodes into account is used. Unstructured overlay networks can, on the one hand, not provide routing based
upon identifiers, but on the other hand, have a more stable structure that does
not depend on the node identifiers of nodes that join or leave the network.
Unstructured overlay networks are not of interest in this thesis, however, the
next section shortly describes the unstructured NICE overlay to make the difference of between structured and unstructured overlay networks clear.

2.5.3.1   NICE

NICE [20] was one of the first overlay protocols for scalable provisioning of
multicast upon the application layer, a concept called *Application Layer Multicast* (ALM). Traditional *IP Multicast* [61] requires support in the underlay—a
requirement that resulted in deployment issues [65], e. g, due to necessity for
provider trust. ALM can be deployed upon the application layer without
support from the underlay.

NICE clusters nodes that are "close" with respect to a latency metric. A cluster leader is elected based upon the graph-theoretic center with respect to latency within a cluster. If the number of nodes within a cluster exceeds $3k - 1$ the cluster is split into two clusters, based on design-time parameter k. Cluster leaders within the single clusters form a higher-layer cluster. This process of cluster splitting is continued recursively, i. e. higher layer clusters made up of cluster leaders are split again and a new cluster leader for the resulting cluster is elected. Data dissemination in NICE is based on forwarding the data to the cluster leader, and forwarding received data to cluster members. This way, a "wave"-like scheme is implemented that distributes multicast data to all nodes in the NICE overlay network.

The NICE protocol has been analyzed extensively, both in terms of behavior under bulk churn [20], as well as realistic real-world churn models [116].

2.5.4   Structured Overlay Networks

Structured overlay networks make use of NodeIDs to build up a structure through arrangement of nodes. Nodes are assigned NodeIDs—e. g. randomly generated 160 bit identifiers—that are used for addressing of nodes and that determine the position in the overlay topology. The use of structure in the overlay is key to a number of services that the overlay can provide, especially routing upon NodeIDs—called *Key-based Routing* (KBR)—or to determine responsibilities of nodes dependent on their NodeIDs for distributed data storage—called *Distributed Hash Tables* (DHT). KBR and DHT are both based on the principle of responsibility for an identifier-range, with respect to a node's own NodeID. Given a distance metric, a node is responsible for an identifier if its NodeID is closest to this identifier with respect to the given metric. While early systems such as Chord [238] did not differentiate between DHT and KBR, in this thesis the architectural view of [54] is used: KBR is an underlying routing mechanism, and DHT a key-value-store built upon KBR.

Structured overlay networks allow for efficient implementation of distributed storage through DHTs, with lookup time in $\mathcal{O}(\log N)$, N being the number of nodes in the overlay. In contrast, early systems for file sharing such as Napster implemented the file index through a central server. Next generation systems as Gnutella used flooding of keys in the complete network to locate files. To implement applications such as file-sharing through DHTs, file hashes or keywords are distributed and stored in the DHT, providing information which node in the network stores the actual file content. This decoupling through indirection enables that only key-value pairs need to be moved to other nodes in case of churn, but leave the actual file content on the node responsible for the key. Importantly, searching for files is implemented in logarithmic number of steps with respect to the network size.

2.5.4.1   Chord

A ring-based structure is built up through the *Chord* [238, 239] overlay protocol that arranges nodes in a clockwise circle with respect to their 128 bit NodeIDs; with circle wrap-around at 0 and $2^{128} - 1$. Originally, Chord was designed as DHT for storing key-value pairs, but can also be used to perform KBR functionality. Chord uses a linear distance metric to arrange nodes. NodeIDs are chosen through uniform hashing, e.g. by hashing the device's IP address. Each node in Chord manages a successor and a predecessor node which are numerically closest in the identifier space. For routing, each node stores a set of so-called *fingers* which form the *finger table*: Connections to further nodes in the overlay with NodeIDs in logarithmic distance to the node's own NodeID. The i'th finger of a node has a clockwise distance of 2^i.

KBR in Chord is based upon logarithmically distributed fingers. Sending a message to the identifier id_i is implemented by forwarding the message to the farthest finger with NodeID preceding id_i. The node where the finger points to is therewith a better suited node as it is closer to the node responsible for id_i. Depending on the routing mode, the node pointed to by the finger either forwards the message further (*recursive* mode), or returns the sender address information of the closer node (*iterative* mode). Through this mechanism, Chord can deliver messages in $\mathcal{O}(\log N)$ steps, with N being the number of nodes in the overlay.

For structured overlays to work efficiently, distribution of NodeIDs must be random at best. If this is not the case, and the distribution is skewed, runtime to locate a key can be higher. Having random NodeIDs, however, means that neighbors in the overlay are with high probability not close in the underlay, resulting in longer underlay routes. To cope with this problem, several approaches have been proposed to make underlay routes more efficient in structured overlay networks [104, 262].

2.5.4.2   Kademlia

The Kad network [231] is a real-world large-scale deployment of the *Kademlia* [164] structured overlay protocol in the eDonkey network. Kad has been subject to analysis in terms of churn [232], and resilience [250] and is one of the few large-scale overlay networks. The structured Kademlia protocol is based upon the *XOR metric* to define distance between NodeIDs. This is in contrast to, e.g., the Chord protocol which uses a linear distance metric to built up its structure of nodes. Similar to Chord, Kademlia allows to locate the node responsible for a certain key in $\mathcal{O}(\log N)$ steps. In contrast to Chord, Kademlia provides better resilience for Churn and failure of nodes, even if a large number of nodes fail concurrently.

Routing tables in Kademlia are made up of so-called *buckets*. A bucket is a list of NodeIDs (together with IP address and port), where each bucket defines a specific distance of all contained NodeIDs towards the local NodeID. Given a NodeID length of 128 bit, Kademlia manages at most 128 buckets, the exact number being a configuration parameter. Each bucket can hold up to k entries—therefore the buckets are often called *k-buckets*. The distance is defined as follows: If a NodeID resides in the n'th bucket, this NodeID has $n - 1$ common bits with the local NodeID, differing in the n'th bit with the local NodeID. Note, that NodeIDs appear in different buckets and redundancy is achieved depending on the value of k (e.g. $k = 20$ in [164]). Furthermore, *k-buckets* are kept sorted by the time a node has recently been contacted. This way the probability that entries at the top of a bucket are reachable is increased. Routing in Kademlia is based upon the *k-buckets*, contacting nodes which are closer to the destination key with respect to the XOR metric.

2.5.4.3 Pastry

Similar to Chord, the *Pastry* [211] protocol by Rowstron and Druschel builds up a ring-based structure of nodes with respect to their NodeIDs and wraparound at 0 and $2^{128} - 1$. Each node maintains three data structures used for routing: *LeafSet*, *RoutingTable*, and *NeighborhoodSet*. Neighboring nodes with numerically close NodeIDs are stored in the LeafSet. In contrast to e.g. Chord, Pastry is a symmetric protocol that stores nodes as neighbors whose NodeIDs are smaller or larger with respect to the local node's NodeID. The LeafSet has a size of e.g. 16 or 32 nodes. Pastry stores NodeIDs of physically closest NodeIDs in the NeighborhoodSet. Mechanisms for underlay measurement are required that are not part of the Pastry protocol. Rather, the authors suggest that the application should provide such underlay measurement functionality.

2.5.4.4 Internet Indirection Infrastructure

The original Internet architecture was developed for unicast end-to-end communication. This model poses several issues in the evolving Internet, e.g. integrating support for anycast, or mobility. Stoica et al. present in [237] the *Internet Indirection Infrastructure* (i3) that provides an abstraction of traditional communication using overlay-based indirection. i3 provides an abstraction in that sources send messages to an identifier rather than a destination IP address, and receivers register for messages sent to such identifiers. Such a registration is called *trigger* in the context of i3, follows a soft-state behavior, and therefore must be refreshed periodically by the receiver. Triggers can be evaluated strict, or with prefix-matching of an identifier—broadening the use cases of i3. The i3 scheme is heavily based on rendezvous mechanisms: i3 decouples senders from receivers and performs delivery through rendezvous identifiers. This way, senders must not be aware of e.g. the number of receivers, or their location—the same holds true for senders. A central role represent i3-servers that manage triggers, and perform matching of messages sent to an identifier with registered triggers. To deploy an i3 system scalable and perform efficient identifier matching, the authors use the Chord [239] overlay protocol that provides KBR functionality to implement a distributed version of an i3 server. Each node in Chord is responsible for a range of identifiers through the DHT. This mechanism is used to determine responsibility for administrating a specific trigger. A source, sending a message into i3, will deliver the messages through KBR to the responsible node that administrates the trigger. KBRs closest-match routing behavior allows for inexact identifiers to be delivered to the correct i3 server in Chord, which can then evaluate the prefix-matching locally. i3 does not store messages but just forwards them—providing a best-effort service similar to IP. In case nodes leave and join the overlay, i3 does not move state to new responsible nodes but employs soft-state for the triggers. i3 clients periodically refresh triggers, and i3 servers delete triggers if they are not refreshed within a deadline. Triggers that normally should be moved to another node when responsibilities change due to churn are deleted at timeout, and the periodic refresh reestablishes the triggers at the new responsible node.

2.5.4.5   Virtual Ring Routing

Based on the principle of KBR, Caesar et al. present in [37] the *Virtual Ring Routing* (VRR) protocol. In contrast to the indirection step taken by protocols such as Chord or Kademlia, VRR performs routing directly upon NodeIDs and does not require an underlay routing protocol such as IP. VRR can be directly implemented upon the link layer, with applicability mainly in the field of MANETs (cf. Section 2.1.1). Nodes are organized in a virtual ring with respect to their NodeIDs. Two routing tables are maintained: First, the *physical neighbor set* (pset) maintains the NodeIDs and MAC addresses of devices it can communicate with directly through the link layer. Second, VRR maintains routing tables for virtual neighbors on the ring—which are mostly not physical neighbors—in the *virtual neighbor set* (vset). Next hops for reaching virtual neighbors are stored as *vset-paths*. A vset-path identifies the local and remote vset-path's endpoint, as well as the next hop. Actual identifier-based routing is performed based on a distance metric. Therewith, no translation from NodeID to underlay identifier is required in VRR. Routing tables are maintained proactively in VRR, which is best suited for the KBR approach as traffic is not only generated locally, but messages can reach a node which has to forward it with respect to the closest virtual neighbor.

2.5.5   Frameworks for Creating Overlay-based Services

Several frameworks exist for development of overlay-based services. In the following, those frameworks are divided into *research-driven*, and *software-driven*. Research-driven frameworks introduce new concepts resulting from research work. The actual software library is therefore mainly a side-product and proof-of-concept. On the other hand, software-driven frameworks have the main goal of providing a fully-functional software library. They, however, often do not provide state-of-the-art algorithms from current research,

e. g. complete decentralization. Examples for research-driven frameworks are SATO [236], Hypercast [151], FreePastry [108], UIA [80], MACEDON [209], ProtoPeer [82], and Overlay Weaver [226]. Prominent examples for software-driven frameworks are JXTA [183], Microsoft's Peer-to-Peer API [169], or Cirrus [5] from Adobe.

In most cases the frameworks provide an abstraction layer to hide complexity of the underlay: Hypercast provides the concept of *overlay sockets* that hide all functionality related to the overlay structure and maintenance through an extension of the Berkeley socket interface. The SATO project has defined the *Ambient Service Interface* for hiding transport complexity in the underlay. An API similar to the *Common API* [54] is provided by Overlay Weaver. The concept of *peer groups* and *pipes* is introduced in JXTA [183]. A peer group represents a logical clustering of nodes, while a pipe provides a virtual communication channel concept that can distribute messages either in a unicast 1-to-1 style, or a multicast 1-to-n style. In terms of extensibility, the frameworks provide different concepts. For integration new overlay structures, Hypercast[183] allows to add new overlay socket types. Services like multicast can be added on top of FreePastry[183] and benefit from its connectivity features. An approach based on finite state machines is provided by MACEDON [209]. ProtoPeer [82] provides an abstraction environment to ease simulation, emulation, and real-world deployment. The abstraction covers important aspects such as time, and network abstraction. Overlay Weaver is a toolkit of loosely coupled tools, namely an emulator for distributed environments, scenario generator, overlay visualizer, and message counter [226].

With respect to functional properties, the frameworks differ much stronger: The basic service provided by all frameworks is end-to-end connectivity, however with different levels of support, especially in face of middleboxes, mobility, multihoming, and protocol heterogeneity. FreePastry, e. g., provides NAT traversal but no support for heterogeneous protocols. This assumption on homogeneous protocols is further adapted by MACEDON and Overlay Weaver. SATO provides some degree of heterogeneity support through the help of the NodeID architecture [8]. Support for heterogeneous protocols is provided by JXTA, UIA, and Hypercast; based on the assumption that an overlay structure can be built up, and messages are routed along the overlay. JXTA requires in practice accessibility to a central bootstrap server hosted in the public Internet, limiting flexibility and spontaneous deployment. All projects implementing an identifier/locator split naturally provide support for mobility. Not all overlay frameworks automatically detect mobility changes and do not necessarily repair connections, i. e. do not handle underlay changes but only simplify overlay development. In face of multihoming, SATO provides cross-layer information to support selection of access links.

Microsoft's P2P API is a software-driven project, but has influences from a research-driven project. Its origins can be assumed in the Pastry [211] protocol. While this is not officially stated by Microsoft, it can be assumed as the Distributed Routing Table sub-API contains the concept of *leaf-sets* which was introduced by Rowstron and Druschel in [211], funded by Microsoft.

2.6   Summary and Discussion

DTNs are a promising way to provide communication if infrastructure is not available, or to offload traffic from infrastructure networks. Performance of DTNs is directly dependent on mobility of devices. Understanding of mobility processes is important for development of protocols, their configuration, and deployment. While most mobility modeling approaches are performed on plain network areas where devices move on straight lines, in reality streets and buildings restrict mobility. While resulting contacts and inter-contacts are well understood, how restrictions impact mobility is insufficiently understood. Chapter 3 will analyze this impact by modeling possible movement paths as graphs, i. e. using street graphs of real-world cities, and synthetic grid-based graphs. In addition to simulative analysis of an underlying graph's impact, a formal analysis is performed based on Random walks, and spectral graph theory.

DTNs alone have limited applicability as their performance is bound by mobility of devices. E. g. in large geographic areas mobility becomes a limiting factor. Most often a certain degree of infrastructure access is available, e. g. through WiFi. In terms of delay/capacity scaling such hybrid networks are beneficial as they allow to overcome long distance through a wired backbone that does not generate wireless interference. Existing protocols and architectures to support hybrid networks have, however, limited applicability. They require additional information, e. g. on the geographic location of devices, or use central components that prevent scalability, and spontaneous and cost-efficient deployment. Chapter 4 will present the Hybrid Routing System that implements transparent hybrid routing through distributed overlay networks. Existing DTN protocols can be integrated, based on a novel categorization. The Hybrid Routing System can be used to collaboratively provide communication in face of few infrastructure access, e. g. in rural areas. In urban city scenarios where a large number of devices are infrastructure capable, the Hybrid Routing System can be used to offload traffic from infrastructure using DTN.

Development and deployment of a distributed system such as the Hybrid Routing System is complex. Available frameworks for overlay-based services are limited in their support of challenges such as mobility, multihoming, and heterogeneity. Chapter 5 presents a Framework for Overlay-based Services that provides seamless development and deployment of distributed services. While the framework has general applicability, it is used in this thesis as enabling platform for the Hybrid Routing System.

3. Mobility Modeling on Graphs

Devices in DTNs are in this thesis assumed to be carried by humans on a daily basis, e. g. smartphones. Such devices are exposed to the mobility of their human owner. This mobility has shown to be non-random in several analysis of real-world traces [43, 136, 208]. Routing protocols for DTNs exploit this non-randomness for building up routing state to perform strategic forwarding/replication of messages, as described in Section 2.1.6. It has been shown, that performance of DTNs is directly influenced by mobility, e. g. Chaintreau et al. [43] showed how the power-law slope of the *inter-contact time* between mobile devices has direct impact on the expected end-to-end delivery delay. The results have been confirmed through simulations by Rhee et al. who showed that inter-contact time directly affects performance of DTNs [207].

Modeling of the mobility process describes and analyzes the movement and contacts of mobile devices on a predefined area. While analytical works often use a circular network area for ease of modeling, simulations mainly use rectangular areas. Besides structure of the network area that bounds movement, movement paths can be further constrained by streets or buildings. Such restrictions can be modeled by an underlying graph that dictates possible movement paths, preventing arbitrary movement. While graph-based models have been used to analyze their impact on DTN *performance* [40, 242], an underlying graph actually impacts *mobility* of devices. Only in a second step this mobility impacts performance of networks, as devices in DTNs can only exchange messages when in mutual communication range. This direct impact of graph structure on mobility is insufficiently understood. Importance of graph-based mobility models has been recognized early: Camp et al. concluded in their well-cited survey on mobility models in 2002 that *"Fur-*

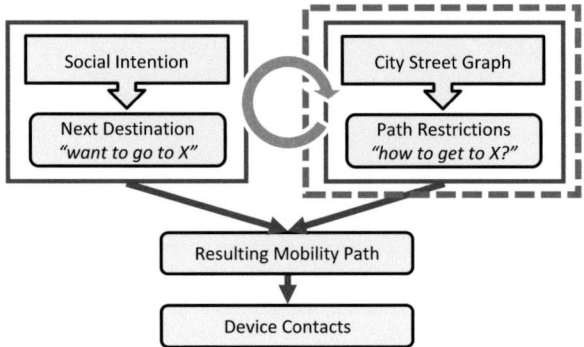

Figure 3.1 Generation of device contacts through social intention and movement restrictions of an underlying graph.

ther development of this model [graph-based mobility model] *(e. g., to use realistic city maps) is desired."* [40, p. 25]. However, there is insufficient insight on the impact of underlying graphs on mobility. This chapter is dedicated to this problem and will answer the question: *How do underlying graphs impact the mobility metric of inter-contact time under random and social mobility models?*

The reader is referred to Section 2.3 for an introduction to stochastic background, and state of the art in mobility modeling. This chapter is structured as follows: An introduction to the problem of graph impact on mobility is given in Section 3.1. Real-world city and grid-based graphs are presented in Section 3.2 that are used for analysis of mobility. Simulation of mobility on those graphs and model fitting of simulation data is presented in Section 3.3, and Section 3.4. As simulation alone does not provide insight into the properties of the graph that generates mobility behavior, Section 3.5 performs an analytical analysis of graph properties through Random walk theory. A correlation of simulative data and analytical models is given in Section 3.6. Summary and concluding remarks are given in Section 3.7.

The work on mobility modeling has been published in [163].

3.1   Impact of Graph Structure on Mobility

A large number of research evolved in the area of mobility modeling, based on the information that was gained from analysis of real-world traces. Chaintreau et al. [43] were the first to analyze the power-law characteristic of inter-contact times. Shortly after, Karagiannis et al. [136] showed that the distribution of inter-contact times not completely follows a power-law, but rather turns into an exponential distribution after a characteristic time of approximate half a day (cf. Section 2.3.2). Several mobility models have been pro-

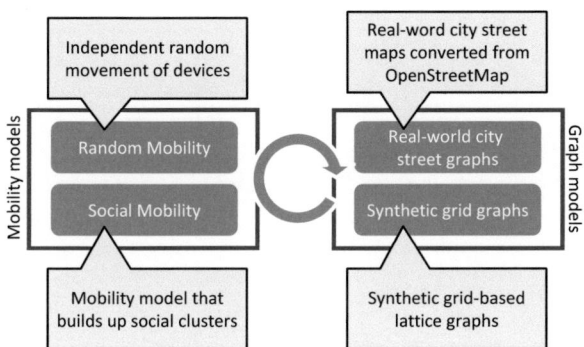

Figure 3.2 Mobility modeling approach based on two kinds of mobility models, and two types of graph sets.

posed that can generate the observed distributions by simulating social behavior of humans (cf. Section 2.3.3). Besides complex mobility models that emulate human behavior it was shown that very simple mobility models like Random walk can produce the characteristic of power-law and exponential decay, when performed on a graph structure such as a ring [136]: While a Random walk on an infinite line $\mathbb{Z}^1$ produces a power-law behavior for the probability of return at time t [256, p. 1], limiting the size of the line using a modulo operation to length k, i.e. Random walk on the modulo space $\mathbb{Z}^1/k\mathbb{Z}^1$, results in a mix of power-law and exponential decay [44, p. 4]. This indicates that the *underlying graph where devices move can strongly influence the mobility behavior*. While in a Random walk model the movement is directly determined by the vertex degree, the question arises how strong a social mobility model is influenced by an underlying graph.

Most analysis of mobility and proposed mobility models are based on *plain* network area where devices can move freely on straight lines towards their next destination. In reality, however, movement paths are restricted by the street graph of a city. There has been work to show the impact of different underlying graphs on performance of MANET and DTN routing protocols [40, 242], however, such protocol performance directly relies on mobility, while mobility relies on the underlying graph that restricts movement. Figure 3.1 characterizes the interplay of social intention and underlying graph used in this chapter: Social intention determines the next destination where the device wants to move to. The underlying graph restricts possible movement paths towards this destination. As this interplay is a per-device process, contacts between devices are a result of each device's social intention *and* the underlying graph that restricts both device's movement paths. This chapter

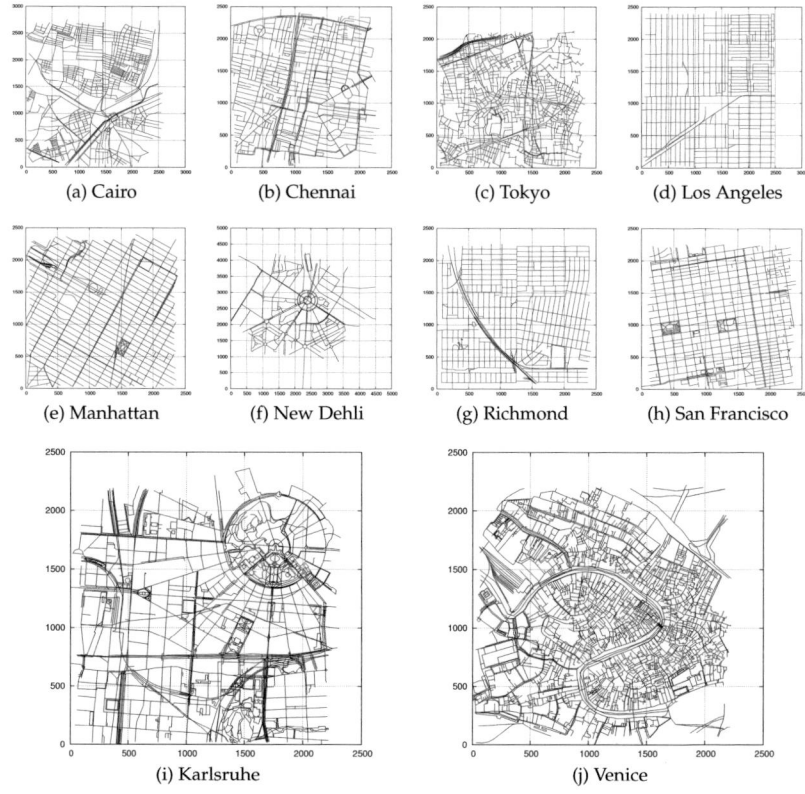

Figure 3.3 Analyzed city graphs based on 10 urban cities.

analyzes how different underlying graphs restrict movement of devices and impact the inter-contact times behavior.

In this chapter an analysis of mobility on graphs is performed, a methodology for correlating properties of the graph with properties of the resulting mobility developed, and analysis of real-world city graphs and synthetic grid-based graphs together with random and social mobility models performed. Figure 3.2 shows the combinations of graphs and mobility models used in this thesis: Real-world city maps of urban cities and synthetic grid-based graphs are used in combination with a social mobility model, and a random mobility model.

City	$|V|$	$|E|$	$L(E)$	$\varnothing L(e)$	$\varnothing \deg(v)$	τ	$1 - \lambda_2$
Cairo, Egypt	1 024	1 580	100 725 m	63 m	3.08	43 613	0.000648
Chennai, India	822	1 255	89 025 m	70 m	3.05	25 016	0.001153
Karlsruhe, Germany	2 902	4 853	129 352 m	26 m	3.34	47 311	0.000569
Los Angeles, CA, USA	480	775	92 624 m	119 m	3.22	10 125	0.002909
Manhattan, NY, USA	1 032	1 852	119 059 m	64 m	3.58	16 702	0.001651
New Dehli, India	387	590	59 814 m	101 m	3.04	6 635	0.004383
Richmond, VA, USA	569	927	80 895 m	87 m	3.25	14 592	0.001998
San Francisco, CA, USA	792	1 287	94 839 m	73 m	3.25	12 665	0.002200
Tokyo, Japan	1 888	2 577	81 661 m	31 m	2.72	32 672	0.000853
Venice, Italy	4 750	6 459	141 002 m	21 m	2.71	80 859	0.000324

Table 3.1 Graph metrics of analyzed city maps [163].

3.2 City and Grid-based Graphs

For analysis of the impact of underlying graphs on mobility, 10 metropolitan city graphs have been selected and converted from OpenStreetMap[1] data. Section A.10 describes the required conversion steps for simulation and analysis of the map data. An area of 2×2 km has been selected around the city center of each city graph to keep the spatial layout constant, and enable fair comparison. This area size is reasonable as movement to every destination is possible within time limit of few hours. The city graphs are shown in Figure 3.3, and graph metrics introduced during this chapter in Table 3.1. The spatial area of graphs is always 2×2 km, overall length of all edges is denoted $L(E)$, average length of edges $\varnothing L(e)$, average degree of vertices $\varnothing \deg()$, Random walk mixing time τ, and spectral gap $1 - \lambda_2$.

Cities have been selected to cover a large diversity of different graph structures of urban cities. There are mainly two types of cities [143]:

- *Planned* cities like Manhattan or Karlsruhe exhibit a well-defined structure that was planned early.

- *Unplanned* cities like Venice or Tokyo exhibit a more chaotic structure that evolved over time.

Interesting analysis of city graphs in terms of social behavior (like crime, or development of slums), and development of the city structure over time can be found in the work of Blanchard and Volchenkov [27, 246]. The New Dehli map in Figure 3.3f shows a most likely incomplete data set[2], however, it will be shown that regardless of this incompleteness the graph exhibits the same inherent properties in-line with the other cities.

A graph $G = (V, E)$ is modeled as follows: Street parts are edges $e_i \in E$ and street crossings are vertices $v_i \in V$. A complete street $s_t \in S$ is made

---

[1]http://www.openstreetmap.org
[2]OpenStreetMap is a community data mapping project with no guarantees on map completeness.

up of several street parts, modeled through a set of connected edges: $s_t = \{e_i, \ldots, e_j\} = \{(v_i, v_j), (v_j, v_k), \ldots, (v_x, v_y), (v_y, v_z)\}$. For simplicity, however, only individual street parts are modeled as the edges of a graph. The length of a street part (i. e. of an edge) is denoted $L(e_i)$, and the length of a complete street s_t as the sum of its edge lengths: $L(s_t) = \sum_{e_i \in s_t} L(e_i)$. Table 3.1 shows the summed and average lengths, as well as average vertex degree. Other metrics shown in Table 3.1 will be described later in this chapter.

Besides real-world city graphs, grid-based graphs are used in the following simulation and analysis. Note, that the spatial layout of all city and grid-based graphs used in this thesis is always 2×2 km. The difference between grid-based graphs is determined by the density of horizontal and vertical edges. A $k \times k$ grid is modeled through a graph $G = (V, E)$ with vertex set $V = \{1, \ldots, k\}^2$, and edge set $E = \{((i, j), (i', j')) : |i - i'| + |j - j'| = 1\}$, i. e. vertices are connected to their direct neighbors. Note, that edges at borders are not wrapped for simplicity, therewith the graphs are not completely regular. This non-regularity will be revisited later. In the following, a $k \times k$ grid is denoted *grid-id k*. As the spatial layout is 2×2 km, the distance between parallel edges in grid-id k is $2 \,\mathrm{km} / (k - 1)$.

3.3 Simulation

Simulation and analytical modeling approaches both have benefits and drawbacks: While analytical methods provide direct insight into a process, simulation enables analysis and easy variation of parameters that are complex to model. In this thesis analytical methods are used to gain insight into the impact of the underlying graph on mobility, and simulative approaches are used as they allow for detail. Such detail—that is complex to model but comparably easy to simulate—is e. g. the wireless communication range of mobile devices. While in an analytical Random walk model two devices are defined to be able to communicate when they reside on the same graph vertex, simulation allows the use of wireless communication range, i. e. two devices are defined to be able to communicate when they are within mutual communication range. Similarly, the spatial layout of a graph is not taken into account in an analytical modeling approach. While mobile devices in simulations have movement speed, and edges a specific length, such details make the analytical modeling approach overly complex. The combination of analytical methods and simulative approach allows the correlation of otherwise hidden characteristics, and—in focus of this chapter—enables to classify the impact of underlying graphs on the mobility of devices.

The analytical part is described in Section 3.5. In the following the simulative approach is described. Figure 3.2 shows an overview of the components in the simulative approach: Two mobility models are used for simulative evaluation, a random mobility model, and a social mobility model. While the social mobility model is used to describe human behavior and is of most importance in this thesis, the random mobility model allows to analyze border cases. Devices move towards their next destination at a uniformly distributed speed between 1–3 $\frac{m}{s}$, depicting human walking speed [78]. The effect of different movement speed is discussed in Section 3.7.

The metric of inter-contact time is of main interest, as conclusions on the performance of DTN protocols are available in literature, as described in Section 2.3.2. Simulation of two devices suffices in random mobility to gather inter-contact time samples, however 40 devices are used to gather more inter-contact time samples more quickly. Under social mobility, several devices are necessary as each device has in itself a different social behavior in relation to the other devices.

Random Mobility

In the random mobility model a device selects its next destination uniformly at random over the complete network area, i. e. an (x, y) coordinate that is uniformly at random with $x, y \in [0\,\text{km}, 2\,\text{km}]$ each. Based on the selected coordinate, a graph vertex is chosen that is closest to the geographic point in euclidean distance. Length-shortest paths are calculated over the graph towards the next destination, and movement speed selected uniformly at random out of the aforementioned 1–3 $\frac{m}{s}$. Selection of the next destination vertex based on the network area is performed to prevent bias in case a larger number of graph vertices lie spatially close. This is e. g. the case for rounded streets that are modeled through several small edges which are connected by a larger number of vertices.

Social Mobility

As social mobility model *Small World in Motion* (SWIM) [142, 166], described in Section 2.3.3, is used due to its ability to run on different graphs without manual configuration. SWIM is a state of the art mobility model that has been studied extensively by its authors and shown to generate realistic mobility behavior found in real-world traces. In contrast to mobility models such as [73], SWIM requires very few configuration. Especially, SWIM does not require configuration that is graph-dependent. Therefore, it can be applied to different underlying graphs. A configuration value of $\alpha_{\text{swim}} = 0$ is used as this generates the strongest power-law behavior in inter-contact times, and enables best analysis of the graph's impact. Parameters for generation of power-law waiting times are taken from recommendations in [166]: power-law slope of 1.45 with cut-off at 12 h.

Simulation Setup

Table 3.2 shows the simulation parameters. City maps described in Section 3.2 are simulated each with random, and with social mobility. Furthermore, grid-based graphs—as described in Section 3.2—are generated and, too, simulated with both random and social mobility models. All scenarios resulting

Category	Value
Mobile devices	$n = 40$
Movement speed	uniformly in $[1,3]$ $\frac{m}{s}$
Ad hoc comm. range	$r = 50\,\text{m}$
Social mobility model	SWIM [166], $\alpha_{\text{swim}} = 0$, wait-time slope 1.45, cutoff 12 h
Network area size	city and grid-based graphs, $A = 2 \times 2\,\text{km}$
Seeds per scenario	30
Simulation warmup	7 days
Simulation reporting	7 days

Table 3.2   Evaluation parameters for mobility simulation.

from these combinations are simulated each with 30 statistically independent seeds using a wireless communication range of 50 m. Simulations perform a warmup phase of 7 days where the social mobility model generates state, and the random mobility model reaches steady state distribution of devices on the graph. The next 7 days are used for actual measurement of contact and inter-contact behavior.

3.4   Model Fitting

The numeric inter-contact time distributions gathered through simulations are non-trivial to compare. Two fitting methods are used in the following for quantitative comparison of inter-contact time distributions for mobility on different graphs:

- To determine a good fit for the complete distribution and understand the evolution of parameters, least-square fitting is used. This is performed through a combination of power-law and exponential distribution, based upon the CCDF of inter-contact times. Goal of this fit is not in determining whether the distribution really is power-law, but rather to see the evolution of the distribution's shape.

- The first fitting method outputs parameters for a distribution made up of power-law and exponential part, but it does not give information whether the distribution really follows a power-law, i. e. whether it really is heavy-tailed. This is evaluated using a maximum likelihood estimator on the inter-contact time samples directly.

Least-square Fit Estimation

As described in Section 2.3.2, inter-contact times can be modeled through a combination of power-law and exponential distribution. In the random mobility model, a continuous shift from power-law to exponential can be observed, while in the social mobility model a more abrupt cut-off from power-law to exponential appears at about half a day. Two different functions are used for model fitting, called f_{random} for data generated by the random mobility model

$$f_{\text{random}}(x; a, b, c) \propto (a \cdot x)^{-b} \cdot e^{-c \cdot x}, \qquad (3.1)$$

and f_{social} for data generated by the social mobility model

$$f_{\text{social}}(x; a, b, c) \propto \begin{cases} (a \cdot x)^{-b} & \text{if } x < 12 \text{ hours} \\ e^{-c \cdot x} & \text{if } x \geq 12 \text{ hours.} \end{cases} \qquad (3.2)$$

The border of 12 hours has been chosen based on the work of Karagiannis et al. [136] who showed based on real-world traces that the exponential drop occurs at the order of half a day. Parameters a, b, and c describe *shift*, *power-law slope*, and *exponential drop*, respectively. Note, that the fitted power-law slope b does *not* give information on whether the distribution really follows a power-law and is heavy-tailed, this will be evaluated using a maximum likelihood estimator as described in the next paragraph. Parameter b can be different from actual power-law slope ω. Rather, least-square fitting in this section is used to analyze the evolution of the complete distribution.

For each combination of graph and mobility models a set of parameters $\{\hat{a}, \hat{b}, \hat{c}\}$ is estimated through least-squares fitting by minimizing the sum of squared errors between the fitted model, and the CCDF data. Goal is to find a configuration $\{\hat{a}, \hat{b}, \hat{c}\}$ so that the sum of squared residuals

$$S = \sum_{i=1}^{n} \rho_i^2 \qquad (3.3)$$

is minimized. Residual ρ_i is defined as difference between data value y_i and value $f(i; \hat{a}, \hat{b}, \hat{c})$ given by the estimated model $\{\hat{a}, \hat{b}, \hat{c}\}$, as

$$\rho_i = |y_i - f(i; \hat{a}, \hat{b}, \hat{c})|. \qquad (3.4)$$

Figure 3.4 shows estimations $\hat{a}$, $\hat{b}$, and $\hat{c}$ for grid-based graphs obtained using least-square fits. In all figures the x-axis shows the grid-id, and the y-axis show the estimated parameters. As first observation, the x-axis and y-axis show a correlation, as the evolution of the estimated values are of general continuous behavior. Main derivation of this continuous behavior is around $x = 40$ to $x = 50$, which will be discussed later.

Estimation $\hat{a}$ shown in Figure 3.4a shows general growth tendency with the grid-id on the x-axis for random mobility, and is comparably constant for social mobility. A larger value $\hat{a}$ shifts the inter-contact time distribution towards smaller values, resulting in decrease of all probabilities $P(X > x)$, and therewith shorter inter-contact times. However, the variation in $\hat{a}$ is small and does not impact inter-contact time behavior noteworthy. The most important

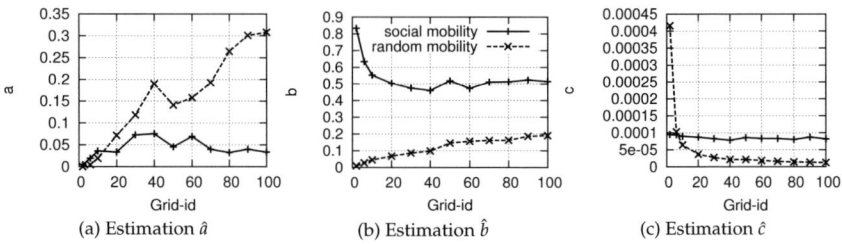

Figure 3.4 Least-square fits for grid-based graphs.

estimation $\hat{b}$—comparable to $\hat{\omega}$—shows a general correlation with the grid-id on the x-axis. $\hat{b}$ decreases until stabilization at around $x \approx 0.5$ for social mobility, while for random mobility $\hat{b}$ increases steadily, i. e. the underlying graph and mobility model impacts the slope of the power-law. An increasing value b makes the slope of the inter-contact time distribution steeper, increasing the probabilities of shorter inter-contact times. Estimation $\hat{c}$ is stable for social mobility, and initially falls quickly for random mobility. However, the actual values of $\hat{c}$ vary only slightly and are negligible in the actual inter-contact time distribution.

Transition from grid-id 40 to 50 is a characteristic point where the general continuous behavior of the estimated values is invalidated. From grid-id 40 on the grid becomes so dense that two devices on parallel edges are *nearly* in mutual wireless communication range. For all grid-ids > 40, devices really are in mutual wireless communication range when moving on parallel edges. So grid-id 40 is a worst case grid where movement has very *high path diversity*, but comparably *few contacts* between devices; compared to a grid-id > 40 with similar path diversity but much more contacts. This behavior can theoretically be observed at further grid-ids where wireless communication across different edges becomes possible. However, the actual derivation in values is relatively small and does not impact the inter-contact times noteworthy.

The estimations $\hat{a}$, $\hat{b}$, $\hat{c}$ for city graphs are shown in Figure 3.5. The ordering of city graphs on the x-axis is based on the graph's spectral gap that will be described in detail in Section 3.5. The value of $\hat{a}$ is overall very small and additionally behaves on a small range. However, the variance is higher for random mobility, and very stable for social mobility, which is in-line with the observation on grid-based graphs in Figure 3.4a. For estimation $\hat{b}$ and $\hat{c}$ a correlation with the given ordering of cities is visible for random mobility. The actual values $\hat{b}$ and $\hat{c}$ are within similar range compared to grid-based graphs. Estimate $\hat{b}$ is higher for social mobility than for random mobility over all graphs, i. e. stronger slope of inter-contact times CCDF. I. e. the probability

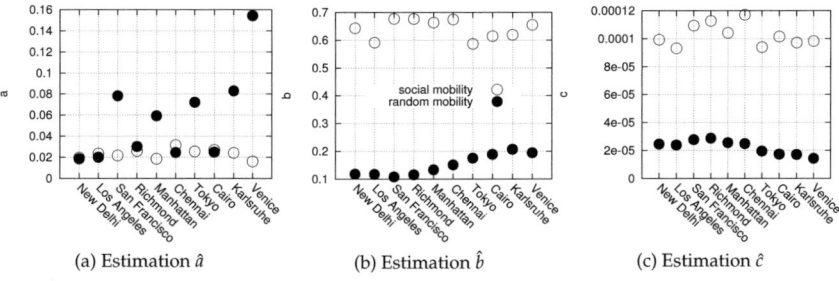

(a) Estimation $\hat{a}$ (b) Estimation $\hat{b}$ (c) Estimation $\hat{c}$

Figure 3.5 Least-square fits for city graphs.

of shorter inter-contact times is higher in social mobility, compared to random mobility. However, *relative* comparison of the values between city graphs on the same mobility model are marginal, indicating that city graphs are not diverse enough to impact inter-contact times within the same mobility model on the same graph model.

Power-law Maximum-Likelihood Estimation

While the prior method gives information on the complete distribution, it does not answer the question whether the data really follows a power-law, and if it does, what is the lower bound x_{min} and the exact power-law slope parameter ω, introduced in Section 2.3.1. The unit of x_{min} is given in minutes and is the smallest inter-contact sample so that the data set of all samples greater x_{min} exhibit a power-law behavior. The methodology of [50] is used[3] for determining the power-law slope through a maximum likelihood estimator, and determining x_{min} through the Kolmogorov-Smirnov test, as described in Section 2.3.1. The estimation is based on the inter-contact time data samples directly, in contrast to the least-square fit that is based on the CCDF distribution. The values of ω are in the following figures decreased by 1 to reflect the CCDF power-law slope comparable to the least-square fits (cf. the relation of power-law slope for PDF and CCDF in Section 2.3.1). The combination of power-law and exponential distribution found in inter-contact times is a special case of the family of power-law distributions. Therefore, the power-law estimation can be employed despite the mixed distribution [50, Sec. 5.2].

Figure 3.6 shows maximum likelihood estimations $\hat{x}_{min}$, and $\hat{\omega}$. Not all combinations of mobility model and graph really exhibit a power-law in inter-contact times. Data items that do not exhibit power-law behavior are not shown. For grid-based graphs the social mobility model exhibits a power-law for grid-id $\geq$ 10, and random mobility exhibits a power-law for grid-id

---

[3]Implementation from Adam Ginsburg available at https://code.google.com/p/agpy/wiki/PowerLaw is used that implements the methods from [50].

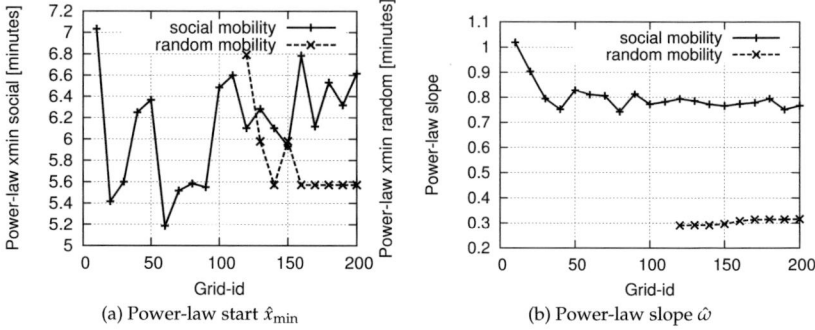

(a) Power-law start $\hat{x}_{min}$ (b) Power-law slope $\hat{\omega}$

Figure 3.6 Maximum-likelihood fits for grid-based graphs.

≥ 120. The power-law values in social mobility are in-line with characteristics found in real-world traces [43, 136]. Figure 3.6b shows that this behavior is irrespective of the underlying density of grid-based graphs. Random mobility shows a power-law for large grid-ids, i.e. high density, however the actual power-law slope $\hat{\omega}$ is small and the CCDF therefore shallow.

The evolution of x_{min} in Figure 3.6a does not correlate with the grid-id. However, the actual values on the y-axis behave in a comparably small range within 2 minutes, i.e. the inter-contact time samples on different graphs differ in a small range with respect to the beginning of the power-law behavior. This variation can be neglected when focusing on the overall inter-contact times distribution.

For social mobility the power-law slope $\hat{\omega}$ shown in Figure 3.6b has a general similar behavior compared to the least-square fit in Figure 3.5b. However, the actual values on the y-axis differ. *Within* one fitting methodology, the variation of the power-law slope between graphs is comparable, confirming the general difference in inter-contact time slope between grid-based graphs. The random mobility model does not generate noteworthy power-law behavior.

For city graphs, the maximum likelihood estimates $\hat{x}_{min}$ and $\hat{\omega}$ are shown in Figure 3.7, but only for social mobility, as random mobility never exhibits a power-law when run on city graphs. The Chennai graph is surprisingly the only city graph that does not exhibit power-law behavior, for reasons unknown. The value of x_{min} in Figure 3.7a differs between city graphs maximal 6 min and can—compared to the inter-contact time samples of hours and days—be neglected. The power-law slope $\hat{\omega}$ shown in Figure 3.7b varies within small range $\hat{\omega} \in [0.89, 0.99]$. For grid-based graphs a strong variation of $\hat{\omega}$ is observed when the grid becomes dense. Due to stability of power-law slope resulting from social behavior it can be argued that real-world city graphs are not diverse enough in structure to impact ω noteworthy. Inter-

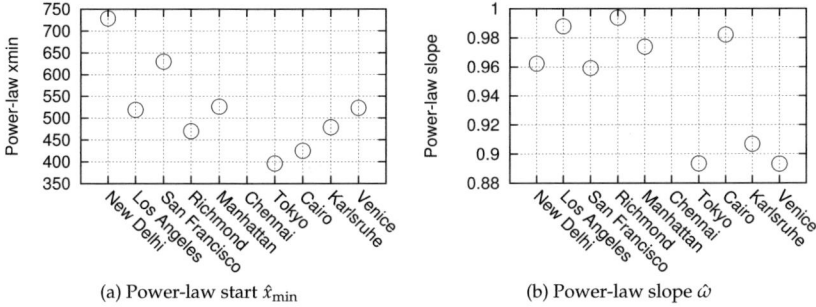

(a) Power-law start $\hat{x}_{min}$ (b) Power-law slope $\hat{\omega}$

Figure 3.7 Maximum-likelihood fits for city graphs.

contact time behavior mainly depends on the social mobility behavior. For evaluation of mobility and Delay Tolerant Networks on city graphs, the inter-contact times between different real-world cities are comparable.

3.5   Random Walks and Spectral Analysis

Goal of this thesis is to provide insight into the impact of underlying graphs on mobility. In Section 3.3 simulative analysis has been performed and fitting of simulation data to models described in Section 3.4. While simulations take into account communication range and speed of devices, i. e. the spatial layout of the graph, they do not provide insight into properties of the graph that generate the inter-contact time behavior. In this section an analytical approach based on spectral properties of the graph is performed. Goal is to derive a graph metric that provides a correlation with parameters of the inter-contact times distribution, and therewith gives direct insight into the properties of a graph that impacts mobility behavior. Both simulative and analytical results are finally correlated in Section 3.6.

Modeling Inter-contact Time in Random Walk

Random walk theory does not cover inter-contact times between pairs of walkers. However, conclusions about inter-contact time behavior are possible for regular graphs. As described by Grinstead and Snell [87, p.17], given a vertex $(0,0) \in V$ of a Random walk on $\mathbb{Z}^2$: *"The paths of two walkers in two dimensions who meet after n steps can be considered to be a single path that starts at (0, 0) and returns to (0, 0) after 2n steps. This means that the probability that two random walkers in two dimensions meet is the same as the probability that a single walker in two dimensions ever returns to the starting point"*. This is formalized in the following. Two definitions are necessary for the theorem:

- A graph is *regular*: $\forall v_i, v_j \in V : \deg(v_i) = k$, with k constant. The graph is called k-regular.

- The Random walk is *simple*: the transition probabilities only depend on the vertex degree, e. g. if the Random walk resides on v_i which has edges to v_j and v_k, the transition probability of the Random walk to move to v_j or v_k is $1/\deg(v_i)$, respectively.

Theorem 1. *Given a regular graph G, the probability that two independent simple Random walks X_t, Y_t on G that start at the same vertex v_i meet again after t steps at v_j equals the probability that a single Random walk starting at v_i returns to its origin v_i after 2t steps.*

Proof. Let X_t and Y_t be two independent simple Random walks, both residing at the same vertex v_i at time t. This means that the probabilities of X_t and Y_t to reside at v_i are equal: $P(X_t = v_i) = P(Y_t = v_i)$. Let G be regular and the Random walk simple, then holds that the transition probabilities are symmetric: $\forall x, y \in V$ with $(x, y) \in E$: $p(x, y) = p(y, x)$. This means that $p_t(x, y) \cdot p_t(x, y)$ can be written as $p_t(x, y) \cdot p_t(y, x)$, i. e. a Random walk that moves from x to y after t steps, and returns from y to x again after t steps. Therewith the Random walk has returned to x after $2t$ steps, i. e $P(X_{2t} = x)$, with same probability that X_t and Y_t meet after t steps.   □

Theorem 1 shows that on regular graphs the probability of inter-contact time at time t can be modeled as probability of return to a starting vertex at time $2t$. The synthetic grid-based graphs in this thesis are regular, but not at the borders of the grid. While vertices *inside* the graph have degree 4, vertices at the border of the graph have degree 3, and four vertices only have degree 2 which are in the four corners. Therewith the average vertex degree for grid-id k is[4] $\deg(k) = 4(k^2 - k)/k^2$, a function that converges quickly to 4, e. g. $\deg(k = 20) = 3.8$, $\deg(k = 100) = 3.96$. The deviation from a completely regular graph with wrapper borders is small and the non-regularity in a strict sense ignored in the following. For a regular graph the return time equals the number of vertices $|V|$, as described in [158]. For grid-id k the number of vertices is $|V| = k^2$. Therewith, the mean return time on grid-id k is k^2.

Spectral graph theory allows to analyze the Random walk in terms of the graphs *eigenstructure*, i. e. its eigenvalues and eigenvectors. Given a Random walk and steady state probability π, it holds that $\pi = (M^T)^t \cdot \pi$, i. e. π is the eigenvector to the eigenvalue 1. Further conclusions on the Random walk behavior on the graph in terms of its eigenvalues can be made. A correlation exists between steady state probability π, the eigenvalues λ_k, and the hitting times of the Random walk. The *hitting time* $H(s, u)$ is the expected number of steps the Random walk requires, starting at vertex s, to reach vertex u. Let

---

[4]Grid-id k has $k^2 - 2k - 2(k-2)$ vertices with degree 4, has $4(k-2)$ vertices with degree 3, and has 4 vertices with degree 2. Summing over all degrees and dividing by the overall number of vertices k^2 gives $4(k^2 - k)/k^2$.

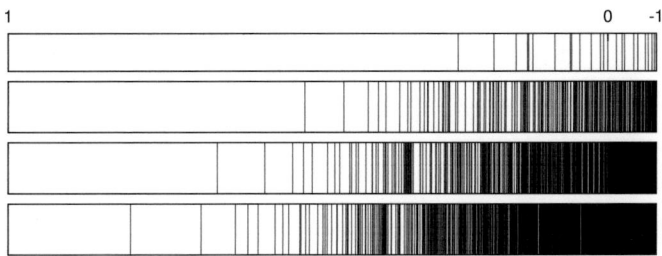

Figure 3.8 Eigenvalues of grid-based graphs with grid-id 10, 30, 50, 70 (top to bottom) shown on logarithmic scale [163].

$\Gamma(s)$ be the set of neighbors of vertex s, then $H(s, u)$ can be defined recursively as [158, p. 15]

$$H(s, u) = 1 + \frac{1}{\deg(s)} \sum_{w \in \Gamma(v_i)} H(w, u). \qquad (3.5)$$

The metric of hitting time provides a more general metric in comparison to return time. Note, that a graph with $|V|$ vertices has the same number of $|V|$ eigenvalues, each with an eigenvector of size $|V|$. The relation between hitting time and the eigenvalues of the graph is given through [158, p. 17]

$$\sum_u \pi(u) H(s, u) = \sum_{k=2}^{n} \frac{1}{1 - \lambda_k}. \qquad (3.6)$$

In this form the eigenvalues λ_k are normalized so that $-1 \leq \lambda_k \leq 1$, with $\lambda_1 = 1$. Eigenvalues are calculated as follows: Let A_G be the adjacency matrix of the graph G and D the diagonal matrix with $(D)_{ii} = 1/\deg(i)$. Define $N = D^{1/2} A_G D^{1/2} = D^{-1/2} M D^{1/2}$. The matrix N has the same eigenvalues as $M = D A_G$ (that was introduced above as probability transition matrix of the Random walk) but is symmetric and its eigenvalues real. From the Perron-Frobenius theorem it follows that the eigenvalues are in the range: $1 = \lambda_1 \geq \lambda_2 \geq \ldots \geq \lambda_n \geq -1$. It can be seen that λ_2 in the denominator of Equation 3.6 has strongest impact on the sum, and therewith is of most importance. This eigenvalue λ_2 bounds the other eigenvalues and therewith gives conclusions on the eigenstructure of the graph which is used to draw conclusions about the Random walk behavior.

Figure 3.8 shows the eigenvalues of four grid-based graphs with different grid densities on log-scale. Each vertical impulse defines the position of one eigenvalue λ_i. The leftmost impulse that is smaller 1 is the value of the second largest eigenvalue λ_2 that bounds the other eigenvalues, and the leftmost

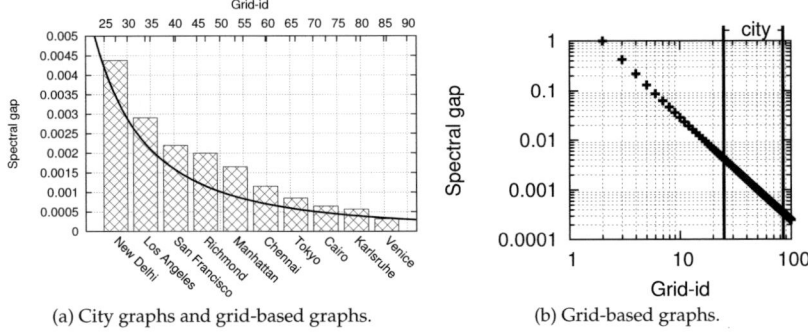

(a) City graphs and grid-based graphs.   (b) Grid-based graphs.

Figure 3.9 Spectral gap for grid-based graphs and city graphs [163].

white space the *spectral gap*, defined as $1 - \lambda_2$. The evolution of the spectral gap for grid-based graphs and city graphs is shown in Figure 3.9. Spectral gap for grid-based graphs is based on grid-id shown as continuous curve in Figure 3.9a, aligned to $x2$-axis. Real-world city graphs are shown as bars in Figure 3.9a, aligned to $x1$-axis. The $x1$-axis and $x2$-axis in Figure 3.9a have been manually aligned. Figure 3.9b shows the spectral gap for grid-based graphs based on grid-id and log-log scales for diverse grid densities. The two vertical lines indicate the borders of the area where spectral gaps of city graphs are. Intuitively, the spectral gap defines how the number of closed paths increases as the path length tends to infinity [160], i.e. a smaller spectral gap results in more closed paths for a given path length.

The city graphs in Figure 3.9a are ordered with respect to decreasing spectral gap, which is the ordering used in prior figures in this chapter. For grid-based graphs, high density of the grid results in a small spectral gap. With respect to the grid-id, the spectral gap falls very fast like a power-law, i.e. the path diversity increases quickly.

For correlating properties of the graphs with inter-contact time of the mobility, the line of arguments is as follows:

1. Inter-contact time can be described as return time on regular graphs where transition probabilities are equal over all vertices. While the real-world graphs used in this thesis are not completely regular the variation of overall degree is small as described above. Section 3.6 will show that a correlation emerges.

2. The hitting time of the Random walk describes the expected number of steps, starting from v_s until v_t is reached. In this step the probability information is lost and therewith only mean inter-contact time can be modeled, i.e. the expected number of steps until two independent Ran-

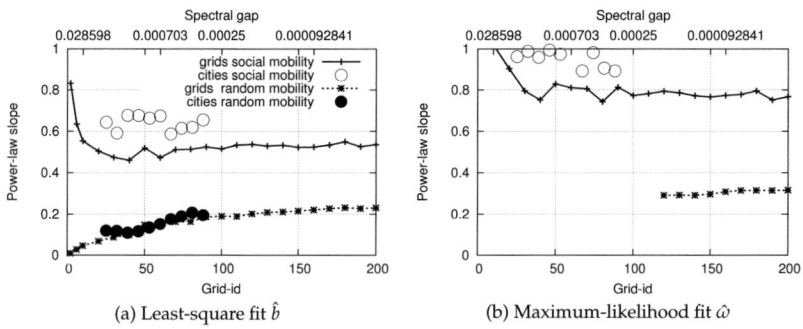

(a) Least-square fit $\hat{b}$ (b) Maximum-likelihood fit $\hat{\omega}$

Figure 3.10 Correlation of spectral gap with power-law slope for least-square fit and maximum-likelihood fit [163].

dom walkers meet. Section 3.6 will show that this mean determines the shape of the distribution and can be used to correlate with the power-law slope of inter-contact time.

3. The eigenstructure of the graph is correlated with the hitting time. Therewith conclusions on the mobility inter-contact behavior in terms of the graphs eigenvalues can be made. Specifically, the second largest eigenvalue λ_2 has strongest impact on hitting times.

3.6 Correlation

Based on the spectral gap—that has been identified in the prior Section 3.5 as important graph metric for mobility—correlations are in the following identified with the fitted models from Section 3.4. Figure 3.9 shows the ordering of graphs with respect to decreasing spectral gap. A higher path diversity generally results in a smaller spectral gap. As the spatial layout of graphs is fixed, more and shorter streets result in smaller spectral gap. For grid-based graphs this ordering equals an increasing grid-id, for city graphs the ordering is New Dehli, Los Angeles, San Francisco, Richmond, Manhattan, Chennai, Tokyo, Cairo, Karlsruhe, Venice. It is intuitive that Venice has the smallest spectral gap due to large number of short streets and the resulting high diversity in movement paths.

Correlation with Inter-Contact Time

Figure 3.10 shows a complete correlation of previously shown data of the inter-contact time power-law slope with the spectral gap for city and grid-based graphs, both for the random and social mobility models. Missing combinations in Figure 3.10b do not exhibit a power-law behavior. Ordering is based on the spectral gap shown in Figure 3.9. Power-law slope b obtained using least-square fit is shown in Figure 3.10a, and ω using maximum-likelihood fit in Figure 3.10b. The x-axis of both Figure 3.10a and Figure 3.10b uses the grid-id of graphs which has been aligned with the $x2$-axis for the corresponding spectral gap. Circles are city graphs which have been aligned with respect to their spectral gap to the $x2$-axis. For the maximum-likelihood fit in Figure 3.10b only combinations of graph and mobility model are shown that actually exhibit power-law behavior. The general tendencies in both figures are comparable, especially the behavior in the power-law slope for random mobility on grid-based graphs. Focusing on the y-axis and $x2$-axis which relate the power-law slope and spectral gap, a correlation can be observed for all combinations of graph model and mobility model except social mobility on city graphs. In this case the social intention is stronger than the forced mobility behavior resulting from the underlying graph.

Correlation with Number of Contacts

While inter-contact time and the power-law slope have important impact on DTN routing performance, as described in Section 2.3.2, the *number of contacts* is of importance, too, especially for finding multi-hop paths in a DTN. While inter-contact time is based on pairs of devices, the number of contacts analyzed in the following counts the number of contacts that a device encounters per hour in average. Figure 3.11 shows the average number of contacts per hour per device, based on successfully built up wireless ad hoc associations. Again, the ordering of graphs is based on the spectral gap, both for grid-based graphs and city graphs. Figure 3.11a shows a decrease in contacts for increasing grid density. Recall that Section 3.5 stated that the spectral gap describes how the number of closed paths increases as the path length turns to infinity. As movement paths of devices becomes more diverse, the number of contacts with other devices decrease. Again, this decrease is until grid-id 40 where path diversity is high but distance between parallel edges prevents communication. For grid-id 50 the number of contacts is disproportional higher with respect to the slightly higher path diversity, compared to grid-id 40.

The number of contacts on city graphs are shown in Figure 3.11b. No correlation with spectral-gap is observed and the number of contacts relatively stable. The general increase of contacts from random to social mobility results from geographical social clustering where devices reside for longer duration. Generally, the graph impacts number of contacts strongly, as shown for grid-based graphs. Again, city graphs are not diverse enough to further impact the number of contacts.

3.7   Summary and Conclusion

While DTNs provide cheap communication, they open up a new dimension of complexity due to non-deterministic mobility of devices. Human mobility

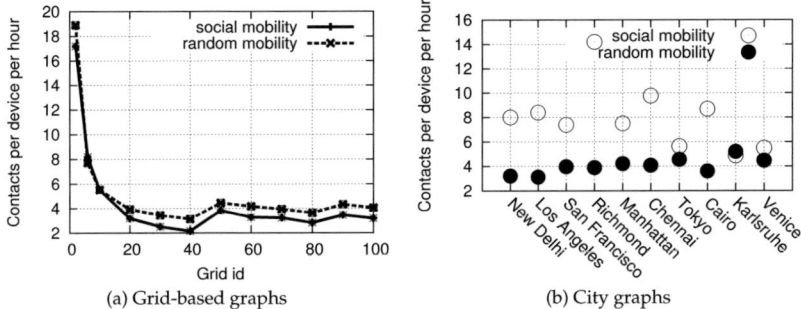

(a) Grid-based graphs   (b) City graphs

Figure 3.11 Average number of contacts per hour for grid-based graphs and city graphs.

is not random, which enables DTN protocols to build up routing state and perform strategic forwarding. Social intention dictates a persons next destination. Movement towards this destination is restricted by the underlying network area, its structure, and spatial layout. This chapter analyzed the impact of such underlying restrictions on mobility using graphs, and developed a correlation based on the graph's spectral gap.

The following conclusions can be drawn from the analysis in this chapter:

- The graph structure has strong impact on the mobility metric of inter-contact time. Graph structure can be analyzed in terms of the spectral gap that provides a correlation with the most important parameters of the inter-contact time distribution, especially with its power-law slope.

- Grid-based graphs strongly impact inter-contact times in social and random mobility over diverse grid densities.

- Real-world city maps—and their resulting street graphs—exhibit no sufficient difference in structure to influence the power-law slope of inter-contact times for a social mobility model.

Diverse street maps have been used in this thesis. They are, however, not diverse enough to impact social mobility. This analysis supports the assumption of Rhee et al. who stated in [207] that *"these tendencies [in mobility] are likely caused by human intentions in deciding travel directions ... but not by geographical constraints such as roads ..."*. While an underlying graph generally *does* impact mobility, this impact is equal over graph structures of real-world city maps under social mobility. This conclusion is important for development and configuration of DTNs in human-centric environments.

The model developed in this chapter has limitations which were introduced to limit complexity. First, the graph structure does not take obstacles like buildings into account. Those limit wireless communication and therewith impact the number of contacts and inter-contact times. Second, the movement speed of devices has been defined as human walking speed. Higher movement speed on the one hand result in shorter inter-contact times and higher number of contacts. However, due to a finite bandwidth model, too short contacts can not be used to build up a communication association, or only allow for very limited message exchange. Both aspects are interesting to analyze in future work. For the aspect of obstacles, this can be modeled into the graph structure directly, i. e. taking reduced wireless communication into account by arranging the graph edges. This allows to use the presented evaluation methodology by performing a first graph preprocessing step. For the second aspect of movement speed, it can be assumed that higher movement speed is not realistic with today's wireless technology to build up ad hoc communications. Therewith, mainly lower movement speed is of interest that results in a generally lower number of contacts. However, it can be assumed that the general trends in inter-contact times and number of contacts observed in this chapter will remain valid.

4. Hybrid Routing System

Delay Tolerant Networks can provide end-to-end communication without infrastructure support at the cost of increased delay and probabilistic delivery guarantees. In reality, however, a mix of infrastructure-based and mobile DTN-based networks exist. Both networks are reality today, however their usage is different: Infrastructure-based networks are the prevailing communication form today, while DTNs are used in a handful of experimental deployments [68, 77, 91, 153, 188, 227]. Generally, the large number of mobile devices like smartphones carried by humans on a daily basis—7 billion expected 2015 [47]—make mobile ad hoc communication opportunities reality today. Those opportunities are, however, not used for DTN communication, i. e. opportunistic device-to-device contacts do exist, they are, however, not used for deploying networks.

Infrastructure-based communication and DTN-based communication both represent extremes, as they either *only* make use of infrastructure, or *only* make use of opportunistic device-to-device communication. The integration of both network types has empirically shown beneficial, as it can enrich DTN communication [122, 123, 156], and offload infrastructure-based networks [98, 99, 253]. Furthermore, such integration is beneficial for wireless interference over pure ad hoc networks in terms of delay/capacity scaling, as described in Section 2.2.1. Actual integration of infrastructure-based and opportunistic DTN-based networks is, however, complex due to different paradigms; e. g. for routing of messages.

This chapter presents the design and architecture of the *Hybrid Routing System* (HRS) that allows for cooperative routing in mixed DTN and infrastructure networks, called *hybrid networks*. On the one hand, HRS can boost DTN

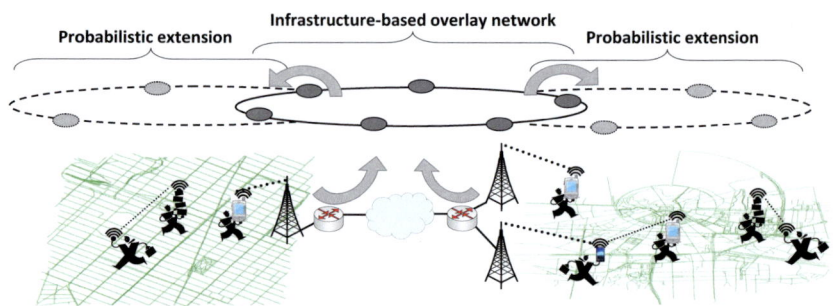

Figure 4.1 Hybrid Routing System as probabilistic extension of overlay-based communication into DTNs. Arrows indicate dissemination of routing information.

routing performance through the help of infrastructure-capable devices, and enable routing in large, or even partitioned and distant geographic areas. On the other hand, HRS can offload infrastructure networks by routing messages preferably in infrastructure-less DTNs.

HRS builds upon a cooperative approach, based on the principles of decentralization and self-organization, without relying on central servers. This allows to deploy HRS flexibly and spontaneously. The main idea of HRS is to extend the reach of overlay-based communication into DTNs by announcing DTN contact information in the overlay, as shown in Figure 4.1.

This chapter is structured as follows: Problem statement and requirements for hybrid routing are discussed in Section 4.1. Section 4.2 presents a model for hybrid networks that is used in this chapter. For integrating DTN protocols through a generic approach, a categorization of DTN protocols suitable for hybrid routing is presented in Section 4.3. The architecture of HRS is described in Section 4.4, before DTN-specific and overlay-specific protocols are described in Section 4.5 and Section 4.6, respectively. HRS provides a generic system for integrating existing DTN protocols of a wide range, which is shown in Section 4.7. Section 4.8 describes how two important use cases can be implemented with HRS: providing communication with few infrastructure, and offloading infrastructure networks through DTNs. Extensive evaluation of HRS is presented in Section 4.9 with focus on the two use cases. The design of HRS is reviewed in Section 4.10 and compared to related work. Section 4.11 summarizes and concludes this chapter.

4.1   Problem Statement and Requirements

DTNs can support communication of mobile devices within a limited geographic area. The network in this area can be defined as "one DTN" if mobility of devices allows for communication through store-carry-forward routing. As mobility is geographically bounded and movement speed limited, DTNs can only work within certain geographic extent and on longer time-scales of delay tolerance. Such limitations prevent widespread applicability of DTNs. In reality, however, infrastructure access is often available at least to a subset of participating devices, e. g. cellular or WiFi access. Empirical analysis has shown that incorporating partial infrastructure access can strongly boost performance of DTNs [122, 123, 156]. However, integration of opportunistic DTNs with infrastructure networks faces several challenges:

Routing DTN protocols for non-deterministic networks are based on opportunistic hop-by-hop routing decisions. In contrast, infrastructure-based networks use link-state, or distance-vector protocols to establish and maintain end-to-end links. Integrating the two routing paradigms is non-trivial: Link-state or distance-vector protocols can not be deployed in DTNs, as described in Section 2.1.3. Deploying opportunistic protocols in infrastructure-based networks results in unacceptable performance due to route instability.

Addressing In infrastructure-based networks, addressing is hierarchical and directly suites the routing process by forwarding messages towards the address-encoded destination network. In DTNs the network graph evolves over time and its instability prevents hierarchical routing. More stable higher-layer structures such as social graphs have been used in DTNs [120]. Most often, however, a flat addressing scheme is applicable for opportunistic DTNs that decouples the device identities from the network structure.

Mobility Wireless ranges are shorter for ad hoc than for infrastructure-based communication, i. e. few 10 m for ad hoc wireless vs. several 100 m for infrastructure-based wireless, resulting in shorter contact durations. Additionally, in DTNs both wireless transceivers are mobile, resulting in more challenging duration and prediction of contacts[1].

Gateways Mobility results in the need for dual-stacked *gateways* that translate between DTN routing and infrastructure-based routing. While gateways can be explicitly deployed through static infrastructure [77, 91], the use of opportunistic gateways through mobile devices themselves—that are DTN-capable *and* infrastructure-capable—allows for more flexibility and self-organizing in hybrid networks.

---

[1]Assuming a plain network area and equally distributed movement angles, shorter contact durations arise when both devices are mobile, compared to one devices being static—i. e. infrastructure—and one mobile. This can be modeled through an equilateral triangle under constant movement speed. If movement directions are within $60°$, distance is kept less or equal over time, than if one device was static. Given movement direction of one device, chances that the second devices moves within $60°$ left or right are $\frac{2 \cdot 60°}{360°} = 33\%$, i. e. DTN wireless links are of shorter duration 66% of times, not event taking into account the shorter range of wireless ad hoc communication.

After problems of integrating infrastructure-based and DTN-based networks, in the following requirements for a hybrid routing system are described.

Unicast End-to-End Routing While multicast and concast communication received considerable attention, still end-to-end unicast communication is the predominant paradigm in today's communication networks. A system for hybrid routing must support end-to-end unicast communication between all participating mobile devices.

Stable Flat Addressing Each device must have a stable identifier that does not change with device mobility. The identifier must be flat and not encode network structure, geographic region, or gateway association.

Heterogeneous Infrastructure Capabilities Mobile devices have heterogeneous infrastructure capabilities. While some devices may have continuous infrastructure access, others may not be able to access infrastructure at all, or only at times. Irrespective of such infrastructure capabilities a hybrid routing system must allow for communication between all pairs of sender/destination devices.

Transparency of Destination Sending a message must be possible with knowledge of the destination device's identifier alone. Information such as geographic area, mobility patterns, current gateway, or infrastructure capabilities must not be required.

Geographic Scale DTNs only work on comparably small geographic scale due to delay introduced by carrying of messages through mobility. Integration of infrastructure enables geographic shortcuts. A system for hybrid routing must make use of infrastructure-based shortcuts to overcome long distance. This enables coupling of geographically remote, or strongly clustered DTNs.

Cooperative Routing Devices in DTNs are cooperative by design and carry messages—sent by, and destined for—other devices. In face of heterogeneous infrastructure access, cooperativeness must be used to establish end-to-end routing, e. g. by sending messages into the infrastructure network on behalf of a device that is not infrastructure-capable.

Opportunistic Mobile Gateways Devices in a DTN are mobile and reduce the duration of contact association for cooperative devices, e. g. providing infrastructure access for another device. Gateway devices must be used in opportunistic ways, both for sending messages to the infrastructure, and receiving messages from the infrastructure. Similar to DTN protocols that route messages towards devices that are more likely to encounter the destination device, messages can be routed towards devices more likely to encounter infrastructure access.

Decentralized, Autonomous, and Scalable To allow spontaneous and flexible deployment, a system for hybrid routing must be decentralized and autonomous. No central unit must be required to configure or control the system, rather, new devices must be integrated into the system in a self-organizing way. Similarly, new infrastructure opportunities must be integrated autonomously. A potentially large number of devices must be supported and the system be scalable.

Generic Applicability The system must not present a point-solution that can only be deployed for one specific DTN protocol. A large number of DTN protocols have been developed [7, 14, 35, 36, 59, 74, 119, 120, 154, 176, 179, 228, 229, 259], all with focus on specific scenarios and environments. At best, the system for hybrid routing must be applicable for a defined category of DTN protocols.

4.2 Network Model

In this section a model for hybrid networks is introduced. A formalism is described that is used in the categorization of DTN protocols in Section 4.3, and later for description of algorithms.

- **Device:** A mobile device is defined d_i, and the set of mobile devices $\mathcal{D}$. A device is exposed to mobility of its human owner.

- **Identifier:** Device d_i has a stable identifier id_i. The identifier has a length of e. g. 128 bit or 160 bit, is flat in its structure and has no semantics. Two devices must not share the same identifier. Generation of identifiers can be random, by hashing of e. g. d_i's MAC address, or cryptographically[2].

- **Message:** Every device d_i has a local process that generates messages m_{ij}. The message's destination device d_j is selected uniformly at random over all devices in the network. Every message has a *Time-to-Live* (TTL) counter that is initialized on message creation. A message is deleted when its TTL expired. Upon replication of a message the value of its TTL counter is copied.

- **Device-to-Device Communication:** Two devices d_i and d_j can exchange messages when in mutual communication range r. Communication range is modeled through the Unit Disk Model [125] that provides an abstraction of wireless channel characteristics and medium access. A device can only take part in one device-to-device communication at a time. The number of messages exchanged depends on the bandwidth, message size, and contact duration. If devices move out of mutual communication range during exchange of a message, the exchange failed and transmitted data is deleted.

- **Copy Mode:** After transferring a message, the copy mode decides how the sending device handles the sent message. In *single-copy* mode the

---

[2]Due to the large identifier space the probability of collision is small. Ensuring collision-free identifiers is out of scope of this thesis.

sending device locally deletes the message, i. e. forwarding. In *multi-copy* mode the sending devices keeps a copy of the message, i. e. replication. In multi-copy mode two copies of the same message result after the message transfer.

- **Device Queue:** Device d_i has a local message queue q_i for storing messages not destined for d_i. Queues are modeled as infinite in this thesis to prevent replacement effects, and to analyze queue size requirements.

- **Infrastructure:** Communication infrastructure provides wireless access to a communication backbone. Devices in communication range of wireless infrastructure can communicate using IP over the backbone.

- **Infrastructure Access:** Devices have different capabilities for infrastructure access. *Permanent* infrastructure access denotes devices that have continuous access to infrastructure. *Temporary* infrastructure access depends on current geographic location and availability of wireless access in this location. Finally, devices can be *not capable* of access infrastructure at all.

- **Infrastructure Access Classes:** Devices $\mathcal{D}$ are classified with respect to their infrastructure access class as $\mathcal{D}_p$ for devices with *permanent* access, $\mathcal{D}_t$ for devices with *temporary* access, and $\mathcal{D}_n$ for devices that are *not* capable of infrastructure access. The probability of a device to be assigned to one of those classed is denoted $P(\mathcal{D}_p)$, $P(\mathcal{D}_t)$, and $P(\mathcal{D}_n)$, respectively. It holds $P(\mathcal{D}_p) + P(\mathcal{D}_t) + P(\mathcal{D}_n) = 1$.

Network Model: A set of devices $d_i, d_j, \ldots \in \mathcal{D}$ with identifiers $id_i, id_j, \ldots$ move on a network area A. Every device $d_i \in \mathcal{D}$ generates messages m_{ij} destined for other devices $d_j \in \mathcal{D} \backslash d_i$. When in mutual communication range r two devices can exchange a limited number of messages. Messages are either deleted on the sending devices, or replicated, called single-copy or multi-copy mode. Device d_i has a local message queue q_i for storing messages not destined for itself. When connected to the infrastructure a device can communicate with all other infrastructure-connected devices. Access to infrastructure depends on capabilities of a device.

Steps in Hybrid Routing: Figure 4.2 shows an exemplary hybrid DTN network. In the most general case of routing, message m_{ak} is generated by d_a and destined for d_k ($d_a, d_k \in \mathcal{D}_n$). The hybrid routing process requires the following three steps:

(a) *Routing in the source DTN towards the infrastructure:* Forwarding m_{ak} from d_a by DTN routing to a device that has, or is likely to encounter, infrastructure access (e. g. over d_b to d_c).

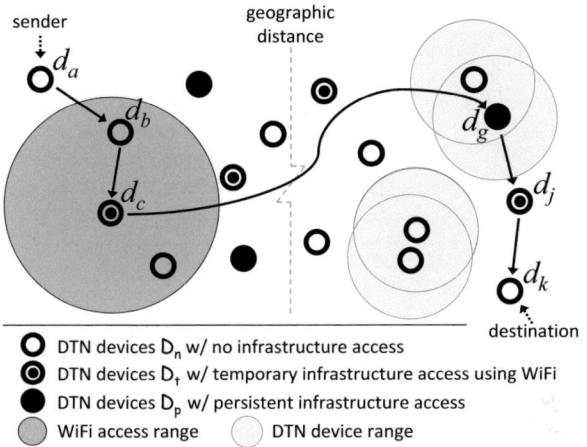

Figure 4.2 Topology of a hybrid network made of up devices from different infrastructure-capability classes, and infrastructure access.

(b) *Routing in the infrastructure:* Forwarding m_{ak} across the infrastructure-based network from d_c to a device with current infrastructure access (e. g. d_g). This device must have a good probability of forwarding the message towards the destination device d_k.

(c) *Routing in the destination DTN towards the destination device:* Forwarding m_{ak} by DTN routing through d_j to the destination device d_k.

By implementing the routing steps (a)–(c) hybrid DTNs can overcome large distance by using infrastructure, i. e. in step (b) of the presented example. Note, that d_a is required to only know the identifier id_k of d_k, neither its geographic location, social cluster, nor infrastructure capability class. While d_a itself does not have infrastructure access, there might exist a multi-hop path that includes infrastructure.

4.3 Categorization of DTN Protocols

Numerous DTN protocols exist that have been developed for specific use cases and environments. A hybrid routing design that can be employed with a larger set of DTN protocols is preferred, allowing the DTN protocol that works best in a given scenario to be employed. However, the different mechanisms that DTN protocols use make a completely generic solution unlikely. Goal of this section is to develop a categorization of DTN protocols that is suitable for hybrid routing, and determine the best suited category. Existing categorizations are described in Section 4.3.1 and analyzed for their applicability for hybrid routing. In Section 4.3.2 a novel categorization is presented that is specifically designed for hybrid routing.

Work	Categorization
Balasubramanian et al. [14, 15]	Storage, bandwidth, routing
Burns et al. [36]	Structure in movement, control of devices
Chaintreau et al. [42]	Stateful vs. stateless
Jones et al. [133]	Replication and knowledge
Nelson et al. [179]	Forwarding and replication
Yuan et al. [258]	Mobile resource, opportunity, prediction
Zhang [259]	Epidemic, history, model, control, coding

Table 4.1 Existing categorizations for DTN protocols.

4.3.1 Existing Categorizations

Often newly proposed DTN protocols come with their own categorization to describe the integration of the new protocol into the set of existing protocols. Table 4.1 gives an overview of existing categorizations for DTN protocols.

Stateful vs. stateless: Chaintreau et al. analyze in [42] the characteristics of real-world contact traces and perform a theoretical study of DTN performance. They differentiate between *stateful* and *stateless* DTN protocols. Stateful protocols collect contact information and infer patterns that are used to predict contacts and route messages. In contrast, stateless protocols do not collect historical data and do not try to infer future events from historical data. Rather, such protocols perform (limited) replication, or apply utility functions to evaluate the benefit of message replication.

Structure in movement, control of devices: Burns et al. [36] focus on vehicles like buses that run on predefined routes. Such devices expose *structure in movement* that can be exploited by a routing algorithm. In contrast, devices which underlie *control* of users, like taxi cabs, are on the other side of extremes. Their movement does not exhibit structure in movement, but can be controlled up to a certain degree.

Epidemic, history, model, control, coding: Zhang [259] provides an extensive survey of DTN protocols. The main categorization is based on *deterministic* vs. *stochastic* routing. The important branch of stochastic protocols is further divided into epidemic, history, model control, and coding. This categorization was used in Section 2.1.5 to given an overview of DTN protocols.

Replication and knowledge: Jones et al. [133] categorize DTN protocols based on *replication* and *knowledge*. *Replication* is further divided into direct-delivery, two-hop relaying, tree-based flooding, and epidemic routing. The *knowledge* category is refined through location-based routing, gradient routing, and metrics of the communication link.

Storage, bandwidth, routing: Balasubramanian et al. [14, 15] categorize DTN protocols with respect to storage, bandwidth, and routing. For storage a differentiation is made of infinite vs. finite device queues. Exchange of messages between two devices is either limited in bandwidth, or unlimited. The routing strategy is classified as replication-based, or forwarding-based; i. e. multi-copy vs. single-copy.

Forwarding and replication: Nelson et al. [179] present a categorization based on number of replicas in the network: *forwarding-based*, and *replication-based*; i. e. single-copy vs. multi-copy.

Mobile resource, opportunity, prediction: Yuan et al. classify in [258] DTN protocols as: *mobile resource-based, opportunity-based*, and *prediction-based*. Protocols in the mobile resource-based category are e. g. data mules that can be controlled and directed to pick up data at specific geographic locations. Opportunity-based protocols work on opportunistic and unscheduled basis. Prediction-based protocols calculate deterministic future contacts, e. g. satellite communication networks.

While existing categorizations have eligibility for the respective works, they are not applicable to the problem of hybrid routing. Especially, they to not exhibit information on the applicability of a device for routing towards another device that could be announced in the infrastructure. This applicability is called *awareness* in the following. A collaborative hybrid routing approach must distribute this awareness information in the infrastructure-part of the network to enable selection of good devices as *proxies* for routing from infrastructure back to DTN.

4.3.2   Categorization for Hybrid Routing

The categorization presented in this thesis for hybrid routing is based on two main ideas: First, the structure of routing information that the DTN protocol maintains, and second, how this routing information is employed in the DTN protocol. DTN protocols are categorized as

- *Destination-aware,*
- *Self-aware,* and
- *Unaware.*

Figure 4.3 illustrates the different categories: Destination-aware protocols maintain destination-specific information, self-aware protocols maintain information about their own general applicability, and unaware protocols route messages based on metadata stored in the messages themselves.

Destination-aware

Protocols categorized as Destination-aware use routing information to decide how well-suited a device is for routing *towards a specific destination device.* Information is gathered locally on device encounters, possibly taking indirect device encounters through a third device—i. e. transitivity—into account. Information is *aged* as a device becomes less valuable over time, and *refreshed* upon new device contacts. Prophet [154] is a well-known Destination-

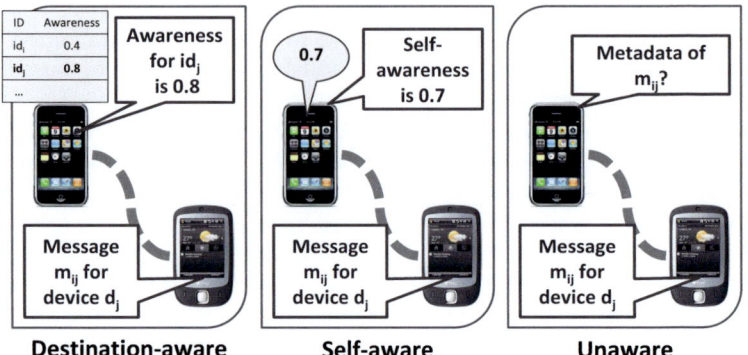

Destination-aware   **Self-aware**   **Unaware**

Figure 4.3 Illustration of the categorization based on awareness.

Category	Description, exemplary protocols
Destination-aware	Device-specific awareness
	Prophet [154], MaxProp [35], Spray&Focus [229], FRESH [69], EASE [90], SEPR [240], NECTAR [59], David et al. [58], CAR [178], RAPID [15]
Self-aware SimBet [55],	Local awareness of device
	Label [119], Bubble [120], PeopleRank [176], EBR [179], MobySpace [150]
Unaware	Forward/replicate message based on metadata
	Spray&Wait [228], RAPID [15], Epidemic [244], Random (Epidemic), Direct Delivery

Table 4.2 Categories with exemplary DTN protocols.

aware routing protocol that builds up probabilities of future device encounters based on historical observation.

Self-aware

Self-aware protocols evaluate the *applicability of a device as forwarder in general*, irrespective of the message's destination. SimBet [55] e. g. locally manages a device-specific rating out of social similarity and betweenness. Similar, EBR [179] uses a locally computed encounter-rate that reflects how frequently the device comes into contact with other devices.

Unaware

The third class of Unaware protocols does not evaluate forwarding quality of devices, but rather performs (limited) *flooding* [228, 244], or *replication on a per-message utility* [15].

Some protocols such as RAPID [15] implement multiple categories. Depending on the metric employed, RAPID is categorized as Destination-aware, or Unaware. Table 4.2 shows exemplary DTN protocols for each category. Building upon the network model from Section 4.2, the categories can be formally defined as follows:

- **Destination-aware:** Every device $d_i \in \mathcal{D}$ manages a table

$$\mathcal{T}_i = \{(id_j, p_i(d_j)), (id_k, p_i(d_k)), (id_l, p_i(d_l)), \ldots\}$$

  for devices $d_j, d_k, d_l, \ldots$ it has come into direct or transitive contact. The *destination-awareness* $p_i(d_j) \in [0, 1)$ reflects the applicability of d_i for forwarding a message to d_j, with $d_i \neq d_j$. For $d_i = d_j$ the destination-awareness is defined $p_i(d_i) = 1$, i.e. the awareness for a device itself is complete and therewith 1.

- **Self-aware:** Each device $d_i \in \mathcal{D}$ locally manages the *self-awareness* p_i that reflects the general applicability of d_i for forwarding messages, irrespective of the message's destination.

- **Unaware:** Each message m_{ij} with sender d_i and destination d_j stores a counter c that reflects the number of replicas allowed for m. Forwarding is based on metadata in m, e.g. replication counter c or TTL counter, irrespective of any awareness.

The DTN routing process can be defined for each category in simplified form:

Definition 1. *Routing m_{ij} from d_i to d_j using DTN is a recursive process based on store-carry-forward. Message m_{ij} carried by d_s is forwarded/replicated to d_t if $d_t = d_j$, or*
- *Destination-aware: $p_t(d_j) > p_s(d_j)$,*
- *Self-aware: $p_t > p_s$,*
- *Unaware: $c > 1$.*

Note, that this is an abstract definition that does not take additional protocol-specific mechanisms into account, but provides a simple way to describe the basic idea behind the proposed categorization and the mechanism of each category. In Table 4.3 exemplary DTN protocols are shown with respective routing information used. This verbally described routing information requires a formalism for actual integration, which is described for exemplary Destination-aware protocols in the following.

An important goal of hybrid routing is to efficiently route messages into the current destination device's geographic area using infrastructure, as described in Section 4.2. To implement this routing step a device needs to be found

Category	Protocol	Information
	Prophet [154]	future encounter probability
Destination-aware	MaxProp [35]	normalized relative encounter
	Spray&Focus [229]	time elapsed since encounter
	PeopleRank [176]	rank in social network
Self-aware	SimBet [55]	similarity/betweenness
	EBR [179]	frequency of device encounters
	Spray&Wait [228]	initial $c > 1$
Unaware	Epidemic [244]	initial $c = \infty$
	Random Epidemic	randomly per contact $c \in \{1, 2\}$
	Direct Delivery	initial $c = 1$

Table 4.3 Categories with exemplary DTN protocols as well as information used for routing.

and selected that is currently reachable through the infrastructure *and* provides good forwarding possibilities to the message's destination device, i. e. a device with a high destination-awareness for the message's destination device. Destination-aware protocols exhibit a strong advantage over self-aware and unaware protocols, since even in case of strong clustering—like remote cities—destination-aware protocols implicitly encode geographic information: iff $p_i(d_j) > 0$, then a time-space path existed between devices d_i and d_j. This further means that d_i and d_j are located in the same geographic area with probability depending on $p_i(d_j)$. If d_i gets connected to the infrastructure network, announcing its applicability for routing to d_j with respect to $p_i(d_j)$, enables other infrastructure-capable *and* potentially geographically remote devices to forward messages with destination d_j to d_i. This is not possible in self-aware and unaware protocols as they do not encode destination-specific information. Destination-aware protocols are used in the remainder of this chapter to implement hybrid routing with focus on unicast communication.

The three exemplary Destination-aware DTN protocols Prophet, MaxProp, and Spray&Focus, shown in Table 4.3, are in the following described from a technical perspective and their mapping to destination-awareness presented. Description of the basic protocols themselves can be found in Section 2.1.6. Table 4.4 shows the mapping for the three protocols from internal data structures towards destination-awareness.

Prophet Prophet [154] maintains encounter probabilities $P_{(i,j)}$ locally on each device. On first device-to-device contact between d_i and d_j the encounter probability is initialized using $P_{(i,j)} = P_{\text{init}} \in (0,1]$ on d_i, and using $P_{(j,i)} = P_{\text{init}} \in (0,1]$ on d_j, respectively. On future encounters the encounter probability is updated through $P_{(i,j)} = P_{(i,j)\text{old}} + (1 - P_{(i,j)\text{old}}) \cdot P_{\text{init}}$. Encounter probabilities are time-variant and aged

Protocol	Mapping
Prophet [154]	$p_i(d_j) := P_{(i,j)}$
	Time-dependent exponential decay, aging parameter defined at design time.
MaxProp [35]	$p_i(d_j) := 1 - \frac{c(i,\dots,j)}{n} = 1 - \frac{1}{n} \cdot \sum_{x=i}^{j-1} \left[1 - (f_{x+1}^x) \right]$
	Normalization of $\sum f_i^j$ on encounter to 1. Calculation of $p_i(d_j)$ based on cost and maximal path length n, e. g. $n = 10$ set in [35].
Spray&Focus [229]	$p_i(d_j) := 1 - \min\{1, \frac{k}{\Delta}\}$
	Linear decrease with elapsed time k since encounter, design-time parameter Δ for time scale.

Table 4.4 Mapping to awareness values. Notation based on original paper of respective DTN protocol.

through $P_{(i,j)} = P_{(i,j)\text{old}} \cdot \gamma^k$, with aging constant $\gamma \in [0, 1)$ and elapsed time k. When two devices are in contact they exchange their encounter probability tables to implement transitivity through a damping factor β using $P_{(i,k)} = P_{(i,k)\text{old}} + (1 - P_{(i,k)\text{old}}) \cdot P_{(i,j)} \cdot P_{(j,k)} \cdot \beta$. Encounter probabilities in Prophet can be directly mapped to destination-awareness values by defining $p_i(d_j) := P_{(i,j)}$.

MaxProp MaxProp [35] handles the problem of ordering messages to replicate, which is necessary under a finite bandwidth model. Each device locally calculates meeting probabilities f_i^j that are—in contrast to e. g. Prophet or Spray&Wait—not time-variant, rather, on device encounters all meeting probabilities are adjusted so their sum is normalized to 1. Therewith, probabilities are more stable, but interdependent. MaxProp distributes meeting probabilities in a control channel on device contacts. This way, devices gather a more complete view of the contact graph used for deciding on message order, based on shortest paths over the contact graph with link costs set to $1 - f_i^j$. For modeling destination-awareness, the local view of MaxProp is used that is a combination of locally encountered devices and meeting probabilities distributed through the control channel. For each destination device the shortest paths are calculated and inverse path costs used as destination-awareness.

Spray&Focus Spray&Focus [229] is based on two mechanism, spraying and encounter ages. Messages have a replication counter c defined at design time. In the "spray" phase messages are replicated and for each forwarded replica the replication counter c decreased by 1. If $c = 1$ the protocol switches to the "focus" phase based on time elapsed since

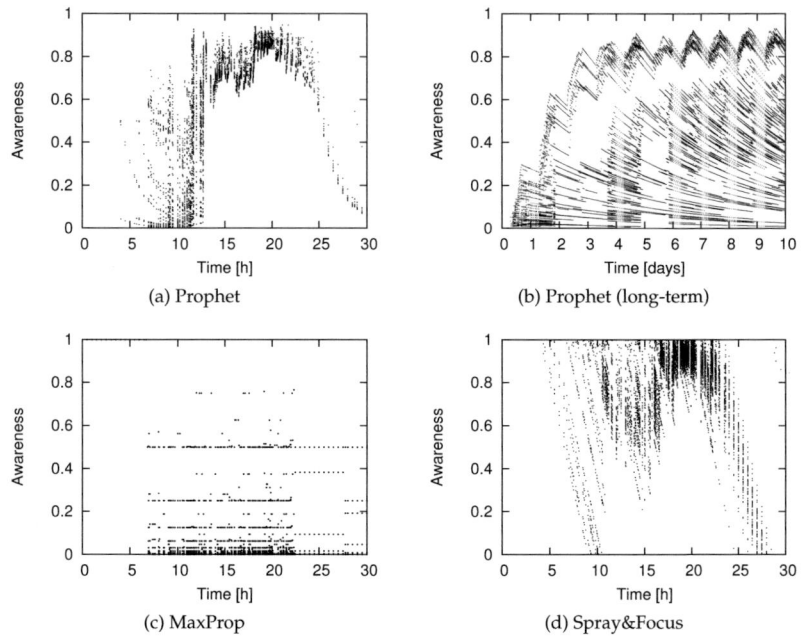

Figure 4.4 Flat representation of destination-awareness from perspective of one exemplary device.

last device encounter, similar to [69]. Messages are recursively forwarded to devices with younger encounter ages. Defining encounter ages as awareness-values, awareness is set to $(1 - \epsilon)$ when the device is encountered, ϵ being a very small value to keep awareness < 1, and decrease it over time. For mapping encounter ages to awareness-values $p_i(d_j) \in [0,1)$, a function that maps time k elapsed since last encounter linearly during a design-time timespan of Δ using $p_i(d_j) = 1 - \min\{1, \frac{k}{\Delta}\}$.

The time-variant characteristics of Destination-aware protocols vary between protocols. Understanding this dynamic behavior is important for the design of hybrid routing that must manage such awareness information. Figure 4.4 shows a flat representation of one device's routing table over a period of 30 h for different destination-aware protocols. For analyzing the awareness behavior the mobility model in Section A.9 is used. It emulates human working day behavior and allows to analyze the increase and decrease of awareness over time.

Figure 4.4a and Figure 4.4b both show the awareness characteristics of the Prophet protocol. While Figure 4.4a is based on the normal Prophet protocol with configuration based on short-term contact behavior, Figure 4.4b uses the parameter-estimation variant from [137] with focus on long-term contact behavior. Prophet's aging function performs an exponential decrease in awareness over time. Devices met more often gain higher awareness. Specifically in Figure 4.4b long-term contact behavior results in a separation of devices met on a regular basis, and devices met rarely—resulting from periodicity of the social-based mobility behavior. In comparison to Prophet that maintains awareness values independently for each device, MaxProp integrates an interrelation in that the sum of all awareness values is normalized to 1. Through this mechanism, MaxProp does not require an aging function, rather, aging is performed on each device contact for all other devices. Figure 4.4c shows the MaxProp behavior, it can be clearly seen that awareness values are more stable, as they are not time-dependent but rather depend on the device's contact rate with other devices. Spray&Focus shown in Figure 4.4d is based on last-encounter time, i. e. elapsed time since the device was encountered. This is $0\,$s at the moment of encounter, i. e. a high destination-awareness of $1 - \epsilon$ which is decreased linearly over time.

A system for hybrid routing must cope with different dynamics in awareness values. Depending on awareness behavior and stability, different variants of hybrid routing might be applicable. Two hybrid routing designs will be presented for different awareness stability in the remainder of this chapter.

4.4   Architecture

Figure 4.5 shows the architecture of HRS, split into two main parts: On the left, the *Overlay part* uses infrastructure-based communication to announce awareness for other devices, and provide communication between infrastructure-connected devices through the *Hybrid overlay protocol*. On the right, the *DTN part* runs the *Hybrid DTN protocol* that uses the *Mixed DTN metric*, and information acquired through an *Existing DTN protocol* to decide which how messages are to be routed.

HRS is not designed to be run as a global routing service to integrate the Internet with all existing DTN-enabled mobile devices. Rather, HRS is designed to be run on a per-application basis to collaboratively support routing within this application. The DTN—made up of mobile devices that participate in the same application—together with the infrastructure-based overlay is called a *HRS-instance*. Such a HRS-instance is application-specific and has an identifier that is used to differentiate between mobile devices in the same, and different HRS-instances.

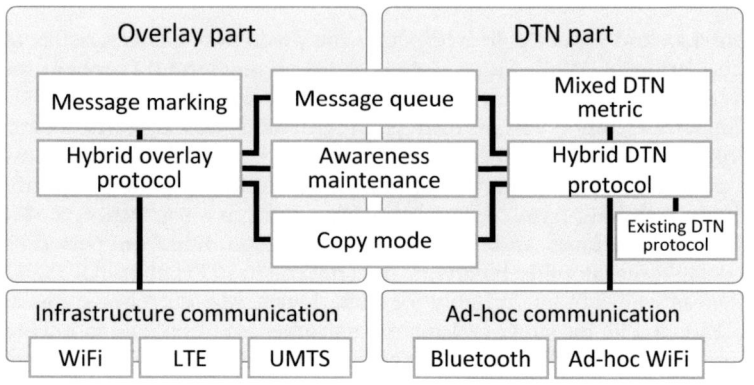

Figure 4.5 Architecture of the Hybrid Routing System.

Ad hoc communication

Mobile devices periodically scan for other devices in their geographic proximity. The HRS-instance identifier is used to only build up associations with devices from the same HRS-instance. This identifier can be encoded in the SSID for ad hoc WiFi, or the service record name in the Bluetooth *Service Discovery Protocol* (SDP). When two devices d_i and d_j from the same HRS-instance are in mutual communication range r an association is built up. During association the devices d_i and d_j can exchange a limited number of control and data message. Ad hoc communication can be implemented, e. g., using Bluetooth, or ad hoc WiFi.

Infrastructure communication

Besides ad hoc communication with other mobile devices when in mutual proximity, devices can make use of infrastructure-based communication, e. g. cellular networks such as UMTS or LTE, or infrastructure-based WiFi. Devices from infrastructure-capability classes $\mathcal{D}_t$ and $\mathcal{D}_p$ can perform infrastructure-based communication. Infrastructure access provides bidirectional communication with other devices that currently have infrastructure access, i. e. Internet connectivity based on IP. Section 5.5 will show how the framework for overlay-based services presented in Chapter 5 provides an enabling platform to implement this communication and how it enables identifier-based routing and addressing.

Hybrid DTN protocol

The Hybrid DTN protocol implements the opportunistic ad hoc routing decision, i. e. it decides which messages to forward/replicate in case of an ad hoc contact between devices. To implement this decision, information from the integrated DTN protocol, and information about the hybrid network are used in a mixed DTN routing metric.

Awareness maintenance

Ad hoc communication between two devices is the basis for maintenance of awareness tables T_i. Through initial exchange of identifiers id_i and id_j, both devices update their awareness table. The exact mechanism for table updates depends on the integrated existing DTN protocol. Besides awareness for other mobile devices, awareness for infrastructure access is maintained to manage a device's applicability for routing towards infrastructure access.

Mixed DTN metric

While pure DTN routing uses the applicability of a device for routing towards the destination device, in hybrid routing the applicability of a device for routing towards the infrastructure is integrated through a mixed metric. Section 4.5 will describe the mixed metric, and Section 4.8 show how it is used for implementing different use cases by trading off awareness for a message's destination device and awareness for infrastructure access.

Message queue

DTN protocols are based on store-carry-forward routing. For storage of messages device have local queues. The hybrid routing approach makes additional use of those message queues for storing messages sent through the infrastructure that are destined for other devices. Devices periodically delete messages from their queue whose lifetime has expired.

Hybrid overlay protocol

The hybrid overlay protocol enables communication between infrastructure-connected devices and implements an *announcement system*. The announcement system allows a device d_i to announce its awareness $p_i(d_j)$ for routing towards another device d_j through ad hoc DTN routing. Device d_i is called *proxy* for d_j. Multiple proxies can announce their awareness for a device. Announcement is performed in the infrastructure-part of the hybrid network and is accessible to all currently infrastructure-connected devices, irrespective of their geographic location. Two distributed designs for the announcement system will be presented in Section 4.6. From an architectural perspective an announcement system must provide mechanisms for managing and looking up announcements.

Copy mode

DTN routing is either single-copy, or multi-copy. Hybrid routing splits the routing process into three *routing parts*, as shown in Figure 4.6. Depending on the current routing part, a message is assigned a different *protocol state* and is handled differently. Those protocol states are:

- Protocol state 1: Routing in the source DTN.

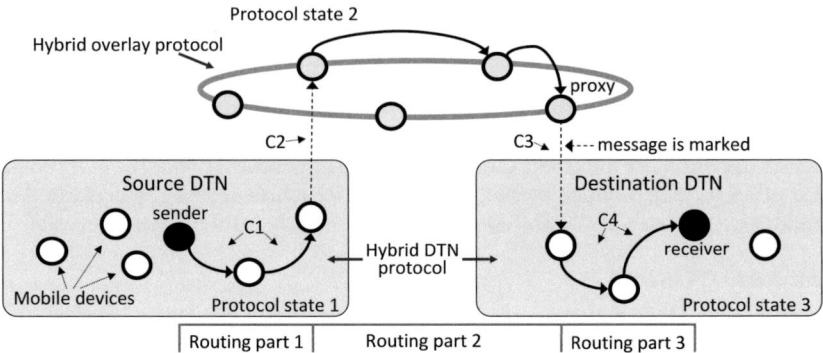

Figure 4.6 Protocol states in hybrid routing.

- Protocol state 2: Routing in the infrastructure announcement system.
- Protocol state 3: Routing in the destination DTN.

Each of the protocol states can be individually configured to perform either single-copy routing, or multi-copy routing. The three states result in four copy decisions:

- C1: Single-copy or multi-copy in source DTN.
- C2: Single-copy or multi-copy when moving messages from source DTN into the announcement system, i. e. keeping a message copy in the DTN, or not.
- C3: Single-copy or multi-copy when moving a message from the announcement system into the destination DTN, i. e. keeping a message copy in the announcement system, or not.
- C4: Single-copy or multi-copy in the destination DTN.

Overall $2^4 = 16$ copy-mode combinations for hybrid routing exist. Depending on quality of information in the protocol states, different combination of copy-modes can be beneficial for trading off performance vs. cost.

Message marking

After a message has been forwarded from infrastructure into DTN the message is *marked*, as shown in Figure 4.6 at point C3. Message marking allows to differentiate between protocol states and implement the aforementioned combination of copy-modes. Additionally, message marking is used to prevent a message being routed through the infrastructure twice. While infrastructure allows to overcome long distance and find a good proxy for routing in the destination DTN, a second infrastructure transfer does not provide additional benefit.

4.5 Hybrid DTN Protocol

The hybrid DTN protocol performs DTN routing based on *awareness for the destination device*, and *awareness for infrastructure access*. The mixed DTN metric used in this protocol is described in the following Section 4.5.1. Section 4.5.2 describes the hybrid DTN protocol run by mobile devices that integrates the mixed metric.

4.5.1 Mixed DTN Metric

For the hybrid routing approach messages must be explicitly routed through ad hoc communication towards devices more likely to encounter infrastructure access. For every device d_i its awareness table $\mathcal{T}_i$ is extended by *awareness for infrastructure access* through a virtual entry $(id_{\mathcal{I}}, p_i(id_{\mathcal{I}})) \in \mathcal{T}_i$, reflecting applicability of d_i for routing a message towards infrastructure $\mathcal{I}$. Based on infrastructure capability classes defined in Section 4.2, $p_i(id_{\mathcal{I}})$ is defined as

$$p_i(id_{\mathcal{I}}) = \begin{cases} 0, & d_i \in \mathcal{D}_n, \\ [0,1], & d_i \in \mathcal{D}_t, \\ 1, & d_i \in \mathcal{D}_p, \end{cases} \tag{4.1}$$

or if the used DTN protocol supports transitive spreading of awareness (e. g. Prophet [154]), defined as

$$p_i(id_{\mathcal{I}}) = \begin{cases} [0,1), & d_i \in \mathcal{D}_n, \\ [0,1], & d_i \in \mathcal{D}_t, \\ 1, & d_i \in \mathcal{D}_p. \end{cases} \tag{4.2}$$

While $p_i(id_{\mathcal{I}})$ is stable for $\mathcal{D}_p$, it is time-variant for $\mathcal{D}_n$ and $\mathcal{D}_t$. Similar to awareness for another device d_j, awareness for infrastructure is maintained by the mechanism of the integrated DTN protocol every time the device becomes connected to infrastructure access.

Based on awareness for mobile devices and awareness for infrastructure access, a mixed DTN routing metric is defined. Given two devices d_s and d_t that are in communication range and can exchange messages, the decision whether a message m_{ij} with destination device d_j should be forwarded/replicated from d_s to d_t is based on the relative normalized awareness-values for destination device d_j, defined as

$$p'_s(d_j) = \frac{p_s(d_j)}{p_s(d_j) + p_t(d_j)}, \tag{4.3}$$

and

$$p'_t(d_j) = \frac{p_t(d_j)}{p_t(d_j) + p_s(d_j)}. \tag{4.4}$$

The relative normalized infrastructure-awareness is calculated as

$$p'_s(id_{\mathcal{I}}) = \frac{p_s(id_{\mathcal{I}})}{p_s(id_{\mathcal{I}}) + p_t(id_{\mathcal{I}})}, \tag{4.5}$$

and

$$p'_t(id_{\mathcal{I}}) = \frac{p_t(id_{\mathcal{I}})}{p_t(id_{\mathcal{I}}) + p_s(id_{\mathcal{I}})}. \tag{4.6}$$

Message m_{ij} with destination device d_j is forwarded/replicated from d_s to d_t based on weight parameter $\alpha \in [0,1]$ if:

$$\Big(\alpha \cdot p'_t(id_{\mathcal{I}}) + (1 - \alpha) \cdot p'_t(d_j) \Big) > \Big(\alpha \cdot p'_s(id_{\mathcal{I}}) + (1 - \alpha) \cdot p'_s(d_j) \Big) \tag{4.7}$$

Equation 4.7 implements a forwarding decision in the DTN that allows to trade off destination-device awareness, and infrastructure-awareness. A value $\alpha \to 1$ puts emphasis on infrastructure-awareness, while a value $\alpha \to 0$ puts emphasis on destination device-awareness. The value of α can be either static, or defined as function. Section 4.8 will present two use cases that are mainly implemented through the choice of α: In one use case α is static, in the other use case α is a function of m_{ij}'s TTL, elapsed lifetime, and additional information about the network.

4.5.2 Protocol Details

Algorithm 1 is run locally by the DTN part of a mobile device to implement the hybrid DTN protocol.

Device Discovery, *line 6*

Device-to-device communication is based on short-range communication such as Bluetooth, or ad hoc WiFi that can provide infrastructure-less ad hoc communication (see [79] for an overview). Mobile devices periodically scan for other devices in their proximity, based upon the unique name of the HRS-instance. In WiFi this name can be implemented as *Service Set Identifier* (SSID), while Bluetooth allows to use the service name of a *Service Discovery Protocol* (SDP) record. A locally maintained ignore list $\mathcal{D}_{\text{ignore}}$, based on MAC addresses, is used to prevent successive communication sessions with the same device. Entries are periodically removed from the ignore list after a preconfigured timeout.

Communication Association, *line 12*

After the point-to-point link has been established, two devices d_i and d_j perform an initial handshake. The point-to-point link allows mutual addressing between the devices through MAC addresses. First, devices exchange their identifiers id_i and id_j and store a temporary association between MAC and identifier for the duration of the communication session.

Algorithm 1: Algorithm run locally by a mobile device to implement the hybrid DTN protocol.

---

1 local device d_i and local identifier id_i;
2 message queue q_i;
3 ignore list $\mathcal{D}_{\text{ignore}} = \emptyset$;
4 infrastructure capability table $\mathcal{C}_i$;
5 **while** *running* **do**
```
     /*Device Discovery*/
```
6     $\mathcal{D}_{\text{scan}}$ = scan for other devices;
7   **if** $\mathcal{D}_{scan} = \emptyset$ **then**
8   ⌊ sleep, continue scanning;
9   **for** $d_j \in \mathcal{D}_{scan}$ **do**
10   **if** *device from other HRS-instance* **or** $d_j \in \mathcal{D}_{ignore}$ **then**
11   ⌊ continue;
```
         /*(Secure) Communication Association*/
```
12   build up communication association;
```
         /*Awareness Exchange and Update*/
```
13   exchange awareness tables $\mathcal{T}$;
14   update awareness for d_j;
```
         /*Infrastructure Capability Exchange and Update*/
```
15   exchange infrastructure capability table $\mathcal{C}_i$;
16   update infrastructure capability for d_j;
```
         /*(Secure) Message Exchange*/
```
17   **for** $m_k \in q_i$ **do**
18   **if** *destination of m_k is d_j* **then**
19   │ send m_k to d_j;
20   **else**
21   **if** *m_k is not marked* **then**
22   │ calculate awareness through mixed metric;
23   **else**
24   ⌊ calculate awareness using destination device only;
25   **if** *d_j has higher awareness for destination of m_k* **then**
26   │ forward or replicate m_k to d_j;
27   ⌊ store received messages in q_i;
```
         /*Session Teardown*/
```
28   teardown communication with d_j;
29   ⌊ add d_j to $\mathcal{D}_{\text{ignore}}$;
30   remove old entries from $\mathcal{D}_{\text{ignore}}$;

Secure Communication Association, *line 12*

Based on the large identifier space (e.g. 160 bit as described in Section 4.2) a secure mutually authenticated association can be designed based on *Cryptographically Generated Addresses* (CGA) [12, 13], and a protocol such as *Transport Layer Security* (TLS) [64]. Every device d_i owns a public/private key pair $\{pub_i, priv_i\}$. Device d_i's identifier id_i is created through a one-way hash function $h(x)$ using $id_i = h(pub_i)$. For 160 bit identifiers $h(x)$ can be implemented using SHA1 [71]. Device d_i can perform a *proof of ownership* for its identifier id_i against a device d_j during build up of a communication association. Device d_j sends a challenge χ to d_i. Device d_i encrypts χ using its private key $priv_i$ and sends back $enc(\chi)$ together with its identifier id_i and public key pub_i. Device d_j validates that $h(pub_i) = id_i$ and decrypts $dec(\chi) = \chi$ using pub_i. Device d_i therewith proves to d_j that it *owns* the identifier id_i through a proof of ownership using $priv_i$. This scheme requires that identifiers can be chosen at random. If this is not possible, *Identity Based Encryption* (IBE) [31] schemes can be used based on a central entity to generate key pairs for arbitrary identifiers. The authentication scheme can be used to build up a confidential and integrity secured communication association, e.g. using TLS. Section 5.2.3 and Section 5.5 give more details on security mechanisms.

Awareness Exchange and Update, *line 13–14*

Devices update their awareness tables with awareness for the other device, i.e. d_i updates $p_i(d_j) \in \mathcal{T}_i$, while d_j updates $p_j(d_i) \in \mathcal{T}_j$. Next, devices exchange their complete awareness tables $\mathcal{T}_i$ and $\mathcal{T}_j$ for protocols that build up transitivity [155], or disseminate a more complete view of the network [35].

Infrastructure Capability Exchange and Update, *line 15–16*

Devices exchange collected information about infrastructure capabilities of other devices in $\mathcal{C}_i$, and exchange information about their own infrastructure capability class $\mathcal{D}_{\{p,t,n\}}$. This information is used in Equation 4.8 to decide for which devices to announce awareness in the overlay.

Message Exchange, *line 17–27*

Messages with final destination for the currently connected devices are exchanged. Messages for other destinations are forwarded (in single-copy mode) or replicated (in multi-copy mode) between d_i and d_j, based on the mixed metric described in Section 4.5.1, and specific mechanisms employed by the integrated DTN protocol.

Secure Message Exchange, *line 17–27*

A device can forge its awareness for another device. Nelson et al. describe in [179] a scheme based on signing of timestamps to prove that another device has been encountered. Devices in proximity mutually sign a current timestamp. This signed timestamp can be used to proof encounter to a third device. The scheme requires loosely synchronized clocks with drift within minutes.

Session Teardown, *line 28–30*

Finally, the communication association is torn down. Devices add each other mutually to their ignore list $\mathcal{D}_{ignore}$ to prevent continuous build-up and tear-down of communication sessions. Quickly recurring sessions have no value as messages and state on devices only change slowly over time.

4.6 Hybrid Overlay Protocol

In Destination-aware protocols every device d_i maintains a table $\mathcal{T}_i$ that reflects applicability of d_i for routing messages in the DTN towards other devices d_j, described by its awareness $p_i(d_j) \in [0,1)$. Devices $\mathcal{D}_p$ and $\mathcal{D}_t$ with current infrastructure access announce such device-specific awareness from $\mathcal{T}_i$ in the announcement system built-up in the infrastructure part of the hybrid network. Other infrastructure connected devices can query the announcement system for devices with high awareness for a message's destination, so-called *proxies*. The main idea is based on the fact that if a device d_i announces its applicability for d_j through its awareness $p_i(d_j)$, a time-variant DTN path from d_i to d_j existed in the past. The value of $p_i(d_j)$ reflects the probability of this path in the future, based upon the requirement of non-randomness in human mobility.

The announcement system is used for lookups to find shortcuts, overcoming long geographic distance even in strongly clustered DTNs. It does not introduce noteworthy delay compared to DTN routing which is driven by comparably slow mobility of devices. Routing a message through infrastructure by making use of the announcement system only makes sense one time. Then, either the destination DTN has been reached, or there exists no infrastructure-enhanced shortcut that could be exploited.

In its simplest form an announcement system can be implemented using a central server. However, such a design is not scalable and does not allow for spontaneous and flexible deployment. Two distributed announcement systems for HRS are presented, based on *virtual nodes* in Section 4.6.3, and based on *indirection* in Section 4.6.4. Both announcement systems are distributed in nature, use different mechanisms, have different overhead, and are applicable for different scenarios, as will be shown later.

Selecting Devices to Announce

It is not feasible for d_i to announce itself as proxy for all devices in $\mathcal{T}_i$, as most of them have a low awareness $p_i(d_j)$. The *virtual-set* $\mathcal{V}_i \subseteq \mathcal{T}_i$ announced by device d_i is defined as

$$\mathcal{V}_i = \{id_j \in \mathcal{T}_i \mid p_i(d_j) > p_{join} \wedge d_j \notin \mathcal{D}_p\}, \text{with } |\mathcal{V}_i| \leq vmax. \qquad (4.8)$$

Let the items of $\mathcal{T}_i$ be sorted by decreasing awareness. The components of $\mathcal{V}_i$ are then:

- $p_{join} \in [0, 1)$ defines the lower bound the awareness value must satisfy, i.e. $p_i(d_j) > p_{join}$ must hold for announcing as proxy for d_j. Device d_i only announces itself as proxy for a device d_j if it has a high awareness for d_j.
- $d_j \notin \mathcal{D}_p$ states that no announcements are to be performed for devices that have permanent infrastructure access themselves. Information about infrastructure-capabilities of devices is exchanged on device encounter and is therefore sure to be known if awareness for a device is > 0.
- $vmax$ defines the maximum number of entries to announce. Based an awareness table $\mathcal{T}_i$, at most $vmax$ entries with the highest awareness values $p_i(d_j)$ are selected. Herewith the load of a proxy device is controlled by itself.

Message Marking

Section 4.5.1 described the mixed metric and how it is used in the hybrid DTN protocol in Section 4.5.2. To prevent messages from being routed *towards* and *through* the announcement system a second time, a simple mechanism called *message marking* is used. Each message has a single bit that states whether this message has already been routed through the infrastructure by using the announcement system.

Given a message m_{ij} with sender d_i and destination d_j, if m_{ij} is not marked:

- The mixed metric is used for DTN routing towards the infrastructure.
- Once m_{ij} arrives at an infrastructure connected device, it is routed through the announcement system towards a proxy device. Upon leaving the infrastructure and entering the DTN, m_{ij} is marked.

If m_{ij} is marked:

- The mixed metric uses $\alpha = 0$, resulting in normal DTN routing that involves only awareness for m_{ij}'s destination device.
- Infrastructure access is ignored and m_{ij} not routed through the overlay.

This simple mechanism allows to differentiate between the routing states. It routes a message initially in the source DTN towards infrastructure-capable devices and through the announcement system. After delivering m_{ij} to one or multiple proxy devices, m_{ij} is routed in the destination DTN while ignoring infrastructure-awareness.

4.6.1   Functional Requirements

This section describes functional requirements for an announcement system. Two distributed designs that implement these requirements are presented in Section 4.6.3, and Section 4.6.4.

Device Registration

Description	Registering a device d_i is based on its flat identifier id_i. A device registers upon access to the infrastructure. Registration ends when infrastructure access ends. During a registration the device has a communication association with the announcement system.
Input	Device d_i, identifier id_i.
Effect	Device d_i is registered using id_i.
Output	Success or failure.

Device Communication

Description	Devices registered at the announcement system can exchange messages using identifier-based addressing.
Input	Message m_{ij}, destination device identifier id_j.
Effect	Delivery of m_{ij} to device d_j if d_j is currently registered.
Output	Success if m_{ij} was delivered to d_j, failure otherwise.

Proxy Registration

Description	Device d_i registers as proxy for other devices $d_j, d_k, \ldots$. A registration is defined as triple $(id_j, id_i, p_i(d_j))$. Multiple devices can register as proxy for one device d_j, each with their specific awareness. Unregistering an active registration $(id_j, id_i, p_i(d_j))$ is performed by d_i using only id_i and id_j as input.
Input	Registration $(id_j, id_i, p_i(d_j))$.
Effect	The announcement system registers id_i as proxy for id_j with awareness $p_i(d_j)$. Multiple proxies can register for id_j.
Output	Success or failure.

Proxy Maintenance

Description	Awareness can increase and decrease over time. Such changes must be reflected in the announcement system. Proxy maintenance allows to update an existing registration. Increasing awareness must be explicitly signaled to the announcement system. Depending on the integrated DTN protocol, decrease of awareness can be implemented autonomously in the announcement system if the aging process is purely time-based (e. g. Prophet [155], Spray&Focus [229]).
Input	Updated awareness $p_i(d_j)$ for device with identifier id_j.
Effect	Update of awareness in proxy registration for id_j.
Output	Success or failure.

Proxy Request

Description	Proxies registered for id_i can be requested from the announcement system. Additionally, a threshold for awareness values or a maximal number of proxies to return can be specified.
Input	Identifier id_i to request proxies for, awareness threshold, maximal number of proxies to return.
Effect	Announcement system collects a maximal number of proxies registered for id_i with awareness higher given threshold.
Output	List of proxies $id_k, id_l, \ldots$ with awareness-values $p_k(d_j), p_l(d_j), \ldots$.

Proxy Forward Request

Description	Device d_i request the announcement system to forward message m_{ij} with destination id_j to one or multiple proxies with highest awareness for d_j. If no proxy satisfies the awareness threshold criteria, the announcement system can store m_{ij} and fulfill the request at a later point in time.
Input	Destination device d_j, message m_{ij}, awareness threshold.
Effect	Delivery to one or multiple proxies that satisfy the awareness threshold, or storage of m_i in the announcement system if no proxy satisfies the awareness threshold.
Output	Message sent, not sent, stored.

4.6.2 Protocol Details

Algorithm 2 is run locally by the overlay-part of a mobile device to implement the hybrid routing overlay protocol. Whenever a device encounters infrastructure access it registers at the announcement system and updates its awareness for infrastructure access (*lines 6–11*). For entries $\mathcal{V}_i \subseteq \mathcal{T}_i$ a registration is sent out (*lines 12–14*). Registrations are updated during association at the announcement system (*lines 15–17*).

Unmarked messages in the local queue contain messages generated locally, or received through DTN routing. If the destination device for a message is registered itself at the announcement system, the message is directly sent to this device (*lines 22–23*). Otherwise, the announcement system is queried for a proxy device that has a higher awareness for the message's destination than the local device (*line 25*). If such a proxy is found, the message is sent to the proxy (*lines 26–27*). If a message is received through the announcement system destined for the local device, it is received successfully and given to the application (*lines 28–30*). If a message is received with destination for another device due to a proxy registration, the message is marked, and stored in the local message queue (*lines 31–33*). Generally, the announcement system is used as lookup system. Lookups are routed semi-recursive [23, Sec. 6.3.1.1] based on identifiers. A lookup includes the sender's underlay address. The system receiving the lookup can send back its own underlay address directly in the underlay. Data messages are then exchanged directly in the underlay. In the remainder of this chapter semi-recursive lookups and routing of data messages in the underlay are used.

If a message is sent out towards the final destination or a proxy device, it is required that the message is not marked, otherwise it has already traversed the infrastructure before. A message is sent through the infrastructure if $\alpha \geq 1$. The value of α can be either defined statically, or as function $\alpha(\cdot)$ of the message's metadata. This allows to influence message routing and is used to implement use cases in Section 4.8.

4.6.3   vHRS: Virtual Nodes-based Hybrid Routing System

Structured overlay networks provide routing based on identifiers, i.e. they allow a message m_{ij} to be routed based on the flat destination identifier id_j to the device with identifier closest to id_j, as described in Section 2.5.4. This so-called *key-based routing* functionality together with explicit placement of *virtual nodes* in the overlay is used for the hybrid overlay protocol presented in this section, called *virtual nodes-based Hybrid Routing System* (vHRS). The main idea of vHRS is to insert additional virtual nodes into the structured overlay at strategic positions in the identifier space to implement proxy registrations. vHRS is completely distributed and does not require a central server or coordinator as each participating device performs autonomous decisions.

Any key-based routing overlay with closest match behavior can be employed for vHRS, if the distance metric used by the protocol allows to calculate identifiers given distance from another identifier. Chord [239] or Pastry [211]—described in Section 2.5.4.1, Section 2.5.4.3—are two such overlay structures that can be employed for vHRS.

Calculating Virtual Node Identifiers

vHRS is based on the idea of inserting additional *virtual nodes* into the overlay, shown in Figure 4.7 as example. The lower graph represents the DTN contact graph and thickness of links describe strength of awareness. The vHRS overlay is shown as ring-based overlay network. Devices d_i and d_j with infrastructure access join the overlay network using their identifiers id_i and id_j. Device d_k is not infrastructure-capable and can not join the overlay. Device d_j often has regular contacts with d_k, resulting in high awareness values, and places a virtual node as proxy in the overlay, close to the identifier position id_k (step ①). The virtual node for device d_k with identifier id_k—inserted by proxy device d_j—is not inserted with id_k as overlay identifier, but with a virtual node identifier id_k^j that reflects d_j's awareness for d_k. With respect to the

Algorithm 2: Mobile device algorithm for the hybrid overlay protocol.

1 local device d_i with identifier id_i, and message queue q_i;
2 awareness table $\mathcal{T}_i$;
3 infrastructure capability table $\mathcal{C}_i$;
4 **while** *running* **do**
      /*Infrastructure Discovery*/
5      $\mathcal{I}_{\text{scan}}$ = scan for infrastructure access;
6   **if** $\mathcal{I}_{scan} = \emptyset$ **then**
7   ⌊ sleep, continue scanning;
      /*Device Registration*/
8   associate with infrastructure access;
9   connect to announcement system;
10   register with id_i at announcement system;
      /*Infrastructure Awareness Maintenance*/
11   update awareness for infrastructure access $p_i(id_{\mathcal{I}})$;
      /*Proxy Registration*/
12   select virtual set $\mathcal{V}_i$ from $\mathcal{T}_i$;
13   **for** $id_j \in \mathcal{V}_i$ **do**
14   ⌊ register in announcement system as proxy for id_j using $p_i(d_j)$;
15   **while** *connected to infrastructure* **do**
          /*Proxy Maintenance*/
16   unregister entries no longer in $\mathcal{V}_i$, register new entries in $\mathcal{V}_i$;
17   registration update for entries in $\mathcal{V}_i$ with strongly changed $p_i(d_j)$;
          /*Send Messages*/
18   **for** $m_k \in q_i$ **do**
19   message m_k destination is d_p;
20   **if** m_k *not marked* **and** $\alpha(m_k) \geq 1$ **then**
21   request destination device d_p;
22   **if** *destination* d_p *online* **then**
                      /*Destination online*/
23   ⌊ deliver m_k to destination d_p;
24   **else**
                      /*Find good proxy*/
25   request proxy for m_k with highest awareness $p_s(d_p)$;
26   **if** $p_s(d_p) > p_i(d_p)$ **then**
                          /*proxy awareness higher*/
27   ⌊ forward/replicate message through infrastructure to proxy d_s

          /*Receive Messages*/
28   receive message m_k through infrastructure;
29   **if** m_k *destination is* id_i **then**
              /*Message for me*/
30   ⌊ send message to higher layer module;
31   **else**
              /*Message for other destination, route in DTN*/
32   mark message m_k;
33   enqueue message m_k into q_i;

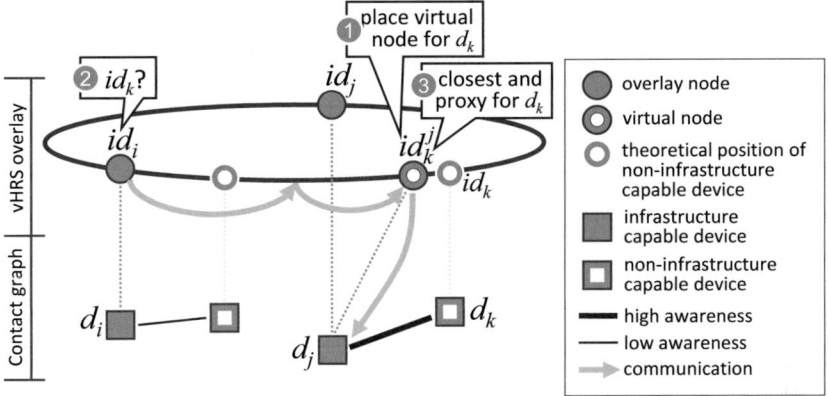

Figure 4.7 Overlay structure of vHRS based on virtual nodes.

awareness of d_j for d_k, the higher $p_j(d_k)$, the closer to the real identifier id_k of d_k the virtual node is placed and it holds:

$$\lim_{p_j(d_k) \to 1} id_k^j = id_k. \tag{4.9}$$

Exploiting the closest-match behavior of key-based routing protocols, a message destined for id_k (step ②) is delivered in the overlay either to d_k itself—if d_k is currently joined in the overlay—or to the closest overlay node at position id_k^j (step ③). This closest overlay node has been placed by device d_j with *best* awareness for d_k—and therewith closest placement of virtual node to id_k in the overlay.

For positioning of virtual nodes a rough approximation on the expected number of nodes N in the overlay is required (design-time, or runtime estimation [222]). Figure 4.8 illustrates the placement of a virtual node: A virtual node for device d_k is placed by device d_j either "left" ($id_k^j < id_k$) or "right" ($id_k^j > id_k$) of the actual node identifier id_k ($\pm$ in Equation 4.10) with distance $\frac{1-p_j(d_k)}{1-p_{join}}$. Denominator $1 - p_{join}$ guarantees better utilization of the overlay identifier space by considering awareness threshold for proxies. This way, granularity of placement in the identifier space is refined. The virtual node identifier id_k^j is calculated as

$$id_k^j = id_k \pm \left(\frac{1 - p_j(d_k)}{1 - p_{join}} \cdot \frac{2^{160}}{2N} \right). \tag{4.10}$$

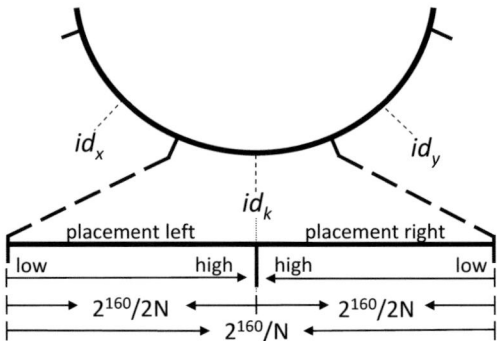

Figure 4.8 Virtual node placement placement for device d_k with identifier id_k
in a ring-based symmetric overlay protocol.

For example, using an identifier space of 160 bit, expected 50 000 nodes, threshold $p_{join} = 0.7$, and $p_j(d_k) = 0.99999$ the resulting distance of id_k^j from id_k in the identifier space is still $> 2^{31}$ due to the large identifier space of 2^{160}. Depending on the key-based routing protocol, placement can be randomly left or right from the actual node position [211], or must specifically be on one predefined side [239].

Sending Message in vHRS

Sending message m_i with destination d_i in vHRS is performed using a lookup based on key-based routing using the identifier id_i of d_i, and in a second step direct delivery of the message through the underlay. The sender of the lookup includes its awareness $p_j(d_i)$, so the receiver can check whether it really has a higher awareness for m_i's destination d_i. This way, the protocol forwarding/replication precondition for destination-aware protocols $p_t(d_j) > p_s(d_j)$, presented in Section 4.3.2, is integrated into the overlay part of hybrid routing. In case the sender has a non-empty virtual-set $\mathcal{V}_i$, sending is performed from the virtual node with identifier closest to the message destination identifier, resulting in shorter key-based routing paths.

Implementing Functional Requirements

The functional requirements presented in Section 4.6.1 are implemented in vHRS as follows.

Device Registration Registration of device d_i is performed by joining the vHRS overlay through an overlay node with identifier id_i. Nodes arrange with respect to a distance metric in the overlay. Unregistering is performed by leaving the overlay structure.

Device Communication Communication between devices is performed using key-based routing. Sending a message from d_i to an identifier d_j

is performed using a semi-recursive lookup for the destination identifier id_j.

Proxy Registration Registering a proxy is performed by joining the overlay with an additional virtual node. The identifier of this virtual node is calculated with respect to awareness: A device d_i registering as proxy for d_j with awareness $p_i(d_j)$ calculates an identifier id^i_j, as defined in Equation 4.10. All communication this virtual node is involved in is actually performed by device d_i. Unregistering is performed by removing the virtual node from the overlay.

Proxy Maintenance Maintaining proxy registration in case of awareness-change requires removing the virtual node from the overlay, calculating a new identifier id^i_j based on new awareness, and rejoining the virtual node. Fine-grained adaptation of awareness is not possible as it induces high churn. Proxy maintenance is only possible within predefined thresholds, i. e. it is only possible to update virtual nodes when awareness-values change remarkably to keep churn manageable.

Proxy Request Performing a proxy request for d_j is implemented by sending a request-message through the key-based routing overlay towards id_j. The receiving node is either d_j itself, the currently best proxy for d_j that is placed closest to id_j, or a node that is not involved with d_j. Device d_k of the receiving node replies with its awareness for d_j, $p_k(d_j)$: 1 if $d_k = d_j$, $p_k(d_j) \in (0,1)$ if d_k has placed a proxy for d_j, or 0 if d_k is not involved with d_j.

Proxy Forward Request A proxy forward request is implemented similar to a proxy request. However, awareness $p_k(d_j)$ is sent back as result to indicate whether destination device d_j itself has received the message, the device that placed its proxy nearest receives the message, or the message can not be processed as the receiving device is not involved with d_j.

Discussion and Applicability

Use of virtual nodes in vHRS has the advantage that state is only managed locally, i. e. besides state of the structured overlay, additional information about proxy devices is not distributed. A proxy can control its load by the number of inserted virtual nodes and is not affected by other proxies. vHRS allows for short overlay paths, as messages accepted by a virtual node are directly received through the respective proxy device. Sending a message across the overlay does not require knowledge whether the destination device itself participates in the overlay, as either the destination device, or a good proxy will receive the message. On the downside, vHRS imposes load as virtual nodes are inserted and removed from the overlay to reflect changed virtual sets $\mathcal{V}$ resulting from time-variance of awareness values. Thresholds are used to prevent fast changes to the virtual set $\mathcal{V}$ in case of slight awareness

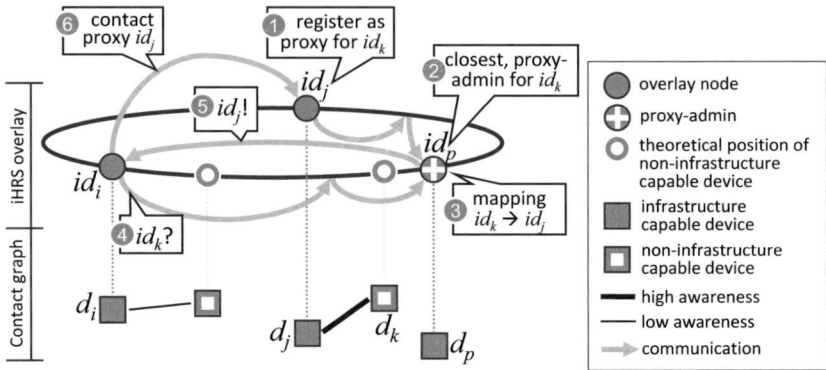

Figure 4.9 Overlay structure of iHRS based on indirection.

changes. vHRS enables hybrid routing in case of awareness values $p_i(d_j)$ that are not subject to heavy fluctuation. This is the case if the DTN protocol build upon long-term contact stability, e. g. [137].

4.6.4 iHRS: Indirection-based Hybrid Routing System

While vHRS generates few state, dynamic awareness results in churn due to coupling of awareness values to virtual node positioning. Using indirection, the *indirection-based Hybrid Routing System* (iHRS) decouples awareness from placement in the overlay. iHRS introduces more state, but is generally applicable, even for short-term contact stability. iHRS implements indirection by means of so-called *proxy-admins*. Whereas in vHRS devices manage their proxy registrations through virtual nodes themselves, iHRS employs proxy-admins that manage proxy registrations on behalf of proxy devices. The general idea of indirection is similar to *i3* [237] (cf. Section 2.5.4.4). Similar to vHRS, any key-based routing overlay can be used; an extensive evaluation of such protocols can be found in [23, Sec. 6].

Figure 4.9 shows the overlay structure of iHRS. Device d_j registers itself as proxy for device d_k, due to high awareness (step ①). This registration is routed to the node closest to id_k in the overlay, i. e. d_p with identifier id_p (step ②). Device d_p herewith becomes proxy-admin and manages registrations for d_k (step ③). Device d_i performs a lookup for id_k (step ④). This lookup either reaches d_k itself, if d_k is joined in the overlay using id_k, or the node closest in the overlay, i. e. d_p with identifier id_p. Device d_p replies with the stored mapping that states id_j as proxy for id_k (step ⑤). Device d_i can now contact the proxy d_j for d_p (step ⑥).

Proxy Registrations and Proxy Admins

Upon joining the overlay, device d_i sends out registrations for its virtual-set $\mathcal{V}_i$, defined in Equation 4.8, through the key-based routing overlay. Building upon the closest match behavior, a registration $(id_j, id_i, p_i(d_j))$ is routed and managed by the node with identifier id_k, being closest to id_j in the identifier space. Device d_k is therewith elected as *proxy-admin* and manages all proxies that register for d_j. Proxy-admins are not predetermined, but rather every node in the overlay dynamically becomes proxy-admin when a registration reaches it. A message from d_l to d_i is sent across the overlay towards id_i, and will reach either d_i directly, or the proxy-admin d_k. Device d_k forwards or replicates the message further in the overlay, based on proxy registrations it has received for id_i. If multiple devices have registered, selection can be performed based on awareness values. If no, or insufficient registrations with appropriate awareness are available, proxy-admin d_k can store the message. This provides time-decoupling, similar to Throwboxes [261], in a decentralized way. If new registrations with appropriate awareness reaches d_k, the message can be delivered to the registering proxy. Actual delivery from proxy-admin to proxies is performed by key-based routing through the proxy's identifier which was sent in the registration.

Managing Awareness

Awareness-values in destination-aware protocols are subject to temporal variance due to aging and refreshing (cf. Section 4.3.2). vHRS must reflect this changes in a device's virtual-set $\mathcal{V}_i$ through joins and leaves of virtual nodes, as awareness directly affects node identifiers. Through indirection, iHRS can handle temporal variance of awareness-values by proxy-admins themselves through simple adaptation of registration-based awareness-values. Aging of awareness-values can be performed by proxy-admins autonomously, if an aging function can be defined. This is, e. g, possible in Prophet [154] but not possible in MaxProp [35]. In case awareness-values need to be refreshed when devices come into contact and the virtual-set $\mathcal{V}_i$ changes, the proxy sends an update to the proxy-admin to update its registration table.

Handling Churn

In case of churn through graceful leave, registration tables as well as stored messages are transferred to a new proxy-admin that is located closest in the identifier space to the destination device identifier. Same is true for a new joining device whose identifier is closer to the destination device. In this case all state and messages are transferred to this new proxy-admin. If the destination device itself joins the overlay, all registrations as well as all messages are automatically transferred, as the new device is closest with zero distance. Registrations are, nevertheless, kept so they can be transferred further in case the destination device leaves the overlay again quickly. If a device leaves ungraceful, registrations are lost. iHRS relies on soft-state behavior where awareness-values are updated due to real-world contacts. To prevent such loss of information, replication stategies [23, Sec. 8.4] can be employed to distribute awareness information to other nodes in the overlay.

Implementing Functional Requirements

Functional requirements introduced in Section 4.6.1 are implemented in iHRS as follows.

Device Registration Device d_i registers in iHRS by joining a node into the overlay with identifier id_i. Unregistering is performed by removing the node from the overlay.

Device Communication Devices d_i and d_j joined into iHRS can communicate through key-based routing.

Proxy Registration Device d_i can register as proxy for d_j by sending a registration in the key-based routing overlay to id_j that includes its identifier id_i and its awareness-value $p_i(d_j)$ for d_j. Device d_k currently closest to id_j is elected proxy-admin and stores registrations for id_j. Unregistering is performed respectively.

Proxy Maintenance Maintenance of awareness information that is distributed in the overlay is performed by sending updates to proxy-admins through key-based routing. In case of decreasing awareness the proxy-admins can perform aging autonomously if the aging function can be defined, depending on the integrated DTN protocol.

Proxy Request A request for proxies with highest awareness for d_j is sent to id_j using key-based routing and received by current proxy-admin d_k with id_k being closest to id_j. The proxy-admin returns the table of registered proxies.

Proxy Forward Request Similar to the proxy request, the proxy-admin can be instructed to directly forward a message to e.g. the proxy with highest awareness, or all proxies with an awareness higher a given threshold. Further, a proxy-admin can be instructed to store a message in case no appropriate registration is available. When new registrations or maintenance updates reach the proxy-admin at later points in time, the proxy-admin can decide to send out stored messages.

4.7   Integration of Existing DTN Protocols

Section 4.5 described the hybrid DTN protocol run by a mobile device. Existing DTN protocols are integrated into the hybrid DTN protocol and define handling and maintenance of destination-awareness, and metadata in messages. In the following the general steps for integration of existing destination-aware DTN protocols are presented:

- Mapping contact information to destination-awareness $p_i(d_j) \in [0, 1]$.

- Integration of awareness for infrastructure $p_i(id_\mathcal{I}) \in [0,1]$.
- Awareness maintenance for iHRS proxy-admins.
- Adaptation of DTN protocol-specific replication for single-copy, and multi-copy mode.

In the following, those steps are described in general and applied to integrate three DTN protocols: Prophet [155], MaxProp [35], and Spray&Focus [229].

Mapping of Contact Information to Destination-awareness

Mapping of contact information to destination-awareness values, has been explained in Section 4.3.2, and an overview given in Table 4.4. The mapping is shortly described now for completeness:

- **Prophet:** For integrating Prophet, the Prophet-probability values can be directly mapped to destination-awareness.

- **MaxProp:** MaxProp builds up a contact graph by disseminating locally gathered contact information. Shortest paths are calculated over this contact graph to determine path costs. Through an inverse cost function, path costs are mapped to destination-awareness, i. e. d_i has a high awareness for d_j if the path over the contact graph is cheap.

- **Spray&Focus:** Spray&Focus uses time elapsed since last encounter, called encounter ages. Encounter ages are mapped to awareness-values by linearly decreasing awareness, i. e. young encounters have high awareness.

Integration of Awareness for Infrastructure

HRS uses awareness for infrastructure in the mixed routing metric, as described in Section 4.5.1, to trade off routing towards devices that often encounter infrastructure access, and routing towards a message's destination device. For integrating infrastructure-awareness, a virtual device $\mathcal{I}$ is defined with identifier $id_\mathcal{I}$, and awareness of d_i for infrastructure access defined as $p_i(id_\mathcal{I})$. Devices maintain this entry autonomously through the integrated DTN protocol.

- **Prophet:** Prophet is extended with a virtual device $\mathcal{I}$ that represents infrastructure-encounter probability, updated upon infrastructure access, and propagated transitively.

- **MaxProp:** MaxProp distributes the local view of the network—including the virtual device for infrastructure access—for deciding on message replication/forwarding. A device locally builds up a more complete view of the contact graph and calculates shortest paths to decide which message has the highest chance to be delivered when it is replicated to the currently connected device. The virtual infrastructure device is integrated and used for calculating shortest paths.

- **Spray&Focus:** Same as with Prophet and MaxProp, a virtual device entry is integrated that represents infrastructure access. This entry is handled through the normal Spray&Focus protocol, being refreshed, aged, and distributed to other devices.

Awareness Maintenance for iHRS Proxy-admins

- **Prophet:** Prophet's aging constant is defined at design-time and aging is time-based. An iHRS proxy-admin can calculate the aging for managed registrations, and autonomously age awareness values.

- **MaxProp:** MaxProp performs contact-driven adaptation of awareness values. Autonomous aging through an iHRS proxy-admin is not possible. If the device contact rate is known the aging function can be derived, however, normally a device needs to update its registration in case of increase and decrease of awareness values.

- **Spray&Focus:** The aging function is defined at design-time and is time-based. An iHRS proxy-admin can compute aging autonomously, similar to the Prophet protocol.

Adaptation for Single-copy and Multi-copy

DTN protocols normally have a predefined replication mode. HRS splits up the routing process into different parts, resulting in 16 possible configurations for copy-modes, as described in Section 4.4. To make full use of those combinations, it is necessary to adapt the DTN protocol to perform routing in single-copy mode *and* in multi-copy mode. Such adaptation might not be intended in the original DTN protocol design, but is recommended for hybrid routing as it provides flexibility for fine-grained performance/cost tradeoff, as will be shown in Section 4.9.3.

- **Prophet:** Prophet replicates message to devices with higher awareness for the destination device, i. e. Prophet runs in multi-copy mode by default. To extend Prophet for single-copy mode, a message is forwarded if the encountered device has higher awareness for the destination device.

- **MaxProp:** In single-copy mode the initial replication boost of MaxProp for messages with young lifetime is removed as it would result in random forwarding. A message is forwarded in single-copy mode if the path cost over the contact graph for delivering the message is smaller through the encountered device than for the device currently carrying the message. The virtual device entry for representing infrastructure is integrated when calculating shortest paths for finding shortcut paths over HRS. For ordering of messages to replicate, path cost is calculated using device awareness alone, and using infrastructure, depending on the value of α.

- **Spray&Focus:** In multi-copy mode Spray&Focus works as by design, in single-copy mode the initial replication counter is set to $c = 1$. The protocol therewith enters the focus phase immediately and performs forwarding based on encounter ages.

4.8 Implementing Use Cases

HRS provides a routing system independent of a concrete use case. In the following, two use cases are described and shown what configuration is required to implement them:

- How HRS can provide communication with few infrastructure-capable devices is shown in Section 4.8.1.
- If a large fraction, or all devices, are infrastructure-capable, Section 4.8.2 shows how HRS uses the DTN for offloading traffic from infrastructure.

Both use cases are implemented by influencing:

1. Routing in the DTN through the mixed metric.
2. Deciding when messages are sent into the HRS overlay.

4.8.1 Providing Communication

HRS can provide communication in face of few infrastructure-capable devices. Using shortcuts through the infrastructure to overcome long distance, HRS allows to provide communication in otherwise unconnected areas. While in this use case every device is DTN-capable, only few devices are infrastructure-capable.

Reasons for partial or complete unavailability of infrastructure are:

- **Isolated areas:** In isolated areas with low population density infrastructure is not deployed due to cost reasons [68, 153, 188][3].
- **Developing countries:** While in the developed world Internet access is widely available, only 21% of the population in developing countries have access to infrastructure-based Internet access[4] [91, 127, 188].
- **Repressive regimes:** In face of repressive regimes infrastructure is often shut down or destroyed to prevent dissemination of incriminating material, e. g. video. Efforts to create parallel networks that can not be shut down by such regimes, based upon wireless mesh technology, are e. g. currently performed by the U. S. government [85].
- **Disaster scenarios:** In disaster scenarios infrastructure can get destroyed or partitioned and is no longer fully functional [131, 179]. HRS can be used in such scenarios for applications that are not time critical, e. g. collecting information about the destruction of streets and buildings.

---

[3]Video about the Saami Network Connectivity project [68] for providing delay tolerant Internet access for a population in Lapland is available at http://www.youtube.com/watch?v=veK77SFgsGo.

[4]Video about the VLink project which evolved from KioskNet [91] for connectivity in rural areas is available at http://www.youtube.com/watch?v=zxohVroSVIE.

HRS can enable communication in face of partial infrastructure through hybrid routing. Mechanisms described above are implemented as follows:

1. **Routing in the DTN through the mixed metric**: Strong emphasis should be placed to route towards infrastructure-capable devices. Even if only a small fraction of devices are infrastructure-capable. The evaluation in Section 4.9 will show that a static value of $\alpha = 1$ provides best message delivery performance.

2. **Deciding when messages are sent into the HRS overlay:** Whenever infrastructure access is encountered a message should be sent through the HRS overlay immediately. This, too, is implemented by setting $\alpha = 1$. Either a proxy with better awareness of the message is found through the overlay, or the current device is affirmed to have the highest awareness. In case of iHRS, additionally replicating the message into the overlay is beneficial as devices accessing the infrastructure at a later point in time can carry the message back into the DTN.

This strategy results in messages being routed in the source DTN towards infrastructure-capable devices first and result in immediate transfer in the HRS overlay. The overlay either provides a shortcut to a device with higher awareness for the destination device, or the lookup will indicate that the device currently storing the message is best suited.

4.8.2   Offloading Infrastructure

In case a large number or all devices are infrastructure-capable, the DTN can be used to offload data from infrastructure. Messages can be routed preferably in the DTN and be delivered in a cheap way without putting load on infrastructure—if increased delay up to a preconfigured TTL can be accepted. If a message could not be delivered before its TTL elapsed, the infrastructure can be used to directly deliver the message to its destination device. The scheme presented in the following has been published in [162].

Reasons to offload traffic from infrastructure networks are:

- **Overloaded infrastructure networks:** Due to strong growth in number of mobile devices, infrastructure networks have to handle a large and growing volume of traffic [180]. Cisco forecasts an increase in mobile data traffic from 0.6 Exabyte in 2011 up to 6.3 Exabyte in 2015—a strong increase with expected exponential growth [47].
- **Low value of data:** Infrastructure access is generally coupled with provider cost, either based on flat rate data plan, or volume-based rates. If, however the monetary value of data is low compared to cost of infrastructure usage, data can be routed in cheap DTN networks. Examples are statistical data obtained through urban sensing.
- **Keeping traffic local:** Infrastructure generally introduces paths often geographically longer than ad hoc communication paths. If traffic is to be kept local, DTN routing can be employed.

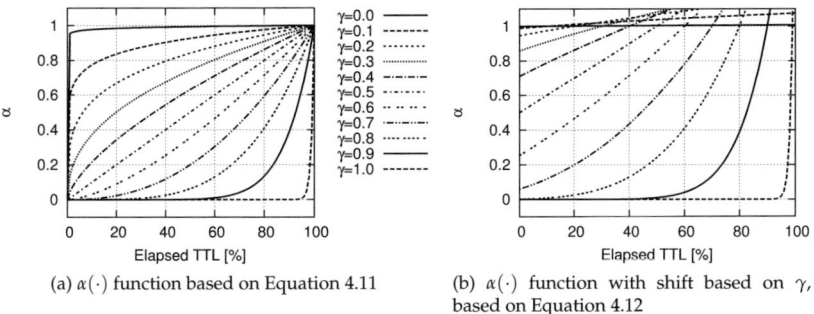

(a) $\alpha(\cdot)$ function based on Equation 4.11

(b) $\alpha(\cdot)$ function with shift based on γ, based on Equation 4.12

Figure 4.10 $\alpha(\cdot)$ function for determining routing strategy [162].

HRS can be used to offload traffic from infrastructure networks by preferring routing in the DTN over routing in the infrastructure. The main idea of the presented scheme is based on assurance that a message can be delivered through the infrastructure in case delivery in the DTN becomes unlikely or fails. The higher this assurance, the longer delivery of a message in the DTN is attempted. This routing strategy is implemented in HRS as follows:

1. **Routing in the DTN through the mixed metric:** Instead of a static α value, an $\alpha(\cdot)$ function is used on a per message basis by taking the elapsed message lifetime and information about the device heterogeneity for infrastructure access into account. Goal is to keep the message for longer duration in the DTN for delivery, and use the overlay if DTN delivery fails.

2. **Deciding when messages are sent into the HRS overlay:** The same $\alpha(\cdot)$ function is applied per message, and a message sent through the overlay if $\alpha(\cdot) \geq 1$.

Let $t_i(m)$ be the TTL of a message m, and $t_e(m)$ the age of the message, i.e. $t_i(m) - t_e(m)$ is the remaining lifetime, and $t_e(m)/t_i(m)$ the elapsed fraction of lifetime. If $t_e(m) > t_i(m)$ the message has expired. The percentage of infrastructure-capable devices in the network is denoted $\gamma \in [0,1]$. For use in the mixed metric, and for deciding when to send messages through the overlay, the $\alpha(\cdot)$ function is defined as[5]

$$\alpha\big(t_i(m), t_e(m), \gamma\big) = \left(\frac{t_e(m)}{t_i(m)}\right)^{\gamma/(1-\gamma)}. \tag{4.11}$$

---

[5]In case $\gamma = 1$, $\alpha(\cdot)$ is defined to be 0 if $t_e(m) < t_i(m)$, and 1 if $t_e(m) \geq t_i(m)$ to prevent division by zero.

Figure 4.10a shows the $\alpha(\cdot)$ function with different degree of infrastructure γ, and elapsed fraction of lifetime on the x-axis. Irrespective of γ, the $\alpha(\cdot)$ function becomes ≥ 1 when $t_e(m) \geq t_i(m)$, as can be easily shown[6]. Depending on γ, additional time needs to be considered for routing towards a device that actually *is* infrastructure-capable. This additional time directly depends on γ, therefore Equation 4.11 is shifted along the x-axis using $(1 - \gamma)$, resulting in

$$\alpha\big(t_i(m), t_e(m), \gamma\big) = \left(\frac{t_e(m)}{t_i(m)} + (1 - \gamma) \right)^{\gamma/(1-\gamma)}. \tag{4.12}$$

This shifted function is shown in Figure 4.10b. The point where $\alpha(\cdot)$ becomes ≥ 1 now directly depends on the fraction of infrastructure-capable devices γ, in contrast to Equation 4.11.

The $\alpha(\cdot)$ function is used to decide on routing through the mixed metric in Section 4.5.1 on a per-message basis in the DTN, based on the elapsed lifetime of a message, and the fraction γ of infrastructure-capable devices. It is evaluated on every routing decision in the DTN, and every time a decision is to be made whether the message is to be sent into the overlay. The value of γ is sampled by every device on its own when in contact with other devices. If $\alpha(\cdot) \geq 1$, the message is sent through the overlay towards its destination.

In case of $\gamma = 1$, i.e. all devices are infrastructure-capable, the strategy results in routing of the message in the DTN until its TTL "nearly" expired, and sending of the message through the overlay if delivery in the DTN was not successful. The value of γ reflects the *assurance* of successful delivery through the infrastructure, which is complete if $\gamma = 1$. The higher this assurance, the longer DTN routing can be performed. For implementation, the time required for sending the message through the overlay has to be accounted. For evaluation in Section 4.9 the message is made artificially older 5 min to account for the overlay transfer.

While DTN protocols often use multi-copy routing, the offloading scheme is built around single-copy mode. In case of multi-copy mode, feedback would be required whether a copy of the message was already delivered successfully. Otherwise, multiple copies of the same message get delivered through the infrastructure.

4.9   Evaluation and Analysis

In this section simulative evaluation and analysis of the Hybrid Routing System using the simulation environment and methodology described in Appendix A is performed. Goal of this evaluation is to analyze suitable param-

---

[6]If $\alpha\big(t_i(m), t_e(m), \gamma\big) \geq 1$, it holds $\left(\frac{t_e(m)}{t_i(m)} \right)^{\gamma/(1-\gamma)} \geq 1$ and therewith $\frac{t_e(m)}{t_i(m)} \geq 1^{-\gamma/(1-\gamma)}$. It must hold $\frac{t_e(m)}{t_i(m)} \geq 1$, and it follows $t_e(m) \geq t_i(m)$. $\square$

eters for configuring and tuning the system, and to give insight into performance and load metrics with respect to the presented use cases.

4.9.1   Assumptions and Simplifications

Wireless Channel   Characteristics of the wireless channel are simplified using the *Unit Disk Model*[7] [125]. Devices exchange messages under a finite constant bandwidth model when they undercut a configuration-specific communication range, and otherwise not. Wireless connectivity is a binary decision, and not subject to noise or interference. A device can have only one concurrent ad hoc communication session. Simplification of the wireless channel is necessary to keep simulation time and complexity manageable. While communication range impacts the number of contacts in DTNs and therewith performance [66], goal of this evaluation is to show the inherent performance gains through hybrid routing.

Overlay Model   Two overlay models are used: A *centralized* model calculates symmetric key-based routing routes. For validation of the centralized model, a *distributed* version based upon simulator coupling with Over-Sim [24] is used, as described in Section A.5. Simulation results presented are based on the centralized model, which is comparable to a symmetric Chord [239] protocol. Stabilization of the central overlay is atomic, i. e. the centralized overlay state is always consistent. Only graceful leave of nodes is assumed. Section 4.6.4 describes mechanisms for handling of ungraceful leave, those are, however, not employed in the simulation model to reduce complexity. Simplifications in the overlay model allow to focus on the inherent trade-offs of hybrid routing without effects from the specific key-based routing overlay protocol.

Device Queues   Devices have local queues for storing messages not destined for them. One queue is employed for DTN routing, in case of iHRS an additional queue is employed for overlay message storage. Both queues are separate and messages not mixed, i. e. the DTN protocol can *not* forward messages from the iHRS queue and vice versa. Unit of queue size is given in number of messages. To prevent effects resulting from limited queue size such as replacement effects, unlimited queue size is used in simulations. This allows analysis of queue size requirements on mobile devices. Evaluation results show, if not stated otherwise, the sum of messages in both DTN queue and iHRS queue to reflect message load on a device.

Infrastructure Access   Section A.4 describes simulator extensions to provide persistent and temporary infrastructure access. Similar to ad hoc communication, the Unit Disc Model is used for communication between

---

[7]Originally called "Unit Disc Graph", the model describes the intersection graph of unit circles, based on euclidean distance in a 2D plane.

mobile devices and infrastructure access. Persistent infrastructure access is assumed to be implemented using cellular networks with perfect coverage. For temporary infrastructure access, WiFi access points are placed uniformly at randomly over the network area. In this case the geographic coverage is used as metric.

4.9.2   Performance Metrics and Setup

Message performance metrics

Most interesting performance metrics are message delivery ratio, and message delivery delay. Note, that the goal of this evaluation is not a comparison of DTN protocols, but rather evaluation of the hybrid routing in general and HRS in special. Performance measures are therefore only comparable within one setup.

- **Message delivery ratio:** The message delivery ratio gives information on communication performance. It is defined as number of unique messages successfully delivered, divided by the number of unique messages generated by sources. Message replication is not accounted in this metric, i. e. only unique messages are of interest.

- **Message delivery delay:** Delay of delivered messages is important for analyzing the potential use cases and applications that can be built upon a hybrid network. Note, that only successfully delivered messages are accounted for delay measure. As messages have a fixed TTL, the TTL value is the upper delay bound a delivered message can have.

Message Cost

DTN routing presents a trade-off between performance and cost. Through replication higher performance can be achieved up to a point where the network gets congested, or wireless interference reduces efficiency. These metrics analyze the cost in the network that results in load on mobile devices.

- **Message Redundancy Degree:** This metric analyzes the average number of replicas per originally sent message in the network.

- **Worst device queues:** Devices have local message queues. This metric analyzes the worst device message queue over a scenario to find a worst-case estimation of queue size requirements.

- **Ad hoc communication per delivered message:** This metric describes the number of ad hoc communications that directly resulted in a successful delivery of a message, divided by the overall message transfers in the network. It gives information on the average communication cost that is required to successfully delivery *one* message.

- **Ad hoc communication per device:** This metric analyzes the ad hoc communication overhead per device in a given time duration. It gives information on the device load in terms of wireless communication.

- **DTN hops:** Similar to communication cost, the number of DTN hops required to successfully deliver a message is of interest. Only successfully delivered messages are included. DTN hops exclude the sender device, but include the destination device, i. e. a hop is counted for every device that receives the message.

Overlay

The overlay schemes developed in this thesis results in additional communication overhead for sending/receiving/forwarding/storing of messages, both for control and data. It is important that the gains of the hybrid approach justify the additional overhead.

- **Overlay size:** Overlay size is defined as number of nodes joined in the overlay. This is an important metric for resulting load and scalability. It is mainly used for cross-checks and validation of other overlay metrics.

- **Key-based routing path length:** Overlay load in terms of message forwarding is directly influenced by the overlay size, and length of key-based routing paths. Typical scalable overlay networks provide logarithmic path length with the number of nodes in the overlay.

- **Overlay load per node:** Devices taking part in the overlay need to handle load in terms of data and control messages that are sent, received, and forwarded. The additional load introduced through the overlay must be justified by increased network delivery performance and be manageable by the mobile device.

- **Overlay stability:** In case of vHRS, virtual nodes are placed in the overlay at strategic positions to reflect awareness. Awareness changes over time and virtual nodes have to be joined and removed from the overlay with adapted node identifiers. This result in churn in the overlay, characterized as number of nodes joining and leaving over time.

Simulation Setup

Parameters used for evaluation are given in Table 4.5. If the mobility model is not explicitly stated, SWIM is used (cf. Section 2.3.3). In case human working day specific behavior is required the mobility model described in Section A.9 is used. If not stated otherwise, 100 mobile devices[8] are simulated

---

[8]Note, that especially the density of devices on the network area is of importance, not so much the overall number of devices. Simulations with a larger number of mobile devices become unmanageable in terms of simulation duration due to the high number of simulation setups evaluated in this chapter.

Category	Value
Mobile devices	$n = 100$
Movement speed	1–3 m/s, uniformly distributed
Ad hoc comm. range	$r = 15$ m
Bandwidth	2.1 MBit/s (Bluetooth v2 EDR)
Infra. comm. range	$r = 50$ m, $b = 50$ access points or variable
Mobility model	○ SWIM [166], wait-time slope 1.45, cutoff 12, $\alpha_{swim} = 0.8$
	○ Working day model described in Section A.9
Message generation	every 15 min–20 min per device process
Message size	○ Providing comm.: 250 kByte
	○ Offloading infra.: 250 kByte up to 8 MByte
Message destination	uniformly at random over all devices
Message TTL	○ Providing comm.: 1 h
	○ Offloading infra.: 1 h, 3 h, 5 h, 10 h
Infrastructure-capable	$P(\mathcal{D}_p) = \gamma \in [0,1]$ of mobile devices
Ad hoc capable	○ Providing comm.: all devices
	○ Offloading infra.: $\delta \in [0,1]$ of mobile devices
DTN routing protocol	Prophet [154, 155], MaxProp [35], Spray&Focus [229]
Network area	map of Karlsruhe, Germany, 2×2 km
p_{join}	0.7
$vmax$	10
Prophet	○ unit 30 s, $P_{init} = 0.5$, transitive $\beta = 0.2$, aging $\gamma = 0.996$
	○ long-term contact stability using $\bar{P}_{target} = 0.7$
Spray&Focus	awareness duration $\Delta = 12$ h, multi-copy mode $c = 10$ [229]
	(multi-copy set according to [229] to $c = 10\%$ of devices)
Seeds per scenario	30
Simulation warmup	7 days
Simulation reporting	1 day

Table 4.5 Simulation parameters.

on a 2×2 km map of Karlsruhe, Germany. Infrastructure-capability classes differ in most scenarios and are described in the respective sections. Message generation is a stochastic per-device process, with a new message being generated every 15–20 min. The message's destination device is chosen uniformly at random over all devices except the sender. Bluetooth v2.0 EDR data rates of 2.1 MBit/s are assumed together with a message size of 250 KByte up to 8 MByte. This results in transfer of approximately 1 message per second between devices in mutual communication range. Figures show mean values based on at least 30 seeds with 95% confidence intervals.

4.9.3   Use Case: Providing Communication

This section presents performance and cost metrics of HRS when used to provide communication, as described in the use case in Section 4.8.1.

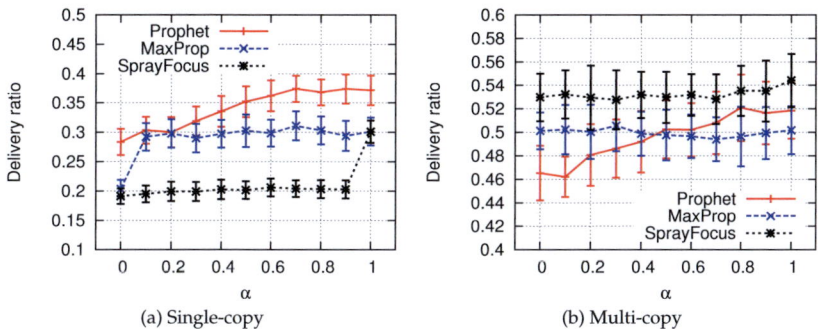

Figure 4.11 Influence of the α parameter on iHRS delivery ratio.

Routing direction

An initial decision has to be made whether to route based on awareness for a message's destination device, or route based on awareness for infrastructure access. This decision is implemented using the α parameter of the mixed metric, as described in Section 4.5.1. Figure 4.11 shows the impact of α on the delivery ratio for iHRS using the three reference protocols in single-copy mode, and multi-copy mode. A mix of infrastructure-capability classes are used with $P(\mathcal{D}_p) = 0.2$, $P(\mathcal{D}_t) = 0.4$, and $P(\mathcal{D}_n) = 0.4$. Using $\alpha = 1$ results in strong focus for routing towards infrastructure-capable devices and immediate transfer of the message through the overlay. While the performance gain is clearly visible in the single-copy case, the increased replication through multi-copy diminishes the effect of α. It can be concluded that initial focus for routing towards infrastructure-capable devices using $\alpha = 1$ is beneficial for the use case of providing communication. Remaining evaluation of this use case employs a static parametrization of $\alpha = 1$.

Performance

Increasing the fraction of devices with persistent infrastructure access $P(\mathcal{D}_p)$ naturally results in higher delivery ratio, as the probability that two devices can communicate directly through the overlay is increased. To analyze this effect, in the following no devices with temporary infrastructure-access are used ($P(\mathcal{D}_t) = 0$), and it is defined $\gamma = P(\mathcal{D}_p)$ and $1 - \gamma = P(\mathcal{D}_n)$, i.e. $\gamma \in [0, 1]$ represents the fraction of infrastructure-capable devices and is shown on the x-axis.

A higher fraction γ increases the chance that source and destination devices are both infrastructure-capable and can exchange messages directly through the overlay. Additionally, cooperative routing works better with more infrastructure-capable devices as routing state distributed in the overlay is kept

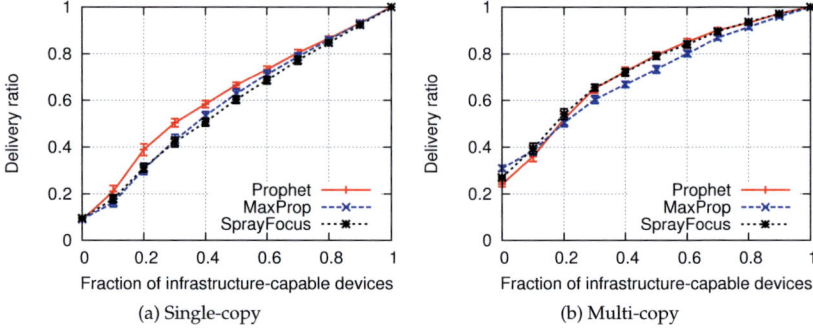

Figure 4.12   Influence of fraction of infrastructure-capable devices on overall message delivery performance in iHRS.

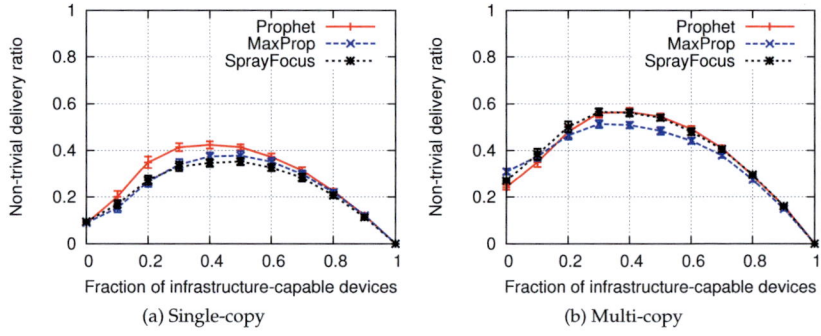

Figure 4.13   Delivery performance without taking communication between both infrastructure-capable sender and destination into account.

more up-to-date. Figure 4.12 shows the message delivery ratio for iHRS on the y-axis with different fraction of infrastructure-capable devices γ on the x-axis. $\gamma = 0$ results in a pure DTN scenario, while $\gamma = 1$ results in a pure overlay-based scenario. A pure DTN scenario has delivery ratio of under 20% in single-copy mode, and under 30% in multi-copy mode for the scenario analyzed. A pure overlay-based scenario has, as expected, a full delivery ratio of 1. Adding a small fraction of infrastructure-capable devices to a DTN scenario increases the message delivery performance of the overall network. Note, that the general performance increase is dependent on the allowed TTL of messages, a higher TTL results in higher absolute delivery performance. This visually pulls the delivery ratio curves into the upper left corner.

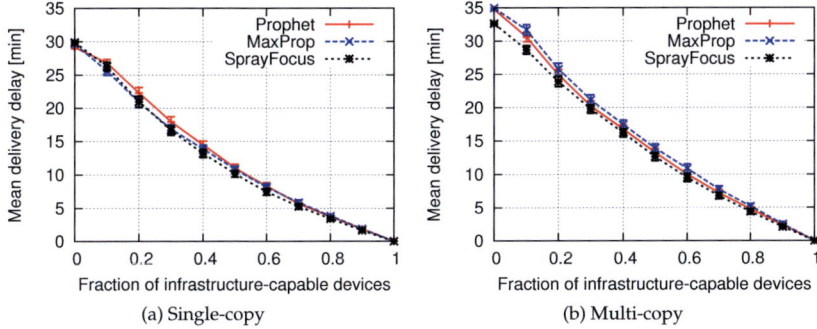

(a) Single-copy   (b) Multi-copy

Figure 4.14 Mean delivery delay in single-copy and multi-copy, based on fraction of infrastructure-capable devices.

Increasing the fraction of infrastructure-capable devices increases the probability that both sender and destination device are infrastructure-capable. This probability that both source and destination devices of a message are infrastructure-capable, and can communicate directly through the overlay, is γ^2, as the message destination device is selected uniformly at random. Communication between such devices can be considered "trivial" from perspective of HRS. Figure 4.13 shows message delivery ratio without taking messages into account that were exchanged between infrastructure-capable sender and destination devices. HRS has an optimal support point where the hybrid approach supports the overall network at best, which is around $\gamma = 0.4$ for the considered scenario. Generally, this best support point is expected to be in the area where heterogeneity in terms of infrastructure-capability is highest.

Figure 4.14 shows the mean delivery delay for single-copy and multi-copy routing, again based on the fraction of infrastructure-capable devices. Note, that TTL counters are used in the metadata of messages to ensure that a message is either delivered within its TTL time bound, or—if delivery was not possible within the TTL—messages are deleted and do not load the network unnecessarily. This mean delivery delay is in the order of TTL/2 for pure DTN scenarios, and decreases as more infrastructure-capable devices are added that allow for faster delivery. Note, that only successfully delivered messages are taken into account for calculating mean delivery delay.

Note, that mean delivery delay in multi-copy routing is higher. Single-copy routing is only able to deliver messages that are "easy" to deliver. Such "easy" messages have a short DTN path and therefore get delivered within short time. Multi-copy routing is able to *additionally* deliver messages that require

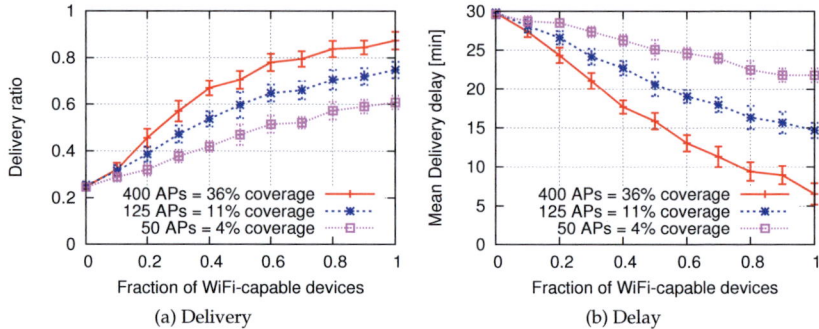

Figure 4.15 Influence of fraction of devices with WiFi access and WiFi coverage.

longer routing paths and therefore have longer resulting delay. Averaging over all messages, the mean delivery delay using multi-copy routing is higher.

The impact of scaling the number of devices $\mathcal{D}_t$ and $\mathcal{D}_n$ with no infrastructure-capable devices $\mathcal{D}_p$ is shown in Figure 4.15 for delivery ratio and delivery delay, using Prophet as DTN protocol and iHRS. Different geographic coverage of WiFi access points is considered, while access points are placed uniformly at random over the network area[9]. Integrating devices $\mathcal{D}_t$ generates two new dimensions of complexity: First, the actual fraction of devices $\mathcal{D}_t$, and second, the WiFi coverage in the network area. Both dimensions are correlated and further have a dependency with the mobility of devices. While increasing *coverage* of access points increases the delivery ratio as shown in Figure 4.15a, increasing the *fraction* of devices that can actually make use of access points, shown on the x-axis, has higher benefits in terms of delivery ratio. It can be stated, that increasing the number of devices that can access infrastructure through WiFi is beneficial in terms of delivery ratio, compared to increasing WiFi coverage: In the analyzed scenario, using a coverage of 4% and $P(\mathcal{D}_t) = 1.0$ results in the same delivery ratio as 11% coverage with $P(\mathcal{D}_t) = 0.5$, or 36% coverage with $P(\mathcal{D}_t) = 0.3$. In the considered setting delivery delay is initially around TTL/2 for a pure DTN scenario. The strength in the decrease of mean delivery delay shown in Figure 4.15b depends on the fraction of WiFi-capable devices and the WiFi coverage. The main reason for the decrease in mean delivery delay is the time-decoupling provided by iHRS. As source and destination devices are not required to be infrastructure-

---

[9]Percentaged coverage includes overlapping, resulting from independent uniform distribution of access point over the network area.

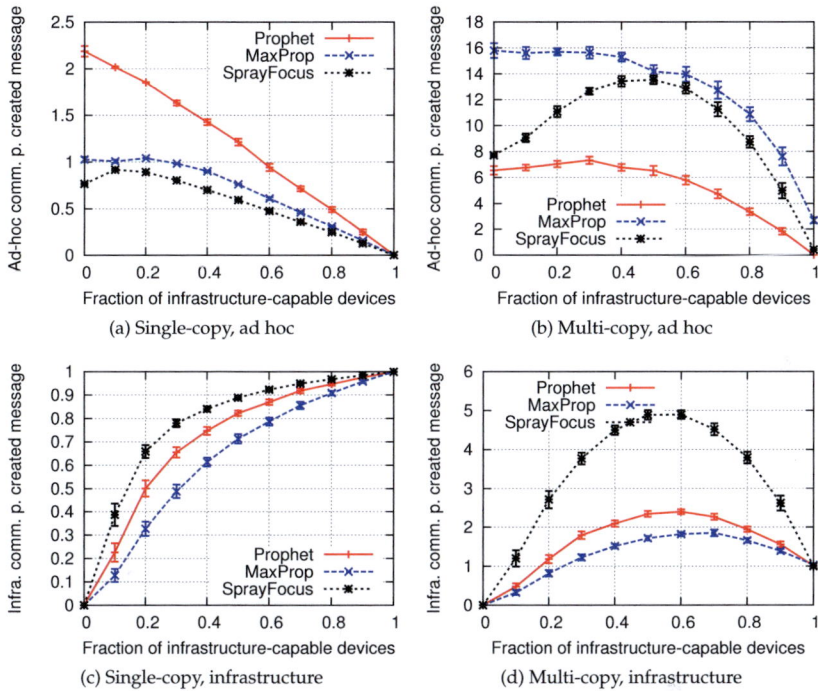

Figure 4.16 Ad hoc and infrastructure communication per created message.

connected at the same time, shorter routing paths can be used with the help of iHRS proxies.

Cost

DTN routing is a trade-off between performance and cost. Cost is in the following divided into communication cost that describes communication efforts, and storage cost that describes device queue size. Increased replication results in better performance, up to a point where the network congests. Replication, however, increases wireless communication cost as multiple copies of the same message are routed in the network. Furthermore, routing multiple message copies increases storage requirements on the mobile devices.

Figure 4.16a and Figure 4.16b show the average number of ad hoc message exchanges in the network, generated per *created* message, dependent on the ratio of infrastructure-capable devices on the *x*-axis. For single-copy routing this cost factor shows a general decreasing behavior with the fraction of infrastructure-capable devices, up to the point where no DTN routing is performed and all messages are delivered through the overlay. Ad hoc communication cost for multi-copy routing shows initial increase due to stronger replication, and then decreases until a pure overlay-based scenario. Compared to single-copy routing, in multi-copy the general ad hoc communication overhead is higher as one created message is replicated into multiple messages, resulting in more messages being routed in the network through ad hoc communication. The DTN protocol itself determines how often messages are forwarded/replicated in the DTN, which is reflected in the different absolute values in Figure 4.16b. From the point of strongest heterogeneity at $x \approx 0.5$ a decrease with increasing infrastructure-capable devices is observed.

In hybrid routing additional cost results from maintenance of the overlay structure, and routing of messages towards proxies. This cost factor is shown for single-copy routing in Figure 4.16c, and for multi-copy routing in Figure 4.16d, again per created message. In case of single-copy routing, the y-axis depicts the absolute, but also the fraction of messages that traverse the infrastructure. Those messages increase strongly, already with small fraction of infrastructure-capable devices, resulting from $\alpha = 1$ in the mixed metric that routes messages preferably towards infrastructure. In case of multi-copy routing a message replica is only allowed to traverse the infrastructure once, however, several copies of the same message might traverse the infrastructure. In case of strongest heterogeneity in infrastructure at around $x \approx 0.5$ a peak in infrastructure load is observed due to message strong replication. In case $x = 1$ a pure overlay-based scenario results, with every message being delivered without replication through the infrastructure directly, both in single-copy routing and multi-copy routing.

Prior cost metrics analyzed cost generated by *additional* messages and are important to understand how the message generation process has impact on device and network load. Cost from perspective of an *individual* device is analyzed to understand load generated on devices, resulting from the cooperative routing approach. Figure 4.17 shows communication cost from perspective of one device as the average number of messages per hour that have to be processed in ad hoc communication, and infrastructure communication.

Ad hoc communication cost in Figure 4.17a and Figure 4.17b shows general small overhead in single-copy mode, while multi-copy mode shows much higher overhead due to replication of messages. Overhead for ad hoc communication decreases quickly for both single-copy and multi-copy, as already a small fraction of infrastructure-capable devices support the overall network strongly. Cost for infrastructure communication grows quickly with small fraction of infrastructure-capable devices. While in single-copy this cost factor grows steadily, in multi-copy routing the highest infrastructure cost is reached at high heterogeneity of the network around $x \approx 0.5$ to $x \approx 0.7$.

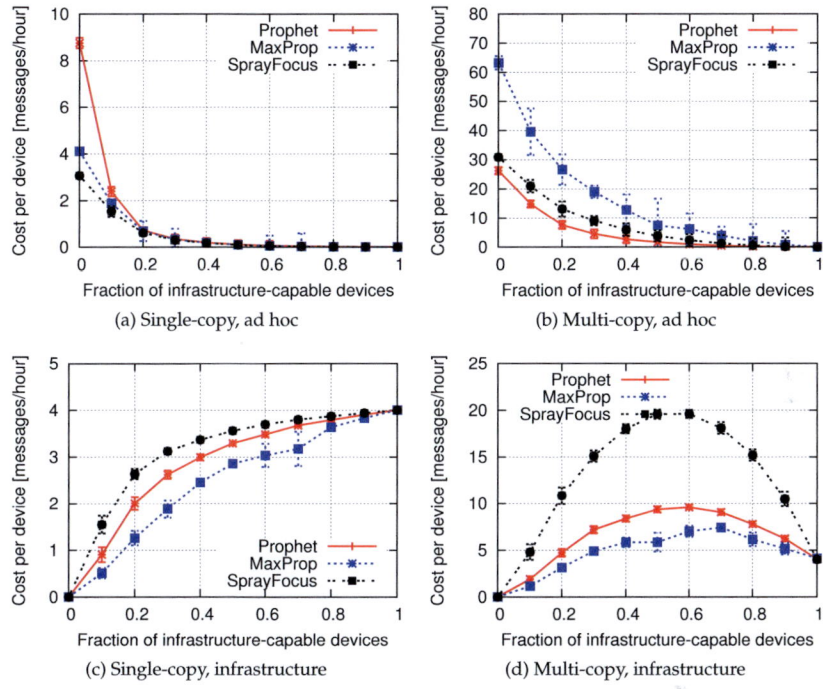

Figure 4.17 Communication cost per device in messages per hour.

From this point on infrastructure cost decreases, converging to a pure overlay-based approach with cost equal to single-copy routing. This resulting infrastructure cost directly depends on the message generation process run by every device.

Cost in terms of queue size is shown in Figure 4.18. Queue size is defined as sum of DTN queue and overlay queue in iHRS, calculated as number of messages. Mean queue size in Figure 4.18a for single-copy and Figure 4.18b for multi-copy behave very different. While for single-copy routing mean queue size decreases linearly with the fraction of infrastructure-capable devices, mean queue size either decreases slowly, or even initially grows for multi-copy routing. In both copy schemes, mean queue size decreases steadily with a larger fraction of infrastructure-capable devices. Worst case queue size are shown in Figure 4.18c and Figure 4.18d, again for single-copy and multi-copy routing, respectively. The general trend of worst case queue size is similar to that of mean queue size, however with much higher actual values. While in single-copy routing worst queue size is up to $70\times$ of mean queue

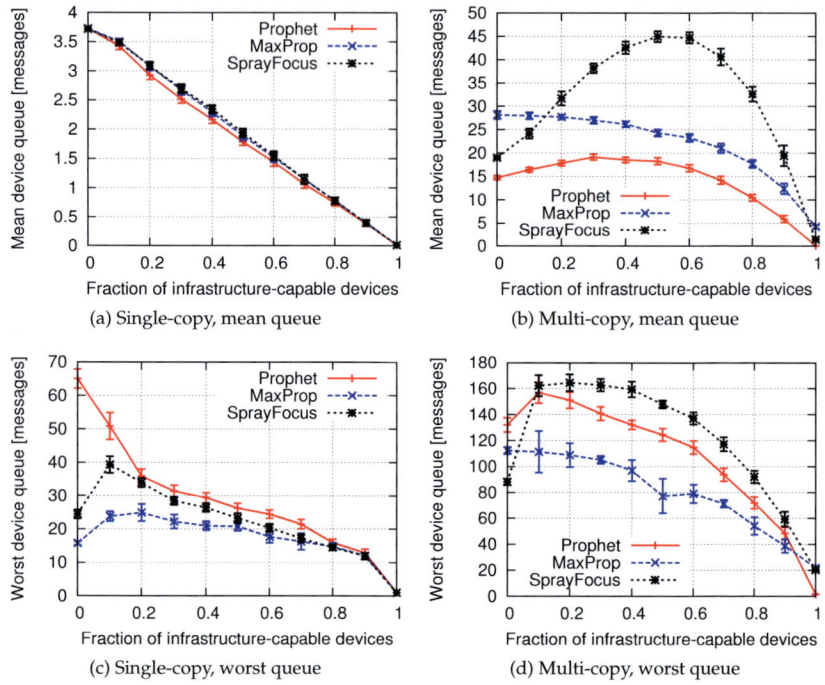

Figure 4.18 Local device queues including DTN and overlay message queue.

size, in multi-copy routing a maximal of 4× of mean queue size is observed. The difference in messages queue size between the protocols depends on the replication strength, and the message delivery ratio. Using a message size of 250 kByte and a worst queue size of 170 messages results in ≈ 42 MByte of storage under the analyzed message generation process and TTL. Given today's smartphones with Gigabytes of available storage, this storage requirement is manageable.

Performance vs. Cost

Section 4.4 described different combinations of copy-modes in hybrid routing. Overall, 16 combinations can be defined, based on single-copy and multi-copy for the different parts of the hybrid routing protocol. Table 4.6 shows IDs of respective copy-mode combinations used in the following. Figure 4.19 uses those IDs to show a performance vs. cost comparison between delivery ratio on the y-axis, and average number of replicas created per message on the x-axis. Every data point describes one of the 16 copy mode combinations. Note, that the y-axis is inverted, so that an optimal performance-cost trade-off is in

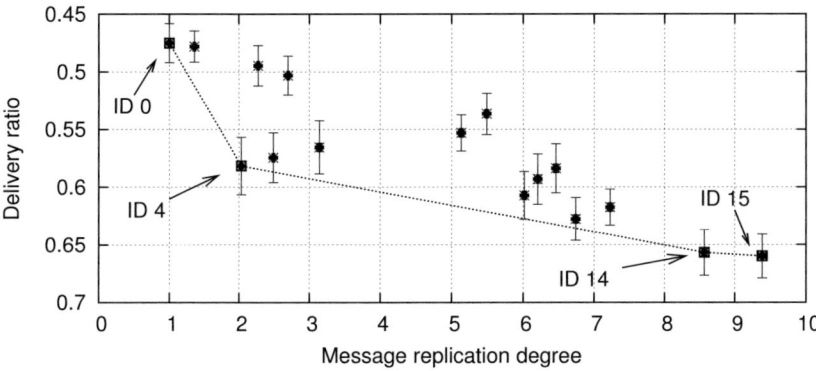

Figure 4.19 Performance vs. cost trade-off in delivery ratio and message replication.

direction of the origin, i. e. 1 replica per message and perfect message delivery ratio of 1. All points closest to the origin are optimal, i. e. they all represent optimal solutions under different conditions. Those points are linked through the dotted line in Figure 4.19, and highlighted in Table 4.6.

No single optimal solution can exist in such a scenario, as scaling of the x-axis and y-axis to another can not be fixed. Copy-mode combination ID 0 is pure single-copy routing, and ID 15 pure multi-copy routing in all steps of the protocol. Based on the notation from Section 4.4, ID 4 describes single-single-multi-single, and ID 14 describes multi-multi-multi-single. Copy-mode combination ID 4 is interesting from the load perspective as it only performs multi-copy when moving a message from overlay to DTN. Generally, it can be observed that single-copy routing in the destination DTN suffices, as the device found in HRS provides a good proxy for routing in the destination DTN. The HRS overlay allows to maintain DTN routing information in an aggregated and up-to-date form, therefore routing decisions in the overlay part of HRS are generally better than in the DTN.

Overlay

Figure 4.20 shows the overlay behavior for iHRS and vHRS, based on multi-copy mode and Prophet as DTN protocol. Prophet is beneficial for iHRS as it allows for autonomous aging in the proxy devices themselves. A mix of $P(\mathcal{D}_p) = 0.5$ and $P(\mathcal{D}_n) = 0.5$ is used, as previous evaluation showed that such strongly heterogeneous scenarios are most challenging. The number of overall devices is increased with the x-axis. Note, that the size of the network area is fixed, therefore increase of number of devices results in increased de-

ID	C1	C2	C3	C4	Delivery ratio	Redundancy degree
0	single	single	single	single	0.47	1.00
1	single	single	single	multi	0.49	2.27
2	single	single	multi	single	0.58	2.03
3	single	single	multi	multi	0.56	3.14
4	single	multi	single	single	0.47	1.35
5	single	multi	single	multi	0.50	2.69
6	single	multi	multi	single	0.57	2.49
7	single	multi	multi	multi	0.58	6.46
8	multi	single	single	single	0.53	5.48
9	multi	single	single	multi	0.55	5.13
10	multi	single	multi	single	0.60	6.01
11	multi	single	multi	multi	0.59	6.20
12	multi	multi	single	single	0.61	7.22
13	multi	multi	single	multi	0.62	6.74
14	multi	multi	multi	single	0.65	8.56
15	multi	multi	multi	multi	0.65	9.38

Table 4.6   Copy-mode combinations and resulting performance/cost. Highlighted rows represent optimal combinations.

vice density. Figure 4.20a shows the overlay load per device in terms of messages per second, including data and HRS control messages. Generally, iHRS has higher load due to the indirection and maintenance of distributed state. A logarithmic growth can be observed, due to the distributed overlay character. The decrease in load for vHRS can be explained due to increased density of devices in the DTN, resulting in a larger fraction of messages being delivered in the DTN directly, without requiring routing through the overlay[10].

Figure 4.20b shows the fraction of successfully delivered messages that have been routed through the overlay. iHRS is able to better help in delivery of messages compared to vHRS, due to additional storage of messages in the overlay and freshness of awareness values that allow for better routing decisions. The decrease of this fraction with increasing number of devices shows that pure DTN routing becomes more successful with increased device density. The size of the overlay in number of nodes is shown in Figure 4.20c. iHRS generally results in smaller overlay size, as vHRS places additional virtual nodes to manage awareness information. The size of the virtual set V_i is configuration-bounded using $vmax$ and the actual size converges to this bound, as increased density of devices results in higher awareness. Under low device density the awareness values do not reach the configured threshold p_{join}, which is required for inclusion into V_i. Figure 4.20d shows the message delivery ratio. The decrease when using iHRS is the result of congestion in the network due to finite bandwidth in ad hoc communication, and increasing device density due to fixed network area size. vHRS shows a dif-

---

[10]With high probability this scaling behavior becomes visible for iHRS, too, however such large simulations were not manageable in reasonable time.

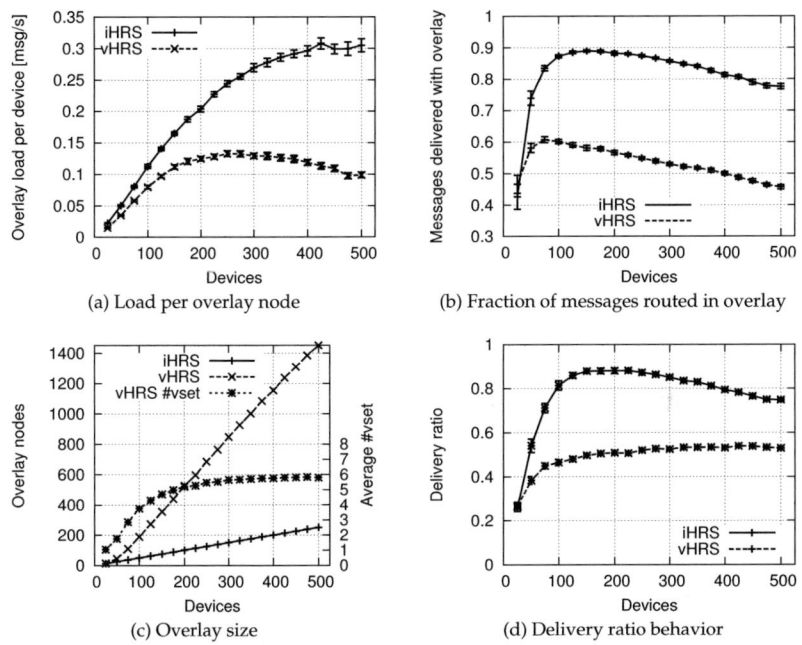

Figure 4.20 Behavior of HRS under scaling the number of devices with fixed network area.

ferent behavior due to fewer replication than iHRS that stores in multi-copy mode a replica of the message in the overlay.

Awareness Stability

As described in Section 4.6, iHRS can work for dynamic, as well as for long-term contact awareness, due to its indirection-based maintenance of awareness values. vHRS, on the other hand, induces churn in the overlay if contact awareness changes and is best suited if contact awareness is comparably stable. Such stability can be achieved if the long-term behavior of the contact graph is considered. Karvo and Ott [137] present awareness-stabilization for Prophet that is used in the following to achieve stable awareness with a target-time scale of one week. For evaluation the mobility model described in Section A.9 is used as it provides deterministic periodicity. It can be seen, that as contact behavior stabilizes and awareness becomes stable, churn is reduced in vHRS, as shown in Figure 4.21a, as adjustment of virtual nodes becomes infrequent. After stabilization of contact awareness churn is reduced to at most 1 join/leave per hour. Delivery ratio shown in Figure 4.21b increases over

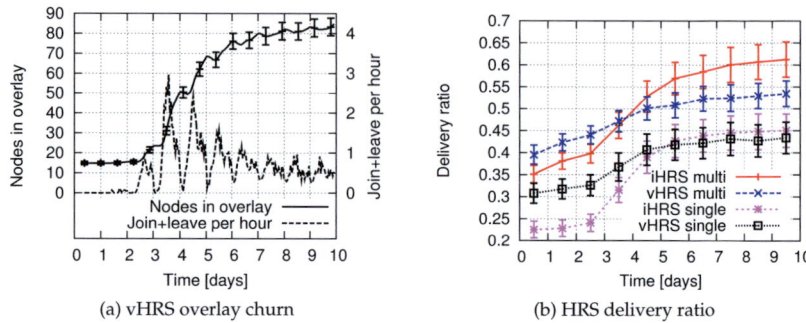

(a) vHRS overlay churn   (b) HRS delivery ratio

Figure 4.21 Overlay behavior and HRS delivery ratio with long-term DTN contact awareness under stabilization.

the course of stabilization: First, the stabilization of contact awareness results in better routing decisions in the DTN routing itself. Second, HRS can perform better routing decisions inside the overlay due to more accurate contact awareness. iHRS generally has a higher delivery ratio due to more replication inside the overlay, and more accurate awareness values through the indirection step. Notably, the single-copy variants of both vHRS and iHRS achieve a strong performance boost resulting from stabilization of contact awareness.

4.9.4 Use Case: Offloading Infrastructure

When a large fraction, or even all, devices are infrastructure-capable, HRS can be used to offload infrastructure networks by routing messages preferably in the DTN. Section 4.8.2 described this use case and how to implement it using a dynamic $\alpha(\cdot)$ function that determines the message routing strategy in the DTN, and determines when messages are sent through the overlay. Goal is to first try to deliver messages in the DTN, and use the overlay if delivery was not possible within the message's TTL. The higher the TTL, the more time is available for routing in the DTN, and the higher the chances that the message can be delivered in the DTN without residing to infrastructure. Four TTL classes are analyzed in the following: 1 h, 3 h, 5 h, and 10 h. Higher TTL values are not of realistic interest, as wired or high-bandwidth wireless access is normally encountered after a period of at most half a day [136].

Note, that infrastructure offloading only makes sense with a larger fraction of infrastructure-capable devices, i.e. $\gamma = P(\mathcal{D}_p) \rightarrow 1$. Two dimensions of heterogeneity are analyzed in the following: Using a different fraction of infrastructure-capable devices $\gamma \in [0,1]$, and using a different fraction of ad hoc-capable devices $\delta \in [0,1]$. The following restrictions are used to keep the analysis manageable and the scenarios realistic:

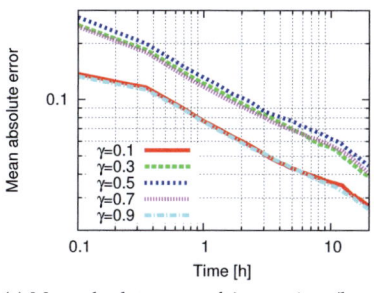 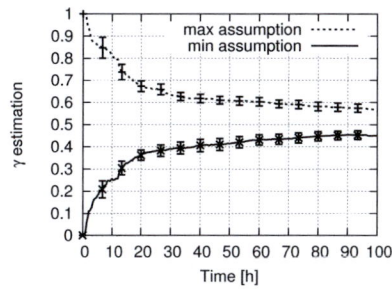

(a) Mean absolute error of $\hat{\gamma}$ over time (log-log axis).

(b) Worst min/max estimation over time for $\gamma = 0.5$.

Figure 4.22 Estimation error of $\hat{\gamma}$ over time [162].

- If *not all* devices are infrastructure-capable, then *all* devices are ad hoc capable: $\gamma \in [0,1) \rightarrow \delta = 1$.
- If *not all* devices are ad hoc capable, then *all* devices are infrastructure-capable: $\delta \in [0,1) \rightarrow \gamma = 1$.

Sampling Infrastructure Capabilities

The routing strategy does not depend on the value of δ, as the main goal is to offload infrastructure. The fraction of infrastructure-capable devices γ, however, is required for implementing the routing strategy through the $\alpha(\cdot)$ function (cf. Section 4.8.2). Devices independently sample the value of γ when in contact with other devices, and build up a local estimation $\hat{\gamma}$. For evaluation of this estimation accuracy simple averaging is used where devices exchange their infrastructure-capability classes during contact, and average over the collected values; defining $\gamma = 1$ for devices $\mathcal{D}_p$, and $\gamma = 0$ for devices $\mathcal{D}_n$.

Figure 4.22a shows the mean absolute error on log-log axis for different network heterogeneity γ, averaged over all devices in the network, i. e. the mean error is calculated as $(\sum_{d_i \in \mathcal{D}} |\hat{\gamma}_i - \gamma|)/\#devices$. This mean error falls very quickly within a few hours after contact with a few devices. Estimation of γ is most challenging with highest heterogeneity in the network, which is at $\gamma = 0.5$. For this scenario, Figure 4.22b shows the two worst case estimates observed over time in the network. At every point in time the γ estimation of all devices is analyzed and the worst case estimates shown, in both positive and negative direction. While worst-case estimation does not fall as quickly as the mean error, an acceptable value of < 0.1 is reached after ≈ 2 days.

Simulations show that it is feasible for devices to sample the value of γ autonomously. Note, that only a simple averaging scheme has been used that already performs acceptably. Using transitive distribution of estimates can

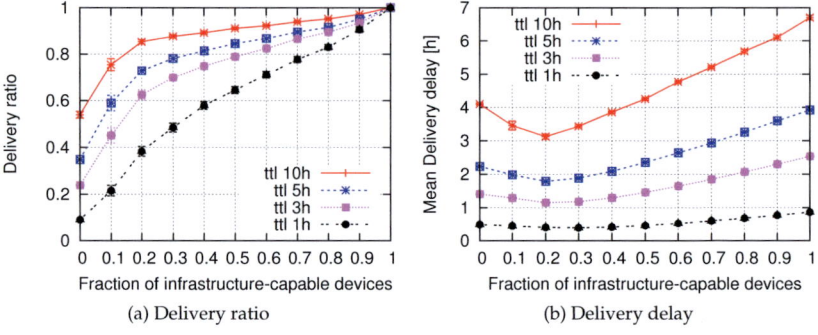

Figure 4.23 Performance metrics for variation of infrastructure access $\gamma \in [0,1]$, all devices ad hoc capable $\delta = 1$ [162].

further decrease convergence time. In the remaining simulations the value of γ is set through an oracle to exclude effects resulting from estimation errors.

Variation in Infrastructure-capability

When varying the fraction of infrastructure-capable devices γ, different $\alpha(\cdot)$ functions result, which are used to find a compromise between offloading of infrastructure under the restriction of acceptable delivery ratio. Figure 4.23a shows the achievable delivery ratio, based on γ on the x-axis, and with different TTL. As not all devices are infrastructure-capable, no full delivery ratio can be achieved. Note, that for the use case of offloading only large γ values are reasonable, i.e. $\gamma \gg 0.5$. For such scenarios a delivery ratio of over 60% can be achieved using a TTL of 1 h, and up to 90% using a TTL of 10 h. The steep initial rise of delivery ratio results in initial drop in delay, as shown in Figure 4.23b, as with increasing infrastructure a larger fraction of devices can be delivered more quickly. Delay rises afterward as more focus is put onto offloading, and therewith longer routing of messages in the DTN. Generally, the scheme guarantees that if a message is successfully delivered, it is delivered within the application-defined TTL.

Offloading and cost metrics are shown in Figure 4.24. Generally, the offloaded fraction is highly dependent on the TTL of messages which determines the time the routing scheme tries to deliver messages through DTN. The fraction of traffic that is offloaded from the infrastructure is approximated in Figure 4.24a. It can only be calculated exactly for $\gamma = 0$, and $\gamma = 1$, and is approximated for $0 < \gamma < 1$. The offloaded fraction is approximated using the fraction of messages delivered purely in the DTN, multiplied by γ for normalization. As the fraction of infrastructure-capable devices γ is increased,

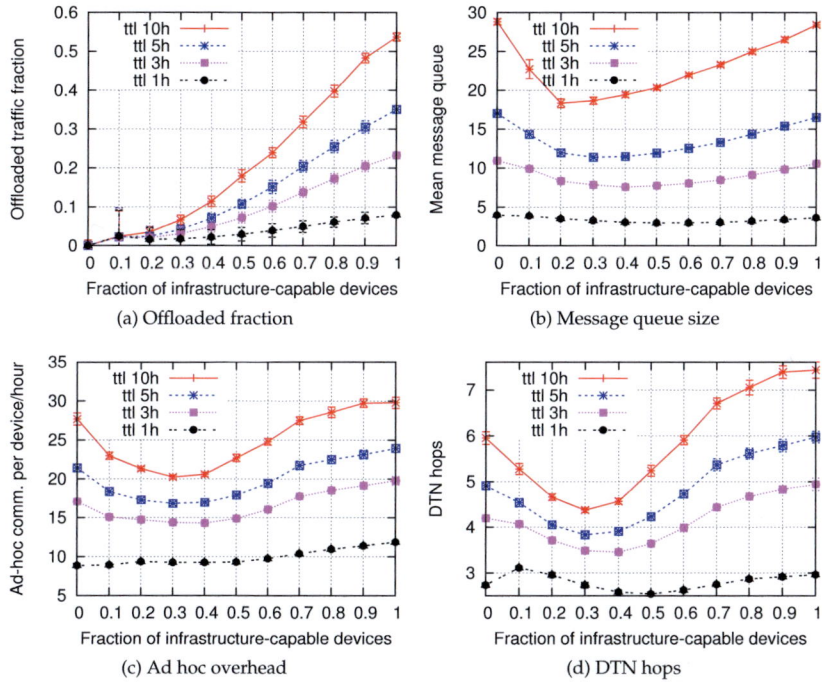

Figure 4.24 Offloading and cost metrics for variation of infrastructure access
$\gamma \in [0, 1]$, all devices ad hoc capable $\delta = 1$ [162].

more messages are successfully delivered which otherwise would not have
been delivered. In addition to this increase in delivery ratio—that depends
on γ—the fraction of offloaded traffic increases due to higher assurance of
delivery through the infrastructure.

Mean message queue size resulting from DTN routing is shown in Figure 4.24b.
Initial decrease results from the strong increase of delivery ratio in Figure 4.23a.
This is the result of messages being delivered within short time and not residing in queues. The following increase is the result of the offloading scheme
trying to keep messages routed in the DTN for longer duration, based on
the γ value on the x-axis. Generally, the mean message queue size is acceptable for mobile devices. A further cost factor is the ad hoc communication
overhead per device per hour resulting from the DTN scheme, as shown in
Figure 4.24c. Its behavior is similar to message queue size, due to same reasons. With increasing TTL messages are routed longer in the DTN and therewith result in more ad hoc communication overhead on mobile devices. With

$\gamma = 1$ the behavior of ad hoc communication cost is comparable to a pure DTN of $\gamma = 0$. Correlated with ad hoc communication overhead is the number of DTN hops a messages has to traverse until successful delivery, shown in Figure 4.24d. Note, that only successfully delivered messages are taken into account. While under short TTL of 1 h the DTN hop count is around 3, under longer TTL of 10 h longer paths over 7 hops are found. While limiting the TTL results in fewer messages being offloaded from the infrastructure, it decreases the ad hoc communication overhead; i. e. a trade-off exists between the cost accepted on the mobile devices, and the fraction of traffic that can be offloaded from the infrastructure.

Bounding Hybrid Routing Control Overhead

The last section presented performance and cost metrics for offloading with heterogeneous infrastructure-capabilities. However, HRS generates additional control traffic in the infrastructure part of the network for coordination, if $\gamma < 1$. This overhead must be small enough to not destroy the desired offloading effect.

Starting point scenario for the analysis is an overlay-based communication system where N infrastructure-capable devices communicate using semi-recursive key-based routing[11]. Delivery of a message is a three-step process:

- First, the sender uses the flat identifier of the destination node to send a message through the overlay using key-based routing. This message includes the sender's underlay address.
- Second, the destination device replies with its underlay address by sending a message directly in the underlay using the sender's underlay address as message destination.
- In a third step, the actual data transfer between source and destination is performed *directly in the underlay*. Per data message this results in $\mathcal{O}(\log N + 1)$ control messages for step one and two, and 1 data message for step three.

Using HRS results in additional control overhead for proxy lookups. The data overhead stays the same as in the starting point scenario, as data messages are transferred directly in the underlay.

- In vHRS the overlay size grows due to virtual nodes. This increases the asymptotic load per overlay node due to longer key-based routing paths and maintenance.
- In iHRS the number of control messages increases for registering, and updating proxy registrations.

It is important to understand that the number of data messages sent through the infrastructure is constant, as single-copy routing is performed and HRS

---

[11]In semi-recursive mode requests are sent through key-based routing and include the sender's underlay address. Replies are sent directly using the underlay address, see [23, Sec. 6.3.1.1]

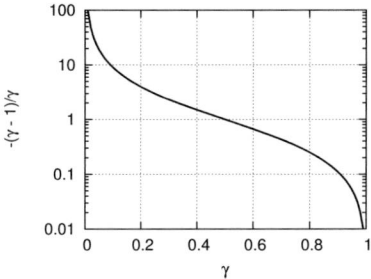

Figure 4.25 Upper bounds $\mathcal{O}(-\frac{\gamma-1}{\gamma})$ on virtual nodes in vHRS (lin-log).

in this case used as lookup system. In case of heterogeneous infrastructure-capabilities, out of an overall N devices, M devices are not infrastructure-capable, and $N - M$ the number of devices that are infrastructure capable; i.e. $M = (1 - \gamma) \cdot N$.

For vHRS the number of additional virtual nodes must be bound by the number of devices not infrastructure-capable to be comparable with the starting point scenario, i.e. maximal M virtual nodes are allowed to be placed in the overlay. As those virtual nodes are placed by the $N - M$ infrastructure-capable devices, every such device is in average allowed to place a virtual-set of size $\mathcal{O}(|\mathcal{V}_i|)$ with

$$|\mathcal{V}_i| = \frac{M}{N - M} \tag{4.13}$$

$$= \frac{(1 - \gamma) \cdot N}{N - (1 - \gamma) \cdot N} \tag{4.14}$$

$$= -\frac{\gamma - 1}{\gamma}. \tag{4.15}$$

This function only depend on γ, which is sampled by devices for determining the $\alpha(\cdot)$ function, as described in Section 4.8.2. Figure 4.25 shows the resulting function that bounds the maximum number of virtual nodes that can be placed per infrastructure-capable device. In case $\gamma > 0.5$ this function becomes < 1. In this case devices have to decide probabilistically whether to place a virtual node. Remember, that virtual nodes are only placed for non-infrastructure capable devices with high awareness for. The number of such devices decreases with an increasing value of γ, and naturally follows the *trend* of this bound.

For iHRS the upper bound is not based on the number of virtual nodes, but rather on control traffic volume. Control traffic results from overlay stabilization. In the starting point scenario every node periodically sends stabilization messages to $\mathcal{O}(\log N)$ nodes. This results in overall $\mathcal{O}(N \cdot \log N)$ control messages in the underlay during one stabilization interval, generated by all nodes in the overlay. If the overall number of nodes in the overlay decreases from N to $N - M$, the control overhead in the underlay per stabilization interval reduces to

$$\mathcal{O}((N - M) \cdot \log(N - M)) = \mathcal{O}(\gamma N \cdot \log(\gamma N)). \tag{4.16}$$

The "saved" control overhead in the underlay is then the difference

$$\mathcal{O}(N \cdot \log(N) - \gamma N \cdot \log(\gamma N)). \tag{4.17}$$

To not destroy the offloading effect, the *additional* control overhead generated by iHRS must be smaller than the *saved overhead* in Equation 4.17.

This bound describes the overall traffic generated in the underlay. As such traffic is only generated by infrastructure-capable devices, it can be distributed over γN devices. This results in an upper bound on the control traffic that *one* infrastructure-capable device is allowed to generate in the underlay

$$\mathcal{O}\left(\frac{N \cdot \log(N) - \gamma N \cdot \log(\gamma N)}{\gamma N}\right), \tag{4.18}$$

which can be simplified to

$$\mathcal{O}\left(\frac{\log(N) - \gamma \cdot \log(\gamma N)}{\gamma}\right). \tag{4.19}$$

iHRS registrations are implemented using key-based routing, which generates logarithmic number of messages in the underlay. The number of such iHRS messages that can be sent is then

$$\mathcal{O}\left(\frac{\log(N) - \gamma \cdot \log(\gamma N)}{\gamma \cdot \log(\gamma N)}\right). \tag{4.20}$$

As worst-case scenario, every infrastructure-capable device performs proxy registrations for *all other* $(1 - \gamma) \cdot N$ non-infrastructure-capable devices. This is worst case as normally social clusters separate devices and due to awareness thresholds only registrations are performed for well-known devices that are encountered regularly. The allowed registrations per infrastructure-capable device are then split up over all non-infrastructure-capable devices $(1 - \gamma) \cdot N$, resulting in

$$\mathcal{O}\left(\frac{\log(N) - \gamma \cdot \log(\gamma N)}{\gamma \cdot \log(\gamma N) \cdot (1 - \gamma) \cdot N}\right) \tag{4.21}$$

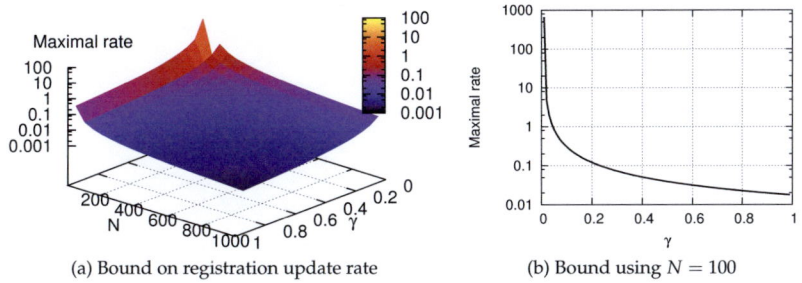

(a) Bound on registration update rate (b) Bound using $N = 100$

Figure 4.26 Bounds on registration update rate (general case left, $N = 100$ right).

iHRS control messages per infrastructure-capable device, per one non infrastructure-capable device. This maximal number of control messages is shown in Figure 4.26a as function of γ and N. The unit of this bound is the number of iHRS registrations per overlay stabilization interval. Figure 4.26b shows an example of $N = 100$ devices with varying fraction of infrastructure-capable devices γ on the x-axis.

For example, let $\gamma = 0.8$, and overlay stabilization interval every 20 s. An infrastructure-capable device is allowed to send iHRS updates for *every* non-infrastructure-capable device every $\left(20\,\text{s} \div \frac{\log(100) - 0.8 \cdot \log(0.8 \cdot 100)}{0.8 \cdot \log(0.8 \cdot 100) \cdot (1 - 0.8) \cdot 100}\right) = 1275\,\text{s} \approx$ 35 min. Note, that this is an upper bound on the registration update rate. Normally a device registers not for all non-infrastructure capable devices, but rather only for few devices it encounters regularly. In this case the update rate can be increased. However, even this upper bound on resulting update rate is sufficient as awareness changes only slowly due to the underlying contact process. If the DTN protocol further allows autonomous aging of awareness through proxy-admins, the update rate further decreases. Note, that this is a bound on the number of *control* messages. When observing this bound, every *data* message that is delivered in the DTN is beneficial for the overall goal of offloading traffic from the infrastructure network.

Variation in Ad hoc Capability
In this paragraph all devices are considered infrastructure-capable, but only a fraction of devices ad hoc capable, i.e. $\gamma = 1$ and $\delta \in [0,1]$. The fraction δ of devices being ad hoc capable does not impact the routing strategy, it rather impacts how well the DTN routing performs and how many messages can be offloaded from the infrastructure. In this case the $\alpha(\cdot)$ function turns into a step-wise function where DTN routing is performed until the TTL *nearly* elapsed.

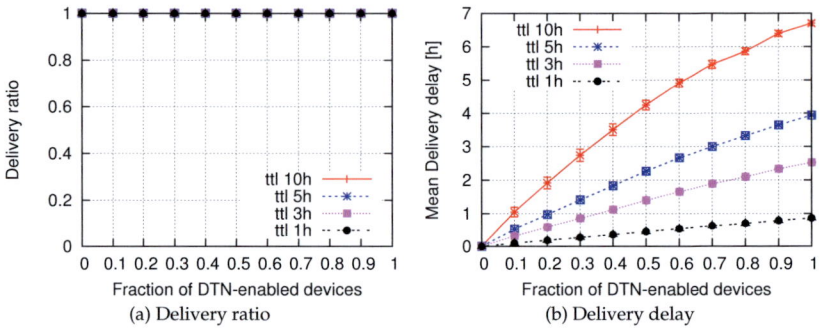

Figure 4.27 Performance metrics for variation of ad hoc capability $\delta \in [0,1]$, all devices infrastructure-capable $\gamma = 1$ [162].

Delivery through the infrastructure is always assured and all messages are delivered successfully as shown in Figure 4.27a. If a devices itself is not ad hoc capable it can not forward messages in the DTN. Such devices immediately send the message through the overlay. This results in average message delay being dependent on the fraction of ad hoc capable devices, as shown in Figure 4.27b. As $\gamma = 1$, DTN routing is performed longest, based on the TTL that then depicts the duration of DTN routing. Message delay increases with δ and is dependent on the TTL, reaching message delay of $\approx 80\%$ of the TTL in case of all devices being ad hoc capable.

Offloading and cost metrics shown in Figure 4.28 all evolve similar to delivery delay—with steady increase as δ grows. The increase in the offloaded traffic fraction in Figure 4.28a behaves exponential over δ, with the exponent depending on the TTL, therewith making offloading more and more interesting for messages that can tolerant longer delay, and over a larger number of ad hoc capable devices. Similar to message delay, message queue size in Figure 4.28b behaves like a square-root function over the number of ad hoc capable devices δ. In contrast, ad hoc communication per device per hour in Figure 4.28c grows exponential, again correlated with the number of DTN hops of successfully delivered messages shown in Figure 4.28d.

Variation in Message Size

Prior simulations used a message size of 250 kByte under a bandwidth model comparable to Bluetooth 2 EDR with 2.1 MBit/s. This results on average in transfer of one message per second over an ad hoc communication connection. With growing message size, successful ad hoc transfer between devices in mutual communication range is only possible if the contact duration between mobile devices is long enough. In the following, message sizes are

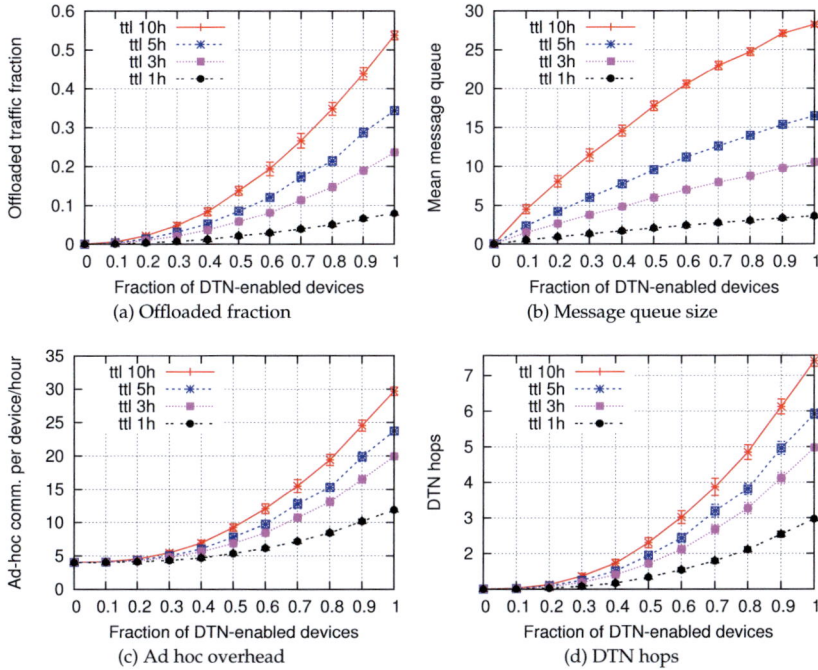

Figure 4.28 Offloading and cost metrics for variation of ad hoc capability $\delta \in [0, 1]$, all devices infrastructure-capable $\gamma = 1$ [162].

considered ranging from 250 KByte up to 8 MByte, requiring from 1 s up to 32 s of contact duration for successful ad hoc message transfer. With growing message size a successful message delivery over multiple DTN hops becomes more and more unlikely, as besides complexity of finding a multi-hop path in the DTN, message transfers fail more often due to shorter contact durations. No fragmentation of messages is considered, rather a message is successfully forwarded if the contact duration is long enough. The fraction of ad hoc capable devices is set to $\delta = 1$, as well as the fraction of infrastructure-capable devices set to $\gamma = 1$. Note, that message delivery ratio is always complete (and therefore not shown), as all devices are infrastructure-capable through $\gamma = 1$. Depending on the message size enough time must be accounted for the overlay transfer, i. e. by making the message *artificially older*, as described in Section 4.8.2.

The DTN hop count in Figure 4.29d gives information on the multi-hop paths that could be found in the DTN. This path length decreases quickly with

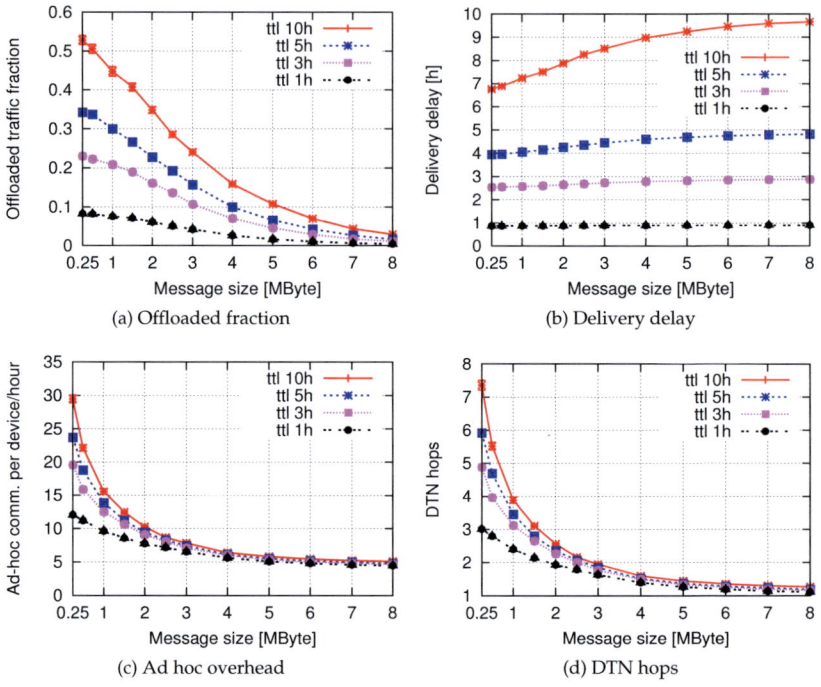

Figure 4.29 Performance and cost metrics for variation of message size, all
devices ad hoc and infrastructure-capable ($\delta = 1, \gamma = 1$) [162].

increasing message size and converges to 1, i.e. messages in the DTN can
only be delivered in a direct-delivery fashion when both sender and destination device meet directly. Further convergence for larger messages can be
assumed to 0 when the message size is too large to even allow for direct-
delivery between source and destination device. While TTL defines the absolute value of DTN hops, it becomes less important with growing message
size. As DTN hop count converges to 1 for the message sizes analyzed, ad hoc
communication overhead per device per hour converges to the message generation process of 4 messages per hour, as shown in Figure 4.29c. In this case
every device performs successful ad hoc communication at maximum with
the destination device directly. As DTN routing becomes more impossible
due to contact duration being too small compared to the bandwidth model,
the fraction of offloaded traffic in Figure 4.29a decreases. Again, the used
TTL becomes unimportant when using large message size, and the offloaded
fraction is very small for large messages. Delay of successfully delivered mes-

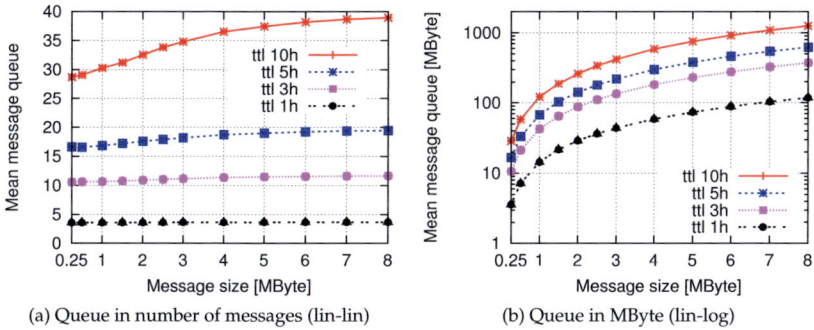

(a) Queue in number of messages (lin-lin)   (b) Queue in MByte (lin-log)

Figure 4.30 Mean queue size, all devices ad hoc and infrastructure-capable $(\delta = 1, \gamma = 1)$ [162].

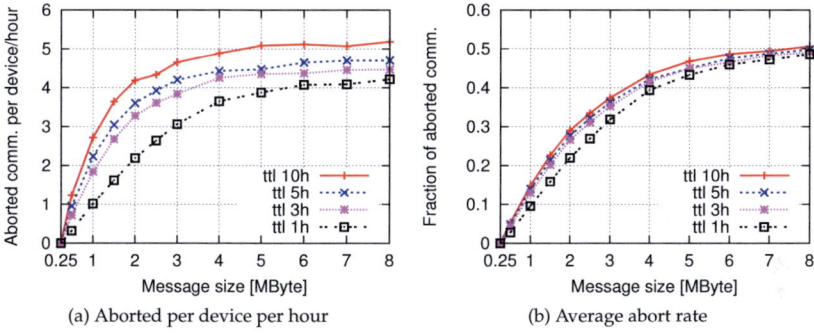

(a) Aborted per device per hour   (b) Average abort rate

Figure 4.31 Aborted ad hoc message transfers $(\gamma = 1, \delta = 1)$ [162].

sages shown in Figure 4.29b varies only slightly for short TTL, and increases maximal up to 30% for the longest TTL analyzed.

Message queues are shown in Figure 4.30a as number of messages, and with respect to the message queue size in MByte. The queue size in number of messages is relatively stable, irrespective of different DTN routing behavior. With increasing message size, the queue size in MByte increases quickly up to several hundred MByte.

The reason for decreasing performance with growing message size is the bandwidth-limited ad hoc communication channel. As contact duration between devices is comparably short, larger messages can only be transferred when longer contact durations occur. Figure 4.31a shows the absolute num-

Work	Unicast End-to-End Routing	Stable Flat Addressing	Heterogeneous Infra. Capabilities	Transparency of Destination	Geographic Scale	Cooperative Routing	Opportun. Mobile Gateways	Efficient Use of Shortcuts for DTN	Decentr., Autonomous, Scalable	Generic Applicability
KioskNet [91, 92, 221]	+	o	o	-	+	o	-	+	o	o
MeDeHa [198–200]	+	o	+	o	+	+	o	+	o	+
Pitkänen et al. [192]	+	n/a	+	n/a	o	+	o	n/a	n/a	+
Throwboxes [17, 261]	+	+	o	+	n/a	+	n/a	n/a	o	+
Banerjee et al. [18]	+	n/a	+	n/a	+	+	o	+	n/a	o
HRS	+	+	+	+	+	+	+	+	+	+

Table 4.7 Related hybrid routing schemes compared to HRS with focus on use case of providing communication ("+" yes, "-" no, "o" partly, "n/a" not applicable).

ber of aborted ad hoc message transfers per device per hour. With growing message size the number of aborted transfers increases quickly. If a message could not be forwarded to a device, the overall number of transfers in the DTN increases, as the message stays in the DTN for longer duration. Due to this increase in overall ad hoc communication attempts, the fraction of failed ad hoc transfers shown in Figure 4.31b has a slightly different form compared to the absolute numbers in Figure 4.31a. In the analyzed scenario up to 50% of ad hoc forward attempts fail at the largest considered message size. This makes DTN routing much more complex, as not only a DTN path has to be found, but additionally parts of this path fail. It can be concluded that message fragmentation schemes, e. g. proposed in [193], are required to route messages of larger size. Such schemes, however, complicate the routing process, as several fragments must be routed through store-carry-forward mechanisms to their final destination.

4.10 Review of Requirements and Comparison to Related Work

Implementation of Requirements in HRS

The requirements stated in Section 4.1 for hybrid routing are now recalled and described how HRS implements them.

Devices participating in HRS have a unique flat identifier. HRS implements *Unicast End-to-End Routing* by only using identifiers of devices, both in the DTN and in the overlay part. Such identifiers are flat in nature and do not expose network structure. This allows for *Stable Flat Addressing*, as mobility of devices, as well as opportunistic gateways are not bound to identifiers. HRS supports devices with *Heterogeneous Infrastructure Capabilities* by tracking infrastructure awareness and employing proxies. The main concepts that allow to integrate all infrastructure capability classes and to provide communication between any device in any class are the mixed metric for routing towards the infrastructure in Section 4.5.1, and the announcement system for routing in the overlay part of HRS, as described in Section 4.6.

A device d_i sending a message to d_j does not require information about the infrastructure capabilities of d_j, neither on the geographic area d_j currently is, enabling *Transparency of Destination*. HRS provides communication between geographically separated areas, e. g. distant cities. It allows for *Geographic Scale* through infrastructure-based shortcuts in combination with implicit geographic information encoded in destination-awareness. The main component of HRS is the decentralized announcement system described in Section 4.6 that provides for *Cooperative Routing*. HRS builds upon probabilistic use of *Opportunistic Mobile Gateways*. The main concepts that support the use of opportunistic gateways are infrastructure awareness, the mixed metric described in Section 4.5.1, and the announcement system in Section 4.6

The mixed metric allows to trade-off between DTN routing towards the destination device, and routing towards the infrastructure through the α parameter described in Section 4.5.1. This allows to route messages preferably towards the infrastructure where the announcement system provides *Efficient Use of Shortcuts for DTN Routing*. HRS is *Decentralized, Autonomous, and Scalable* from two perspectives: First, HRS does not rely on central servers in the infrastructure. Rather, an overlay-based approach is used to implement a flexible and easy to deploy the announcement system in Section 4.6. Second, devices are not required to have infrastructure access themselves. Integration of new devices and new infrastructure possibilities is autonomous without requiring manual configuration.

To allow for *Generic Applicability*, existing DTN protocols can be used with HRS, based on the categorization in Section 4.3, and the integration steps described in Section 4.7.

Comparison to Related Work

Table 4.7 gives an overview of related work in hybrid routing that has been described earlier in Section 2.4.1, and Section 2.4.2. Most related to HRS is KioskNet [91, 92, 221] developed at the University of Waterloo. Compared to KioskNet, HRS uses mobile devices themselves as opportunistic gateways. HRS uses stable flat addressing, compared to KioskNet where a mobile device

Work	Message direction	Mobile device capabilities
MADNet [98, 99]	Infra. → mobile device	All infra.-access, all DTN
Push-and-Track [253]	Infra. → mobile device	All infra.-access, all DTN
Lee et al. [147]	Infra. ↔ mobile device	All WiFi and cellular capable
Wiffler [16]	Infra. ↔ mobile device	All WiFi and cellular capable
HRS	Mobile device ↔ mobile device	Heterog. infra.-access/ad hoc

Table 4.8 Related offloading schemes compared to HRS with focus on use case of offloading infrastructure [162].

has a well-defined association at a static kiosk. While this association needs to be known in KioskNet and is used for addressing, HRS does not require a static association of mobile device to gateway.

Table 4.8 gives an overview of related work for infrastructure offloading presented in Section 2.4.4. HRS is most related to the work of Han et al [98, 99], and the work of Whitbeck et al. [253]. Main difference is that HRS's goal is to support unicast end-to-end routing between mobile devices themselves, compared to content dissemination from infrastructure to mobile devices used in related work. While related work only uses homogeneous device capabilities for ad hoc communication, and infrastructure communication, HRS works across heterogeneous device capabilities.

Deployment and Need for Incentive Systems

Both use cases build upon cooperative behavior of mobile devices. The main cost factor resulting from this cooperativeness is energy for ad hoc communication. For the use case of providing communication the overall goal is to enable end-to-end communication between all participating mobile devices. The benefit of the cooperativeness therefore pays back to the mobile devices directly. For actual deployment an incentive system is required that provides fairness between the mobile devices. Such systems e. g. allow to trade energy against a virtual currency to enable a balance between the mobile devices. Examples for such schemes are "MobiCent" [45], or incentive-aware DTN routing [225].

For the use case of offloading infrastructure, cost is spent by the mobile devices in terms of energy. The actual benefit of offloading, however, pays off for the infrastructure provider as his network has to carry less traffic. As result, the infrastructure provider has to give incentives to the mobile devices to participate in the ad hoc communication. An incentive system that has been developed for such scenarios is e. g. "Win-Coupon" [263].

4.11   Summary and Conclusion

The *Hybrid Routing System* (HRS) presented in this chapter allows for cooperative routing in mixed DTN and infrastructure-bases networks with heterogeneous device capabilities. While today's networks are either infrastructure-based, or DTN-based, HRS integrates the different routing paradigms employed in such networks and can route transparently over hybrid networks. Through a novel categorization existing DTN protocols can be integrated. HRS is a general routing system, its application for two use cases has been shown: In face of few infrastructure-capable devices, HRS provides communication in otherwise disconnected areas through a cooperative routing approach. In face of a large number of infrastructure-capable devices, HRS can be used to offload infrastructure networks by preferably routing messages in DTNs. Extensive evaluation has shown the performance and cost trade-offs, both from the perspective of mobile devices, and from perspective of the overlay network.

5. Framework for Overlay-based Services

Today's Internet evolved from a small network of computers with the initial goal of sharing hardware resources. Due to the high cost of hardware, sharing was essential and the protocols developed therefore targeted to address *systems*. Routing has been based on the *Internet Protocol* (IP) [195] through numeric hierarchical IP addresses which are uniquely assigned to network interfaces built into systems. De-multiplexing to specific services running on a system is not defined within the scope of routing and therefore provided by higher-layer protocols like the *Transmission Control Protocol* (TCP) [128, 196]. Today, the strong growth of systems in the Internet leads to an exhaustion of the 32 bit IP address space that was decided on in the late 1970's[1], and current transition to the new IPv6 [62] protocol that provides a larger address space of 128 bit. While such a transition is not feasible through a hard changeover— a so-called *flag-day*—the transition is continuous. As the two IP versions are, however, not compatible, connectivity problems arise.

The problem of incompatible network protocols is exemplary for today's Internet and its growing complexity. While the initial design was clean and the network small, its growth and popularity resulted in a multiplication of mechanisms, and add-on protocols that make development and deployment

---

[1]Vint Cerf gave an explanation of the 32 bit nature of IP addresses at the Google IPv6 Conference in 2008 [177]. The decision to use an address space of 32 bit was mainly ad hoc to solve the dispute between different engineers who had different opinions on whether the IP address size should be 32 bit, 128 bit, or variable length. As the initial network and protocols were thought of as an experimental test and proof of concept, it was believed that once the tests had been performed, the protocols and networks could be fixed towards a production version before public release. The huge success, however, prevented a further revision of the protocols.

of novel services complex [100]. To build new networks with novel characteristics and functionality on top of existing networks, *overlay networks* have been widely used in the past (Section 2.5.1 gives a historical view). To relief the developer from the complexity of today's networks, this chapter describes a *framework for overlay-based services* that aims to provide an abstraction from the network underlay with the help of overlay networks. The framework helps to develop new *service overlays* [48] that provide novel functionality not provided by the underlay. An application can select a set of such service overlays to implement its logic, irrespective of the underlying network.

The framework aims for seamless development and deployment of novel services and applications[2] through distributed overlay networks: It uses overlay networks itself for abstracting from underlays, and enables developers to build new overlay networks upon this abstraction. The framework hides complex network issues and provides a homogeneous abstraction where developers can easily develop and deploy novel services. The following benefits are provided from a developer's perspective:

- Abstraction from underlying networks and transport protocols.
- Support for mobility, and multihoming through separation of identifier and locator.
- Mechanisms of self-configuration, and self-organization to allow for flexible deployment.
- Distributed and cost-efficient deployment.

While several of the mechanisms and concepts used in this framework are available as standalone solution, they are hard to use and integrate. Goal of the framework presented in this chapter is to provide an *integrated approach* that can be used easily from the developer perspective. For the focus in this thesis, the framework is the enabling platform for developing and deploying the Hybrid Routing System from Chapter 4.

This chapter is structured as follows: A review of today's problems and resulting functional and non-functional requirements for a framework are derived in Section 5.1. The architecture of the framework for overlay-based services is presented in Section 5.2, and its interfaces for developing novel services and deploying legacy services are described in Section 5.3. Implementation details are given in Section 5.4. Integration of the Hybrid Routing System with the framework is describes in Section 5.5. Section 5.6 summarizes and concludes this chapter.

Work presented in this chapter has been developed within the *Spontaneous Virtual Networks* (SpoVNet) project and published in [28, 109–113, 115, 247].

---

[2]In the following the term "service" is used interchangeably with "application".

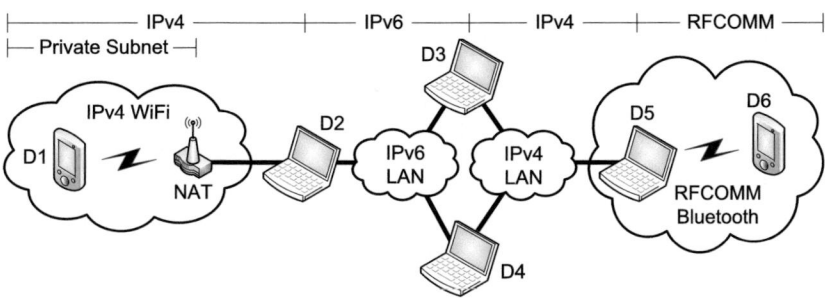

Figure 5.1 Exemplary network topology that poses several challenges to for development and deployment of services [110].

5.1 Problems and Requirements

The complexity of today's networks is challenging for development and deployment of the Hybrid Routing System. In the following, requirements for a framework for overlay-based services are derived, based on problems posed by today's networks, and with focus on the Hybrid Routing System. Requirements are split into *functional* and *non-functional*. Functional requirements in Section 5.1.1 describe *functionality* the system must provide, non-functional requirements in Section 5.1.2 describe *properties* of this functionality[3].

A variety of mechanisms and protocols have been integrated into the Internet to satisfy the changing service requirements that go beyond its initial design [100]. The resulting complexity is the main reason for the complicated development and deployment faced in today's Internet; and faced by the Hybrid Routing System. Figure 5.1 shows—exemplary for this diversity of mechanisms and protocols in today's networks—a network topology that poses several challenges for development and deployment of services:

- **Challenge:** Heterogeneous network protocols like IPv4 and IPv6 are incompatible. They complicate development due to different developer interfaces, and complicate end-to-end-communication through different protocol support in the network.
  → **Example:** Devices D2 and D5 can not communicate as there is no homogeneous network that connects them.

- **Challenge:** Point-to-point protocols such as Bluetooth RFCOMM are becoming increasingly ubiquitous, e. g. in mobile devices like smart-

---

[3]The IEEE defines the term *functional requirement* as *"A requirement that specifies a function that a system or system component must be able to perform."* [197], and *non-functional requirement* as *"A software requirement that describes not what the software will do, but how the software will do it, for example, software performance requirements, software external interface requirements, software design constraints, and software quality attributes."* [67].

phones, but do not allow for seamless integration into networks in an end-to-end manner without complex manual configuration.
→ **Example:** D6 can only communicate with D5. Extending reachability of D6 requires complex manual configuration.

- **Challenge:** Reachability of devices is complicated through middleboxes like NAT.
  → **Example:** D1 is not directly reachable from outside the private subnet built up through the NAT middlebox that provides the IPv4 WiFi.

- **Challenge:** Mobility of devices results in changes of their network attachment and complicate seamless connectivity.
  → **Example:** Movement of D6 into the IPv4 WiFi results in new locators for D6 and breaks current connections.

- **Challenge:** Multiple network attachments result in multihoming of devices that makes communication complex due to multiple connections that the developer must choose from.
  → **Example:** D4 can reach D3 through either the IPv4 or IPv6 LAN.

While individual solutions for the aforementioned challenges exist, the goal of the presented framework is to provide an *integrated solution* that can be deployed flexibly and spontaneously without relying on central servers.

5.1.1   Functional Requirements

Handling middleboxes

Network Address Translation (NAT) [72] introduces private networks which are connected with the Internet through a gateway. All devices behind the NAT gateway are assigned addresses from a private IP range [205] and can not be reached directly from the public Internet. NAT is a convenient way to provide Internet access for a dynamic network of internal systems. Internet access for mobile devices through an infrastructure-based mobile network is often based on private subnets of the provider, and therefore NAT-based Internet access. Generally, the use of such *middleboxes* hinders end-to-end connectivity and makes development and deployment of services complex. Exemplary, the Internet telephony provider Skype has put tremendous effort into making it's service run out-of-the-box for end-users [22], where often both parties of a *Voice over IP* (VoIP, see e. g. [101]) conversation are behind NAT gateways. Handling of NAT gateways can often be overcome by manual configuration, which is, however, error-prone and complex. NAT traversal mechanisms (e. g. STUN [210]) are available to allow a system inside a NAT to detect the presence and type of NAT, as well as its publicly reachable IP address. Such systems, however, require additional infrastructure and application logic. Handling of middleboxes is an essential requirement for the framework to ease service development and deployment.

Heterogeneous protocols

The systems targeted with service overlays are based on *groups of users*, i. e. multiple users who want to cooperate through a given service. Communication between all devices inside this group requires support from the underlying networks, and support of the devices run by users. Heterogeneity of protocols can arise if a device runs only a subset of protocols in its network stack, e. g. due to hardware or power constraints. Furthermore, if the underlying networks where devices are attached to run different protocols, end-to-end communication of devices is prevented. The framework must support protocol heterogeneity transparently through cooperation of devices.

Mobility support

To enable scalability of routing systems, Rekhter's law states that *"Addressing can follow topology or topology can follow addressing. Choose one."* [204][4]. However, in today's IP-based networks this does not hold as semantics of IP addresses are overloaded as *identifier*, and as *locator*. An identifier describes the identity of a device, while a locator describes its location and attachment in the network, i. e. the locator encodes topological information. The identifier is mainly used by the application, the locator is mainly used for routing. Quoting [168]: *"As a result, it is difficult (if not impossible) to make a single number space serve both purposes efficiently"*.

Early hardware systems were large and bound to their geographic location. Resulting, they were stable systems in the network topology and the twofold semantics of IP addresses was unproblematic. Today's mobile devices like laptops or smartphones, however, have reached size and weight that allow its users to carry them around easily, therewith causing problems in the routing system that overloads the semantics of IP addresses for identity and topological network location. Through mobility of such devices, the access technology and/or access network changes, resulting in assignment of new IP addresses and breakage of communication sessions. Mobility is not supported by IP directly, but must be added through additional mechanisms, e. g. *Mobile IP* [189] that uses dedicated systems—so-called *home-agents*—that have stable public IP addresses, and stable topological network location. Home-agents, however, require manual configuration and dedicated systems. The framework must provide support for device mobility and can, if required, employ devices from the same service-instance for cooperation.

Multi-homing support

The problem of overloaded semantics of IP addresses results in further problems. Similar to the problem of mobility where identifiers change due to their interconnection with locators, multi-homing describes a system with multiple

---

[4]The source of the original quote could not be found. In Section 5.8 and Section 6 of [204] Rekhter gives those recommendations. The quota can e. g. be found in [168].

locators that is forced to have multiple identifiers, despite being the same system. Such a setup is classically used for redundancy reasons to have multiple network attachments. Today, however, even mobile devices have a multitude of network interfaces, e. g. cellular, WiFi, or Bluetooth, that can be easily switched on and off. In such dynamic scenarios, supporting multi-homing from the service perspective is complex and the accessibility of the system through each of those locators might be different. Depending on its locator the device might be accessible globally from the Internet, locally in the subnet, or geographically local, e. g. in case of near-field communication such as Bluetooth. The framework must provide support for multi-homing in a transparent way, and decouple device identity from network locators.

Bootstrapping

Initial integration of a node is commonly referred to as *bootstrapping*. In a *centralized system* with a well-defined server the bootstrapping problem is based on a unique domain name of the server which must be resolved to its IP address through a lookup system, e. g. the *Domain Name System* (DNS) [172]. In a *distributed system*, however, such a unique entry point may not be available due to the dynamic set of participating devices. Services can rely on caches of earlier connected devices, or manual configuration. While caches have been shown to be feasible for large-scale systems [248], they are not applicable for small-scale systems which furthermore may get deployed spontaneously and for a limited lifetime. The framework for overlay-based services must provide mechanisms for bootstrapping in decentralized scenarios, with focus on finding other devices in local network proximity.

Interface for novel services and legacy support

The de-facto standard for developing networked services is the Berkeley sockets API [234] which is implemented in all major operating systems. However, this API does not integrate well with today's programming paradigms, resulting in a larger number of libraries that provide easier to use APIs on top of the Berkeley sockets API, e. g. Asio [141]. Using the Berkeley sockets API or one of its abstraction libraries, developers still need to handle underlay address formats, such as IPv4/IPv6, explicitly. A framework for overlay-based services must provide convenient interfaces that abstract from the underlying network, but still provide means of control.

Besides developing novel services, a large set of services exist today, mainly based on IPv4. At best, it should be able to deploy these so-called *legacy* services on top of the framework transparently. This way, legacy services can still benefit from features provided by the framework, like e. g. mobility support.

Requirements-oriented interfaces

Control provided by above-mentioned interface must not be *explicit* in terms of protocols, or features that are *directly* exposed by the framework. Rather, such control should be given to the developer in terms of stating *requirements*. Selection of actual protocols and mechanisms must be implemented in the framework itself and be transparent to the developer. This allows for easy integration of new protocols and mechanisms into the framework—without changing existing services—and relieves developers from selection of explicit mechanisms and protocols.

Virtual network per service instance

The target scenario of overlay-based services are *groups of users* that want to collaborate. The framework must provide separation from other groups of users that run an instance of the same, or different service. Multiple instances of the same or other services must be able to run in parallel with separation.

Utility functionality and framework

Besides the above mentioned requirements, a framework requires a complete and self-contained set of functionality where developers can integrate their services easily. Therefore, not an API where users build their services *upon* must be provided, but rather a framework where users build their services *into*. This requires a set of utility functionality that eases, e. g., threading, provides easy to use built-in types for identifiers and locators, and aforementioned bootstrapping.

5.1.2   Non-functional Requirements

Scalability

Scalability of a service describes its property of handling a growing number of users in a graceful manner. Traditionally, services are based on a client-server model. Such centralized services can only be scaled with (at least) linear increase of resources. The cost to achieve scalability are high, mainly resulting from the fact that the increasing number of clients do not contribute resources by themselves. Distributed overlay networks have the beneficial property to scale logarithmically with the number of clients, as *clients themselves contribute resources*. Several real-world networks have taken advantage of this beneficial property to flexibly handle a large and growing number of systems, e. g. the Kad network [231], or Amazon's Dynamo [60]. The framework must be scalable, and allow for easy development of distributed systems.

Self-configuration and self-organization

Manual configuration is complex and error-prone. The framework must provide self-configuration and self-organization to allow the service to run with little configuration and to adapt in case of changes to e. g. the underlying network, errors and failures, or churn.

Security

Security was not intended in the original design of the Internet protocols, but rather was added later during the rise of the World Wide Web and its commercialization. This made—and still makes—security hard to implement as it is not directly exposed by the underlay but rather through protocols that require additional efforts to integrate for developers. Today, *"Security is probably the biggest imminent problem facing the Internet"*, as stated by Handley in his seminal article [100]. While the general topic of security is very broad, focus in the framework is on communication security in terms of protocols and mechanisms that provide confidential and integrity secured communication with authenticated node identities.

Especially in context of overlay-based networks new possibilities arise to implement security. In contrast to current networks where security is implemented through additional protocols *upon* the underlay, the framework allows to integrate security *inside* the framework directly; providing security as a property of the network abstraction. This way, applications and services can benefit from security transparently. Properties of communication links in terms of confidentiality or integrity can be built into the requirements-oriented interfaces directly. This decouples the developer from actual implementation of security mechanisms which has shown complex and prevented widespread use.

Extensibility and Usability

Support for protocols and mechanisms of the underlay must be integrated into the framework without changes to services. The framework must provide a modular architecture and interfaces that do not expose direct access to the underlay. A broad usability must be ensured by supporting development of novel services, as well as transparent deployment of legacy services.

Isolation

Isolation directly results from the functional requirement of *Virtual network per service instance*. The degree of isolation depends on the underlying network. A complete isolation is only possible with in-network virtualization technology. In normal environments like plain IP-based networks, services must be isolated on a best-effort basis.

5.2   Architecture

None of the existing frameworks for overlay-based services presented in Section 2.5.5 satisfies all functional and non-functional requirements. This section introduces an architecture for a framework for overlay-based services that implements all requirements and is the basic architecture for implementing the Hybrid Routing System.

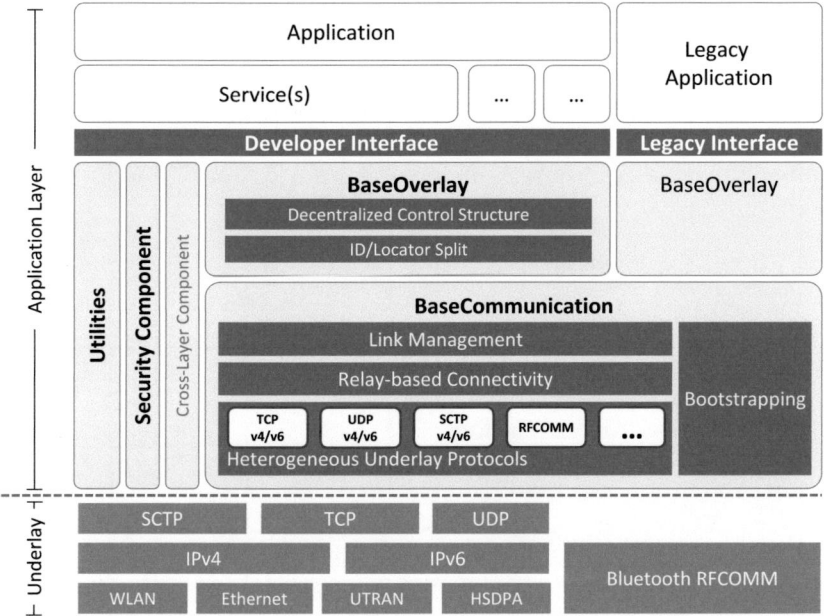

Figure 5.2 Architecture of the framework for overlay-based services [28].

Goal of the framework described in this chapter is to provide an architecture for seamless development and deployment of overlay-based services in today's and the future Internet. The framework itself is built through the use of overlay networks, that have proven beneficial due to scalability, self-organization, and robustness. Per instance of a service—that provides the context for a group of users—a virtual overlay network is established that provides a natural separation from other instances of the same, or different services. In the following, such an instance of a service is called *service-instance*. It is addressed using a flat identifier called *InstanceID*. A *device* runs the framework and can take part in one or multiple instances of the same, or different service-instances. A communication endpoint within a service-instance is called a *node*. Multiple nodes can run on top of one device and take part in the same or different service-instances. Each node has a unique flat identifier, called its *NodeID*. This NodeID is from a large address space, e. g. 160 bit used in this thesis, and is stable for the node—at least for its runtime within a service-instance.

Component	Feature	Mobility Support	Heterogeneity	End-to-End Connectivity	Support for multi-homing	Scalability	Self-conf. & maintenance	Extensibility	Usability	Security
BC	Heterog. Underlay Proto.	×	×	×	×		×			
	Link Management	×		×	×			×	×	×
	Bootstrapping						×		×	
BO	ID/Locator Split	×			×					×
	Decentr. Control Structure			×		×	×			
	Distributed Hash Table						×		×	
SC	Security Component									×
UT	Utilities		×		×	×	×	×	×	
IF	Developer Interface							×	×	×
	Legacy Interface								×	

Table 5.1 Overview of the framework components and the features they support [28].

Figure 5.2 shows the architecture for the framework presented in this chapter. Its main components—that will be described in the following—are:

- Section 5.2.1: The *BaseCommunication* (BC), that provides end-to-end communication between device over heterogeneous protocols. Its interface provides the abstraction of *virtual links* that describe an end-to-end link, irrespective of the transport protocols used to realize the link.

- Section 5.2.2: The *BaseOverlay* (BO), that allows *NodeID*-based addressing and routing based on identifiers, rather than underlay specific locators. It provides the context for a group of users through a common overlay network.

- Section 5.2.3: The *Security Component* (SC), that implements security functionality to provide authenticity, confidentiality, and integrity. Focus in this thesis is on self-certifying cryptographic identifiers to implement security without central infrastructures. An overview of the Security Component can be found in [106].

- Section 5.2.4: A set of *Utilities* (UT), that complement the framework and allows for easy development and deployment.

NodeID
0x73ef71a951bbfb3af192b9093af0d04a2459487f

Endpoint Descriptor	
layer 4	tcp{45002};udp{45085};
layer 3	ip{192.168.1.7|129.13.1.3|2001:53:cc2c::2:36};
layer 2	rfcomm{8};bluetooth{00:26:5E:BB:F9:F7};

Table 5.2 Exemplary endpoint-descriptor of underlay addresses, and NodeID [28, 115].

- Section 5.3: The *Interface* (IF), that provides access for implementing novel services through the developer interface. Furthermore, the legacy interface allows to run legacy services unchanged and transparently on top of the framework.

Table 5.1 gives an overview of the framework's components and the features they implement. Each of the components is described in the following.

5.2.1 BaseCommunication

Most overlay protocols assume direct end-to-end connectivity between all participating devices to build up their overlay structure. This assumption, however, does not hold in real-world scenarios where protocol heterogeneity, middleboxes, mobility, and multihoming complicate this build-up process of the overlay structure. The BaseCommunication enables end-to-end communication links between devices in face of such challenges and provides the basis for the BaseOverlay. To an upper layer—in this case the BaseOverlay—the BaseCommunication provides the abstraction of *virtual links* that are addressed through locally valid *LinkIDs*. A LinkID is a flat identifier, similar to a NodeID, with no semantics in its structure and validity scope on the local device only. It identifies an end-to-end communication link that can be used to exchange messages between two devices. Depending on the capabilities of the communication partners—and the network between them—a virtual link can be established with the help of other devices. Such a virtual link is assembled of multiple piecewise connections.

The BaseCommunication operates upon addresses exposed by the underlay. The set of underlay addresses of a device is called its *endpoint-descriptor*. Table 5.2 shows an exemplary endpoint-descriptor made up of layer 2–4 addresses, and an exemplary NodeID of 160 bit length. The endpoint-descriptor is used for establishing virtual links. Two devices exchange their endpoint descriptors thought the BaseOverlay—described in the next section—and build up underlay connections in both directions.

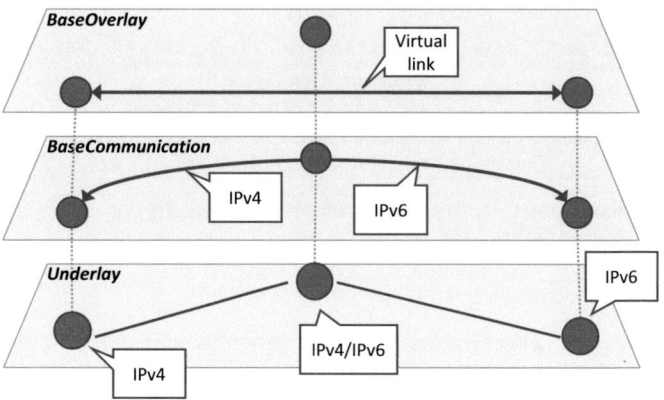

Figure 5.3 Virtual links maintained by the BaseCommunication.

Heterogeneous protocols

The problem of heterogeneity is solved in the BaseCommunication through *cooperation*, i. e. the BaseCommunication establishes paths to provide for communication with the help of third systems that can relay communication. Such third systems are participating devices, rather than dedicated infrastructure systems. With the help of third devices the BaseCommunication establishes end-to-end virtual links between two devices that have no common underlay protocols, as shown in Figure 5.3. A virtual link is made up of piecewise underlay connections, and addressed using a locally valid LinkID. The ordered set of devices making up the path is called *relay path*, and intermediate devices called *relays*. A relay path is not necessarily built over protocols in the same network layer. Different protocols from different layers can be employed, as long as there exists a relay path that can be established based on mutual protocols between pairwise devices. An example are two devices that run different version of the IP protocol, e. g. IPv4 and IPv6. A multi-homed device that runs both IPv4 and IPv6 protocols in its protocol stack can be used to build up a relay path that provides end-to-end connectivity between the two devices. Such a relay path is maintained internally and abstracted through a virtual link that is addressed through its LinkID. Details on the algorithm to find and establish relay paths are not within the scope of this thesis. The reader is referred to [170, 171].

Link management

The BaseCommunication provides the abstraction of virtual links that are addressed locally on a device through a LinkID. The BaseCommunication hides the internal—and potentially piecewise—connections that make up the virtual link. Virtual links can be created either explicit, or implicit. On explicit creation, the upper service is responsible for closing the link. Implicitly created links are setup on demand, i. e. if a message is sent to a node without providing a LinkID. Such *auto-links* are maintained automatically and closed after a preconfigured idle timeout. Establishing of virtual links is performed by passing an endpoint-descriptor that contains a set of underlay addresses to the BaseCommunication. The BaseCommunication tries to establish connections with the remote device through all given protocols for which addresses have been passed in the endpoint-descriptor. Compared to other overlay-based systems that mainly route messages along the overlay, virtual links are built up directly between two devices in the underlay, if possible.

Bootstrapping

Centralized services build upon well-known server names that provide a central system to join other devices; called the *bootstrapping* process. In a decentralized system bootstrapping becomes more complex, as there exists no central well-known device that can be used to join the system. While in most decentralized systems the bootstrapping process is seen as out of scope, the presented framework provides a number of *bootstrap modules* that ease the process of bootstrapping in decentralized scenarios. These in-built bootstrap modules especially help small-scale systems to detect other devices to join the distributed system.

A bootstrap module provides functionality to announce service-instances it is joined to, and to receive such announcements that can be used to join other service-instances. Depending on the type of bootstrap module the announcement must be either periodically refreshed, or is persistent. The "key" for registering such bootstrap information is the name of the service-instance, the respective "value" is bootstrap information in the form of NodeID and endpoint-descriptor.

Exemplary bootstrap modules are based on *Multicast DNS*, Bluetooth *Service Discovery Protocol*, and UDP IPv4/IPv6 broadcasts.

5.2.2   BaseOverlay

To provide a common context that represents a service-instance, the *Base-Overlay* joins all nodes that participate in the same service-instance into a distributed scalable overlay network. Each overlay network that is built up by the BaseOverlay implements exactly *one* service-instance. This results in a natural separation of service-instances through closed contexts. The overlay network is used as control structure and for signaling.

Identifier/locator split

The framework decouples the identifier of a node from its locators. This *identifier/locator split* is an enabler for multiple of the requirements stated in Section 5.1: In face of heterogeneous underlay protocols, locators are different in structure and semantics, whereas identifiers are stable and allow for homogeneous addressing of nodes. Device mobility can result in changes to one or several locators due to association to a different network—and therewith break connectivity. Identifiers, on the other hand, remain stable as they are not bound to the underlying network. A device can have multiple locators due to multi-homing.

A NodeID can be generated by hashing of the device's IP address, as proposed in [239]. Such hashing schemes are necessary to achieve consistent distribution of NodeIDs in the identifier space. However, using the IP address as input for the hashing function binds the identifier to its locator and therewith prevents the separation of identifiers and locators. The BaseOverlay provides different ways to generate NodeIDs through

- random generation,
- hashing of a user name, or
- cryptographically generated self-certifying identifiers.

Section 5.2.3 describes cryptographic generation of NodeIDs and InstanceIDs.

Decentralized control structure

One of the BaseOverlay's main goals is to provide a common context that integrates participating nodes in a common service-instance. One such service-instance is identified through its InstanceID. The number of participating users can become potentially large, therefore the BaseOverlay must provide a scalable overlay structure. Structured overlay networks introduced in Section 2.5.4 provide beneficial properties as they allow graceful growth with the number of participants, i. e. they *scale*. Furthermore, they do not require central servers, i. e. they are *distributed*. Such overlay protocols are used to implement the basic control structure of the BaseOverlay. From a requirements perspective, the BaseOverlay needs a protocol that provides *Key-Based Routing* (KBR) functionality, e. g. [211, 239], to route messages based on NodeIDs.

Distributed Hash Table

A centralized system naturally uses a central server for rendezvous functionality, i. e. to allow participants to search/find for other nodes. In a distributed system there is no well-defined system that provides this functionality. Every participant is subject to churn and therefore no stable rendezvous point available. Built upon the KBR functionality, the BaseOverlay implements a DHT that can be used by services to register nodes for special responsibility tasks using well-defined keys.

5.2.3 Security Component

The Security Component has been developed with colleagues in the Security Task Force of the SpoVNet project. Its goal is to provide basic cryptographic support and protocol building blocks that can be used by the Base-Communication and BaseOverlay, as well as services developed upon the

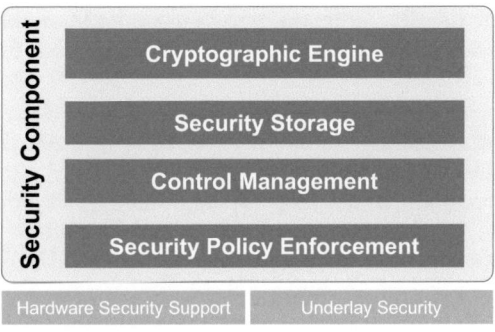

Figure 5.4 Security Component [106].

framework. Focus in this section is on the conceptual use of cryptographic identifiers for autonomous provision of node authenticity and authorization, as well as integrated use of identifiers into a key-exchange protocol. For the general concepts of the Security Component, the reader is referred to [106].

Modules of the Security Component are shown in Figure 5.4. The *Cryptographic Engine* provides access to ciphers, signatures, random number generators, and hash functions. It can be implemented through a cryptographic library such as Crypto++[5]. The *Security Storage* allows to store cryptographic material such as keys, but also protocol state. It can be provided by hardware modules such as a *Trusted Platform Module* (TPM). *Control Management* implements concepts for trusted third parties, and mechanisms for resilience. *Security Policy Enforcement* implements access control, e. g. for running authorization restricted overlay instances. Similar to the goal of abstracting from the underlay, the goal of the Security Component is to provide easy access to general cryptographic operations, and allow the framework to implement security mechanisms transparent for services, directly in the framework. One such specific security mechanism is the use of cryptographically generated NodeIDs and InstanceIDs—which is the focus of this section—for providing authentication, authorization, and integration with key-exchange protocols.

Crypto-Based Identifiers

Crypto-Based Identifiers (CBID) [174] use *Public Key Cryptography* [213, Sec. 2.5] to provide self-certifying identifiers/addresses. Such identifiers allow for proof of identifier-ownership without the help from a trusted third party. The general idea behind self-certifying identifiers is to derive the identifier directly from a public/private key pair. This inherently bind the identifier to the key pair and does not require a trusted third party for binding. In

---

[5]http://www.cryptopp.com

the following the naming, notation, and concepts of Montenegro and Castel-luccia [174] are described in the context of the framework for overlay-based services.

Cryptographic generation of addresses has first been described by O'Shea and Roe for authenticating mobile IPv6 binding updates [185], and developed in parallel by Montenegro and Castelluccia [173] in general form. Since then, several protocols have been presented that exploit large address sizes, mostly for IPv6, for determining addresses and identifiers through crypto-graphic generation, e. g. *Secure Neighbor Discovery* (SEND) [9], *Site Multihom-ing by IPv6 Intermediation* (Shim6) [182], or *Host Identity Protocol* (HIP) [95]. Aura described in [12] the general model of *Cryptographically Generated Ad-dresses* (CGA) with focus on IPv6. In case of IPv6 the number of free bits in the interface identifier is relatively small to achieve collision resistance. The model by Aura integrates the network routing prefix into the hash generation and uses hash extensions to prevent dictionary attacks; which precompute all possible interface identifiers and corresponding public/private key-pairs[6]. Hash extensions increase the generation cost of valid cryptographic addresses by requiring a defined number of bits being zero's in the beginning of the address. Depending on the length of this predefined pattern, the generation time of valid cryptographic identifiers increases quickly, therewith prevent-ing precomputation of dictionaries.

Crypto-based identifiers have the property of being self-certifying, therefore no *Public Key Infrastructure* (PKI) or trust anchor is required. In a PKI a certifi-cate is generated that cryptographically binds an identity to a key-pair. Such a certificate is called *Identity Certificate* (ID Certificate). This binding is certified by a *Certification Authority* (CA) using its private key, and can be validated using its public key. The trustworthiness of a CA is again provided through a signature of a Root CA. A Root CA is self-certified and its certificate must be inherently trusted. Such Root CA certificates are e. g. shipped with the operating system directly. Because in normal identity certificates the certified identity is not related to the key-pair, a third key-pair must be used to crypto-graphically bind it. Crypto-based identifiers are directly *generated* out of the public key. Therewith the binding is inherent and no trusted third party or PKI required.

Given a pair of private key $priv_i$ and public key pub_i, the crypto-based iden-tifier cid_i is created based on [174, Sec. 5.3] from the public key pub_i, and additional information mod using

$$cid_i \;=\; hmac\big(h(mod), h(pub_i)\big) \tag{5.1}$$

$$\;=\; h\Big(h(mod) \otimes opad \;||\; h\big(h(mod) \otimes ipad || h(pub_i)\big)\Big). \tag{5.2}$$

---

[6]Note, that a dictionary attack requires only to find *any* public/private key-pair that generates the victim's interface identifiers. It is not required to find the exact victim key-pair to launch an attack.

Function

- $hmac(\cdot)$ is a *Hash-based Message Authentication Code* (HMAC) [145] with constants[7] $ipad$ and $opad$,
- $h(\cdot)$ a one-way hash function like SHA1 [71],
- $\otimes$ defines bitwise XOR, and
- $||$ denotes concatenation.

In case the output length of $h(\cdot)$ is longer than the required number of bits l, the leftmost l bits are used [57, Sec. 5.1].

While in a normal HMAC *mod* is secret and only known to the HMAC creator and verifier, is can be used in different ways for crypto-based identifiers: either as secret known only to the communicating nodes, information about the node that can be obtained through additional mechanisms, or publicly known. When publicly known, *mod* is used to complicate dictionary attacks. When *mod* must be derived through additional mechanisms, the group of possible attackers is limited to nodes able to acquire this information[8].

Crypto-based identifiers can be used to implement ID certificates without the use of a PKI. A node can prove that it *owns* cid_i by using $priv_i$—which is only known to itself—to provide a signature on challenge data. If the signature can be validated using pub_i, and cid_i generated out of pub_i, the node must know the private key $priv_i$. This binds pub_i to cid_i without the use of a PKI.

Besides ID certificates, crypto-based identifiers can be used to implement *Attribute Certificates* (AC) [76]. Compared to an ID certificate, an attribute certificate does not bind an identity to a public key—it binds an attribute to an identity. As attribute certificates attest the attribute to an identity, additional identity certificates are required. One use of attribute certificates used in this section is to implement authorization. While normally a *Privilege Management Infrastructure* (PMI) is required to implement authorization using attribute certificates, crypto-based identifiers can be used to autonomously implement attribute certificates, as described in [174, Sec. 10.2]. A *Source of Authority* (SOA) uses the private key of its crypto-based identifier to provide an authorized user a signature over authorization privileges, and the user's crypto-based identifier. The user can provide this crypto-based authorization certificate to a third instance to prove that the Source of Authority signed its authorization.

Crypto-Based NodeIDs and InstanceIDs

As described in Section 5.2 an overlay instance is identified through an InstanceID, and a node identified through a NodeID. Both identifier types have a length of 160 bit and are flat in nature, i. e. they do not encode topological

---

[7]Based on [145] $ipad$ is defined as $0x36$ repeated B times, and $opad$ defined as $0x5C$ repeated B times, e. g. $B = 64$ for SHA1.

[8]E. g. if it is required to be on the same LAN segment to acquire the necessary information, only devices which are on the same LAN segment can know *mod*.

or semantic information. Compared to the usage of cryptographic addresses through the interface identifier of IPv6 addresses, length of NodeIDs and InstanceIDs does not require hash extensions to provide collision resistance. Still, the use of hash extensions can be used to prevent generation of larger numbers of valid identifiers; e. g. to make generation of large numbers of sybil nodes more expensive.

NodeIDs and InstanceIDs can be generated based on crypto-identifiers. In case of NodeIDs every node can generate its crypto-identifier autonomously. Node i generates a public/private key-pair $pub_i/priv_i$, randomly selects mod, and generates cid_i according to Equation 5.1. It uses cid_i as its NodeID which is used for addressing and routing in the overlay. The modifier mod can be changed to use the same key material for different identities, e. g. for generating different NodeIDs as private person, or business person using the same key material. A node can authenticate its NodeID by performing a challenge-response protocol where it proves that it knows the corresponding private key whose public key was used to generate the NodeID, as described in the next paragraph.

Cryptographic InstanceIDs are generated by the entity initiating the overlay instance. This entity has a special role as Source of Authority. It generates a public/private key-pair for the overlay instance $\bar{k}$, i. e. $pub_{\bar{k}}/priv_{\bar{k}}$, and generates the overlay identifier $cid_{\bar{k}}$ (modifier mod is not used in the following). This entity uses the private key $priv_{\bar{k}}$ to issue a signature

$$\{cid_i, cid_{\bar{k}}\}_{priv_{\bar{k}}} \tag{5.3}$$

to an authorized node i, i. e. attests node i with crypto-based identifier cid_i that it is authorized to join the overlay instance $\bar{k}$ with InstanceID $cid_{\bar{k}}$. This process is performed out-of-band. It is important to understand that the Source of Authority is not necessarily an overlay node, it can e. g. be an administrator setting up the overlay instance, and providing the authorization signature to a first node.

Validating a node's authorization to join the overlay can be performed by any node that knows the InstanceID $cid_{\bar{k}}$ and public key $pub_{\bar{k}}$; both public information known to joined nodes. This allows to implement authorization validation in a distributed way by every node in the overlay, under the assumption that successfully joined and authorized nodes are honest and do not allow unauthorized nodes to join. If the Source of Authority is an overlay node, it can prove that it initiated the overlay by authenticating the InstanceID using a challenge-response protocol, i. e. a proof of InstanceID ownership, as described in the next paragraph.

Authentication

Crypto-based identifiers are used for proof-of-ownership, e. g. in IPv6 Secure Neighbor Discovery a node can prove that it owns its IPv6 address. Actual

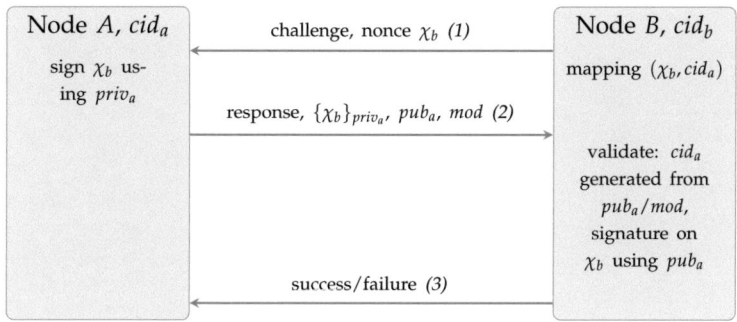

Figure 5.5 Authentication of Node A using crypto-based identifier.

authentication in not provided in such cases as the IPv6 address does not give information on the node's identity that is authenticated. The framework for overlay-based services presented in this chapter provides routing based on identifiers. Such identifiers are used for routing, *and* used to describe a node's identity. Performing proof of ownership on this routing information inherently authenticates the identity of the node.

Figure 5.5 shows a simple challenge-response authentication protocol using crypto-based identifiers where node A authenticates against node B.

(1) Node B sends an authentication request to node A together with nonce χ_b. Node B stores the mapping χ_b, cid_a to remember that the nonce χ_b was sent to authenticate node A with identifier cid_a. Node A signs χ_b using its private key $priv_a$.

(2) Node A sends back the signed χ_b, its public key pub_a, and its modifier mod. Node B validates that pub_a and mod generate the sender address cid_a using Equation 5.1, and validates the signature on χ_b using pub_a. If both the signature is valid and the address generation is correct, Node A authenticated against Node B.

If the overlay instance was initiated by an overlay node cid_i, a slightly modified protocol, shown in Figure 5.6, can be used to challenge the initiator to prove its initiator role, i.e. the initiator cid_i proves that it really initiated the overlay instance $cid_{\bar{k}}$. The InstanceID $cid_{\bar{k}}$ and the public key $pub_{\bar{k}}$ are known both to the initiator and the challenging node. Node cid_c challenges the initiator using a nonce χ_c. The initiator provides a signature on this nonce and its own identifier using the private key of the overlay instance $priv_{\bar{k}}$, i.e. $\{\chi_n, cid_i\}_{priv_{\bar{k}}}$. If the signature can be validated using $pub_{\bar{k}}$, the initiator must know the private key $priv_{\bar{k}}$ of the overlay instance. This ensures that it is the

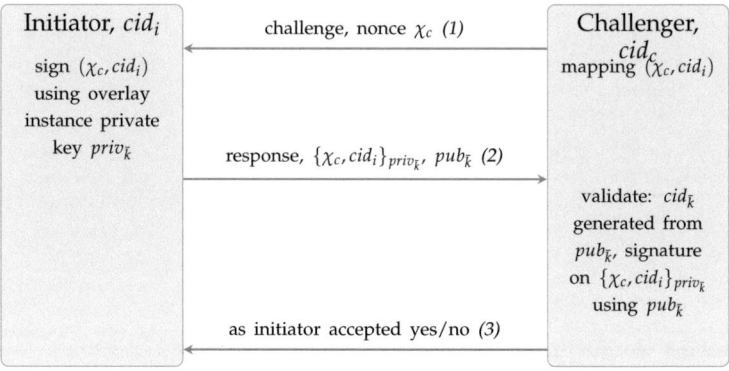

Figure 5.6 Proof of initiation of overlay instance $\bar{k}$.

initiator of the overlay instance with InstanceID $cid_{\bar{k}}$ that was generated out of the public key $pub_{\bar{k}}$. To ensure authenticity of the node that claims to be initiator, its crypto-based NodeID cid_i is integrated into the signature. This way, the challenged node proves that it is initiator, and additionally binds its NodeID to the proof.

This protocol can be used by a node to ensure that it is really talking to the initiator of the overlay instance, e. g. if it wants to prove its authorization only to the initiator, or query information about the overlay's configuration from the initiator.

Authorization

The initiator of the overlay instance can issue certificates to nodes which are authorized to join. Signature $\{cid_i, cid_{\bar{k}}\}_{priv_{\bar{k}}}$ provided by the Source of Authority—knowing $priv_{\bar{k}}$—to node cid_i states its authorization of joining the overlay instance $cid_{\bar{k}}$. This authorization certificate can be validated by any other node that is already joined in the overlay. Such joined nodes know the crypto-based overlay instance identifier $cid_{\bar{k}}$, and the corresponding public key $pub_{\bar{k}}$ used to generate $cid_{\bar{k}}$. Additional information can be encoded in the attribute certificate, e. g. a timestamp to limit the allowed authorization time [126, Sec. 3].

Prior authentication is required to successfully validate the authorization of a node. As described in the prior paragraph a node may wish to only authorize against a node that can prove its initiator role.

Identity-Based Encryption

Generation of identifiers is based on hashing. The hash function's output is consistently distributed over the identifier space, i. e. uniformly distributed over $[0, 2^{160})$ in this framework. Other input to the hash function can be used that is not based on cryptography, e. g. human-readable names. Given the human-readable name of a node or overlay instance, its NodeID or InstanceID can be generated through hashing. This simplifies addressing if humans are involved that have to remember or type such names.

In case of crypto-based identifiers the input to the hash function is a public key. Compared to a human-readable name a public key is equally bad to type or remember as the resulting 160 bit identifier. *Identity-Based Encryption* (IBE) [32, 224] allows generation of a private key, given an arbitrary public key. Such public keys can e. g. be human-readable names. Using IBE allows to use crypto-based identifier by regaining the benefit of human readable names. As drawback, IBE requires a central authority, the *Private Key Generator*, that generates the private keys corresponding to given public keys. This is in contrast to a pure crypto-based identifier scheme where nodes generate their identifier autonomously. Despite of initial centralized private key generation, protocols and mechanisms described in the following work equally for IBE generated keys.

Confidentiality and Integrity

The presented mechanisms for authentication and authorization can be integrated into a key exchange protocol that allows confidentiality and integrity for virtual links. The *Transport Layer Security* (TLS) [64, 206] protocol provides a flexible suite for authenticated key exchange, originally developed for securing web traffic, and today a standard protocol for providing secure end-to-end communication. In the following, the integration of crypto-based identifiers for authentication in the TLS handshake is described. While TLS is employed upon end-to-end TCP connections, the general concepts of TLS are valid as key exchange protocol and can be integrated for securing virtual links in the framework for overlay-based services presented in this chapter.

The Most important part of the TLS protocol suite is the handshake protocol that implements key exchange. Crypto-based identifiers can be implemented into TLS as authentication module. Using TLS's *cipher suites* such a new module can be integrated into the protocol seamlessly. Besides traditional server-side authentication, TLS implements client-side authentication when explicitly triggered by the server-side. This mechanism is in the following used to implement mutual authentication using crypto-based identifiers[9].

Figure 5.7 shows the TLS handshake with mutual authentication that is in the following used for authentication, based on crypto-based identifiers. Key generation is performed using pre-master secrets generated by node A. Both node A and node B have crypto-based identifiers cid_a/cid_b, generated from public keys pub_a/pub_b with corresponding private keys $priv_a/priv_b$.

---

[9]Mutual host-to-host authentication using TLS is shortly described in [206, Sec. 7.15].

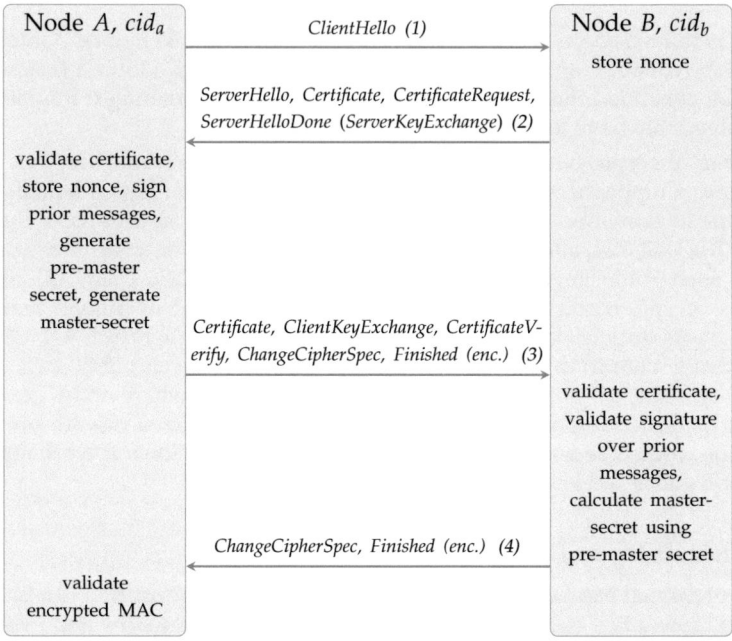

Figure 5.7 TLS key exchange with mutual authentication [206, Sec. 4.3].

(1) Node *A* generates nonce χ_a and sends it to node *B* with a list of supported cipher suites (*ClientHello*). The new cipher suites are defined to support authentication using crypto-based identifiers.

(2) Node *B* replies with the selected cipher suite and nonce χ_b (*ServerHello*), its crypto-based identifier cid_b and public key pub_b (*Certificate*), a request for the client to authenticate (*CertificateRequest*), and indicates the end of its messages (*ServerHelloDone*). If confidentiality is *not* required, an additional *ServerKeyExchange* message is necessary, as described later.

(3) Node *A* validates that pub_b was used to generate cid_b, and generates a pre-master. It sends back its crypto-based identifier cid_a and public key pub_a (*Certificate*), and pre-master secret encrypted with pub_b (*ClientKeyExchange*). To prove that its authentication data is fresh and valid, node *A* sends a signature using $priv_a$ over all prior messages which includes *B*'s nonce χ_b (*CertificateVerify*). Node *A* calculates the master secret using the pre-master secret, χ_a, and χ_b. It indicates that all following messages are sent encrypted (*ChangeCipherSpec*), and sends a MAC over all prior messages, encrypted with the master secret (*Finished*).

(4) Node B validates that cid_a is generated out of pub_a, and validates the signed data sent by A using pub_a. It decrypts the pre-master secret using its private key $priv_b$, and generates the master secret using pre-master secret, χ_b, and χ_a. Using the pre-master secret, node B validates the encrypted MAC sent by node A. It then indicates that all following messages are sent encrypted (*ChangeCipherSpec*), and sends an encrypted MAC of all prior messages (*Finished*).

In this protocol node A proves to node B that it owns $priv_a$ by signing of prior messages in *CertificateVerify*. Those prior messages include the nonce χ_b sent by node B in *ServerHello*. In the other direction, node B proves to node A that it owns $priv_b$ as it can decrypt the pre-master secret sent by node A which is encrypted using node B's public key pub_b. If node B can not successfully decrypt the pre-master secret, generation of the master-secret fails.

If *no* confidentiality is required, authenticity of node B can not be validated, as it depends on node B being able to decrypt a pre-master secret, which does not exist in this mode. In such cases—described in [30] for password-based authentication—a *ServerKeyExchange* message is sent by node B in step (2). It contains a signature over χ_a and χ_b, besides other information. If node B can provide such a signature over its own nonce χ_b and node A's nonce χ_a, then it *must* know $priv_b$. This verifies node B's authenticity, even if no confidentiality is required.

5.2.4 Utilities

Besides the architectural components described so far, the framework provides a set of loosely coupled components, described as *Utilities*. Utilities are mainly provided to ease development tasks and provide a self-contained framework where novel services can be built into:

- Addressing functionality for handling the different locator formats.
- Configuration mechanisms that provide access to configuration files.
- Logging functionality.
- Message serialization and deserialization.
- Threading mechanisms and startup functionality.
- Simulation support for running services source-code compatible in a simulation environment.
- Data types for instance identifier, node identifier, link identifier.
- Visualization mechanisms to visualize a service-instance's overlay.

5.3 Interfaces

While several libraries exist that allow to abstract from operating system API access for networking, as explained in Section 5.1.1, the framework for overlay-based services aims at abstracting not only from the API, but from the network itself. It provides two interfaces for developing novel services, and for

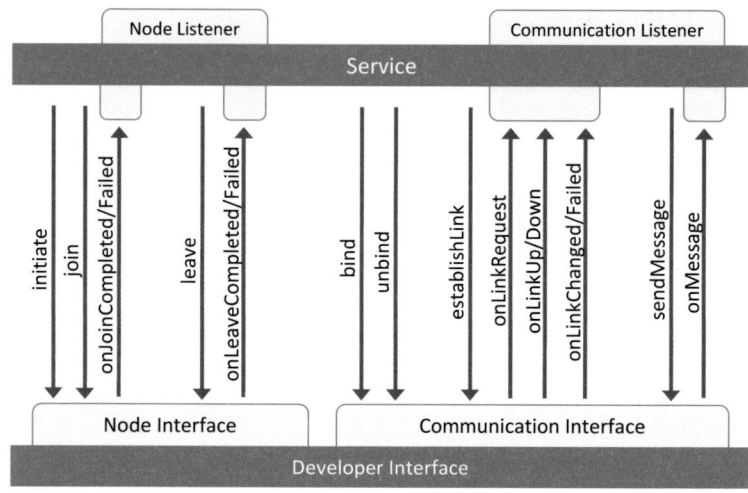

Figure 5.8 Overview of the developer interface usage and event callbacks.

supporting legacy services: The *Developer Interface*, described in Section 5.3.1, provides a programming interface that is used to implement novel services, based upon an object-oriented event-driven paradigm. Existing legacy services can be run on top of the framework through the *Legacy Interface*, as described in Section 5.3.2.

5.3.1 Developer Interface

The Developer Interface is intended for novel services developed upon the framework presented in this chapter. It consists of a stable set of interface functions, types, and event functionality. Table 5.3 gives an overview of the Developer Interface, Figure 5.8 shows the order of calls and events. The Developer Interface is split into *communication-specific*, and *node-specific* interface groups. Both groups provide functions and respective callbacks. The communication-specific interface group is mapped to exactly one *Service Identifier* (ServiceID), which is registered by a service, whereas the node-specific interface is bound to exactly one *Instance Identifier* (InstanceID). While the ServiceID is used for demultiplexing incoming messages to the correct service, the InstanceID is used to distinguish between different overlay instances.

An important characteristic of the Developer Interfaces is its event-driven character. While traditional Socket-based programming requires the developer to constantly poll or block for new data, the Developer Interfaces provides an event-based interface for calling `onMessage` functions of a service. This eases development and simplifies implementation of protocols.

	Function	Description
Node	`initiate`	Create a service-instance
	`join`	Join the service-instance
	`leave`	Leave the service-instance
	`onJoinCompleted`	Indicate join success
	`onJoinFailed`	Indicate join failure
	`onLeaveCompleted`	Indicate leave success
	`onLeaveFailed`	Indicate leave failure
Communication	`bind`	Bind a service through its ServiceID
	`unbind`	Unbind a service
	`establishLink`	Establish a virtual link to another NodeID
	`dropLink`	Drop a virtual link
	`sendMessage`	Send message, if required build up link
	`onLinkUp`	Indicate successful setup of virtual link
	`onLinkDown`	Indicate successful dropping of virtual link
	`onLinkChanged`	Indicate link mobility
	`onLinkFailed`	Indicate that the link has dropped
	`onLinkRequest`	Indicate incoming link request
	`onMessage`	Incoming messages on a virtual link

Table 5.3 Overview of the developer interface [28, 115].

5.3.2 Legacy Interface

Porting existing socket-based services to the Developer Interface is expensive. While novel services can be implemented more easily through the presented Developer Interface, it is desirable to run existing *legacy services* transparently on top of the framework. This way, legacy services can benefit at least from a subset of features, e. g. multi-homing, or mobility support. In focus of this thesis, legacy services are assumed to require an IPv4-based network interface—which is true as of today for all commonly used networked services—e. g. through a socket abstraction. Besides sockets which are used for sending and receiving datagrams or streams, DNS name resolution is required by applications to allow users to work with more easily readable names, rather than numeric IPv4 addresses.

The Legacy Interface is implemented through a simulated layer 3 network interface, a so-called *Tunnel Software Network Interface* (TUN Interface). It allows to capture traffic from the legacy service, and inject traffic back into the legacy service. A naming scheme in the form `nodename.service-instance.ariba` is used:

- `nodename` describes a human readable name for a node. The hash value of `nodename` is used as NodeID.
- `serviceinstance` describes a human readable name of a service instance. The InstanceID is generated through hashing.

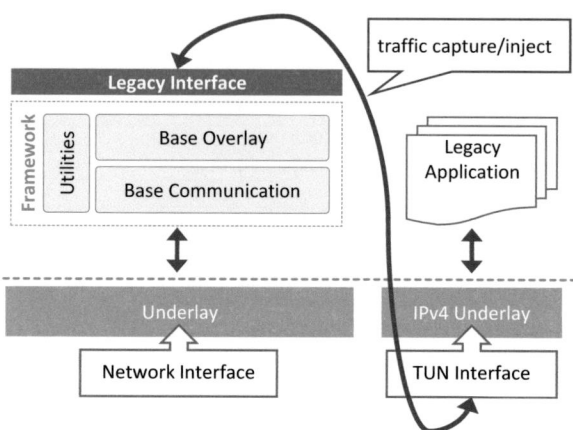

Figure 5.9 Transparent integration of legacy services into the framework.

- ariba describes framework-specific addressing (*ariba* is the implementation of the framework and described in Section 5.4).

Upon receiving a service-specific DNS request, the legacy interface returns a locally valid IPv4 address for the requested node with name nodename. This mapping is stored locally so that subsequent traffic towards this locally valid IPv4 address is forwarded to the node with NodeID being the hash of nodename. DNS requests are resolved within the local machine by setting up local mappings. Before returning the DNS request to the legacy service, a hello-message is sent to the respective node in the service-instance to see if it is existent and responding. Respectively, a DNS reply is generated locally and passed back to the legacy service through the TUN interface. All DNS requests are filtered and traffic towards the locally valid IPv4 address redirected to the service-instance.

Figure 5.9 shows an architectural view of the legacy support [111]. A TUN interface is used to capture and inject packets. The Legacy Interface runs on top of the framework as stub and handles the coordination with the TUN interface. The framework itself runs unchanged and provides properties such as mobility support transparent to the legacy application. Actual implementation of the DNS resolver and TUN interface was performed with the help of OCALA [134].

5.4 Implementation

The concepts and mechanisms presented in this chapter have been implemented as part of the *Spontaneous Virtual Networks* (SpoVNet) [28, 29, 109,

110, 112–115, 247] project in the software library *ariba*[10]. *ariba* is implemented in C++ on the Linux operating system with focus on the widespread Ubuntu distribution. The modular design of the architecture allows high re-use of functionality and easy exchange of functionality, e. g. to implement new underlay protocols or overlay structures. Through an event-driven design the implementation of novel services upon *ariba* requires filling in service-specific functionality. Development of *ariba* is an ongoing effort. *ariba* has been ported to several platforms, currently Linux, OpenWrt, iOS, Maemo, and Android. *ariba* has been presented as demo at several conferences:

- With focus on heterogeneous networks *ariba* has been presented at ACM SIGCOMM 2009 in Barcelona [109] and was awarded "Honorable Mention" [110].

- How *ariba* can support legacy application was shown in a demo at IEEE INFOCOM 2010 in San Diego [111].

- The developed perspective of *ariba* was shown in a demo at the GI/ITG KiVS 2011 conference in Kiel [113] and won the "KuVS Communication Software Award" [112].

ariba has been released as Open Source under the FreeBSD license. For source code, documentation and further technical information the reader is referred to the *ariba* website: http://www.ariba-underlay.org.

5.5 Enabling Platform for HRS

This section discusses the use of *ariba* as enabling platform for HRS described in Chapter 4.

Architectural Integration

Figure 5.10 shows the architectural integration of *ariba* as enabling platform for HRS. *ariba* serves as underlay abstraction for both overlay-based, and ad hoc communication. While ad hoc DTN communication and overlay-based communication are separated in *ariba*, HRS integrates both paradigms by infrastructure-based overlay communication, and DTN-based ad hoc communication. On the one hand *ariba* provides an enabling platform for HRS, on the other hand HRS is a probabilistic extension of *ariba*'s overlay-based routing into DTNs.

---

[10]The name *ariba* is derived from the Spanish word "arriba", meaning "over"/"above", describing the overlay character the ariba library provides build up, hiding the underlay network and its challenges.

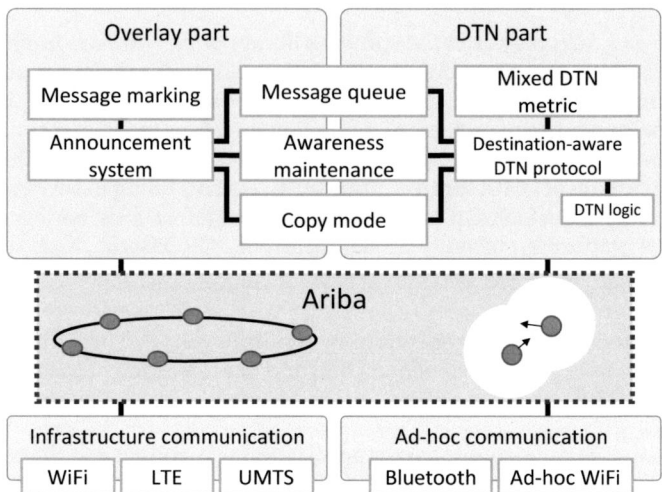

Figure 5.10 Integration of *ariba* as enabling platform for HRS.

Distributed Overlay Instance

Both presented HRS variants build up a distributed overlay network per HRS-instance in the infrastructure part of the hybrid network. This integrates well with *ariba* that builds up an overlay network per service-instance.

Identifier-based Addressing

Addressing in HRS is based on flat identifiers in the DTN, and using the same identifiers for addressing in the overlay. *ariba* provides identifier-based addressing in the overlay and implements key-based routing, based on a structure overlay protocol. HRS directly uses the addressing scheme of *ariba* and especially the KBR routing with closest-match behavior.

Security

The Hybrid Routing System is implemented as a service on top of the framework presented in this chapter and can make use of the crypto-based identifiers described in Section 5.2.3. For iHRS, the use of crypto-based identifiers is possible, in contrast to vHRS that can not be used with crypto-based identifiers. In vHRS virtual nodes are placed in the overlay at strategic positions to represent proxy registrations. NodeIDs of such virtual nodes are explicitly calculated using awareness information. Such explicit identifier calculation is not supported by crypto-based identifiers—and neither using Identity-Based Encryption—as hashing of the public key is still required to achieve consistent distribution in the overlay's identifier key space.

Node authentication using crypto-based identifiers in iHRS allows proxy-admins that manage awareness information in the overlay to prove that they are legitimate proxy-admins. Without the use of crypto-based identifiers, an attacker can place itself strategically in the overlay to affect routing towards a specific victim device.

Node authorization using crypto-based identifiers allows to build up closed hybrid routing contexts where only legitimate devices participate in the overlay, as well as the DTN. Note, that the hybrid routing scheme uses the same identifiers for routing in the DTN *and* routing in the overlay. This enables use of crypto-based identifiers in the DTN. Use of authorization and build-up of closed contexts is not only possible in the overlay network, but additionally in the DTN network. Devices can validate whether an encountered device is authorized to participate in the DTN. This prevents outsider attacks where attackers trick other devices in communication range to forward them messages, or where attackers inject large numbers of fake messages to flood the network.

Crypto-based identifiers do only validate legitimacy of nodes in the overlay, and devices in the DTN. They can not protect against insider attacks, e. g. blackhole routing in the DTN where rogue devices fake their awareness for other devices. Solutions for such attacks exist in literature, e. g. Nelson et al. [179] present a signature-based scheme where encountered devices mutually provide signatures over current timestamps. This enables to proof that the other device was encountered, and allows recalculation and validation of awareness values. Use of crypto-based identifiers integrates nicely with such a scheme, as public/private key pairs are available.

Crypto-based identifiers allow for end-to-end confidentiality of messages by encrypting them with the public key of the destination device. Similar, ad hoc communication between devices can be secured by building up authenticated and confidential channels for message exchange.

Mobility Support

HRS integrates mobile devices with different infrastructure capabilities into hybrid networks. Such devices are subject to mobility through their human owner, resulting in changing infrastructure access association. *ariba* hides mobility through an identifier/locator split that decouples dynamic network addresses from stable node identities. *ariba* therewith relieves HRS from complex mobility handling for the infrastructure-part of the network.

Middlebox Handling

Infrastructure access is often implemented through private subnets and a gateway to the Internet. Such *Network Address Translation* (NAT) middleboxes complicate connectivity, especially in distributed overlay networks where end-to-end reachability is assumed by most protocols. *ariba* does not rely on end-to-end reachability, but rather establishes such reachability itself in a lower layer of its architecture. It therewith relieving HRS from complex handling of middleboxes.

Heterogeneity Support

Access through infrastructure-based mobile networks can be based on different underlay protocols. *ariba* provides an abstraction layer that hides underlay heterogeneity and provides communication through a decentralized and collaborative approach. HRS can make use of heterogeneity support in *ariba* to enable infrastructure-based communication through a diverse set of infrastructure access and protocols.

Ad hoc Communication

ariba supports several communication modules, based on infrastructure communication, but also based on ad hoc communication such as Bluetooth. It can support both communication requirements for HRS, and provide a flexible platform that is, on the one hand, used for the overlay part of HRS, but additionally for the ad hoc communication part.

5.6   Summary and Conclusion

Distributed implementation of scalable services has a complexity orders of magnitude higher than centralized services. The Hybrid Routing System presented in Chapter 4 represents such a distributed service. The SpoVNet project has developed an architecture that allows for easy development and deployment of novel distributed services and applications in today's Internet. Through several levels of abstraction SpoVNet hides challenges posed by the underlay and provides a consistent and homogeneous network to the developer. The SpoVNet architecture has been implemented in the *ariba* C++ library and ported to several platforms.

Focus in this thesis was on the security aspects, which have been built directly into the framework, and allow for transparent provision of security properties to services. For development and deployment of the Hybrid Routing System the framework presented in this chapter provides several benefits: It simplifies development of such distributed systems, hides underlay heterogeneity and mobility, and integrates security transparently. From perspective of HRS, the framework allows for easy development of the overlay-part of HRS. From perspective of the framework presented in this chapter, HRS represents a probabilistic extension of the overlay into disconnected DTNs.

6. Summary and Perspectives

The strong growing number of mobile devices results in exponential growth of traffic volumes in infrastructure-based mobile networks [47]. On the other hand this large number of mobile devices is an enabler for infrastructure-less opportunistic networks [51]. Such Delay Tolerant Networks [259] are made up solely by mobile devices and exploit opportunistic device contacts for store-carry-forward routing. While Delay Tolerant Networks on their own have limited applicability due to probabilistic message delivery and long delay, their integration with infrastructure-based networks is promising [122, 123, 156]. The vision pursued in this thesis is the seamless and self-organizing interplay between today's infrastructure-based networks, and Delay Tolerant Networks based upon mobile devices.

Goal of this thesis was the seamless integration of infrastructure-based networks with infrastructure-less Delay Tolerant Networks into hybrid networks. It was shown through extensive evaluation that the developed Hybrid Routing System can provide end-to-end communication if infrastructure access is sparse by extending the reach of Delay Tolerant Networks through overlays. On the other hand, if infrastructure access is widely available, the Hybrid Routing System can offload traffic from infrastructure-based networks by preferably routing traffic through Delay Tolerant Networks.

Integration of the two network types was non-trivial, e.g. due to different routing paradigms: While infrastructure-based routing builds up and maintains paths in proactive or reactive manner, Delay Tolerant Networks perform opportunistic per-hop routing decisions based on probabilistic models. Integration required the following contributions:

- **Mobility Modeling on Graphs**, Chapter 3: Delay Tolerant Networks introduce complexity due to stochastic mobility of devices. Understanding of mobility and inter-contact behavior in different urban environments is critical for development, configuration, and deployment of opportunistic networks. To improve understanding of mobility on graphs, simulative and analytical models have been developed.
- **Hybrid Routing System**, Chapter 4: A system for hybrid routing that can integrate infrastructure-based overlay networks, and infrastructureless Delay Tolerant Networks. The developed routing system is applicable for existing Delay Tolerant Network routing protocols that have been developed for different scenarios, and allows transparent addressing of devices through a self-organizing system.
- **Framework for Overlay-based Services**, Chapter 5: A framework that supports implementation and deployment of the Hybrid Routing System by abstracting from complexity of today's networks, and reducing complexity of distributed systems.

6.1   Results of this Thesis

Mobility Modeling on Graphs

This thesis contributes to the understanding of mobility by analyzing impact of underlying graphs on mobility, with focus on the important metric of inter-contact time. Real-world city graphs and synthetic grid-based graphs have been analyzed through simulation and analytical models. Different model fitting methods have been used to analyze the inter-contact time behavior over different graphs from simulative data, both for determining the overall evolution of the inter-contact time distribution, and for analyzing specific power-law properties.

While simulations give insight into the resulting mobility behavior and allow to easily integrate real-world conditions like spatial layout and communication range, they provide no insight into graph properties that generate this behavior. For this understanding an analytical model has been developed, based on Random walks and spectral graph theory. The spectral gap of a graph has found to give insight into power-law behavior of inter-contact times and used for correlation with fitted data generated through simulations. It was shown how the power-law slope of inter-contact times varies with underlying graphs, both under social, and under random mobility models. Under social mobility the difference in power-law slope for real-world city graphs is small, indicating that social intention is a stronger factor for determining paths over real-world cities than the underlying graph itself that restricts movement.

The contributions are summarized as follows:

- Simulative evaluation of impact of real-world city graphs, and grid-based graphs on inter-contact time.

- Quantization of simulation data through model fitting to provide numeric comparison.
- Analytical analysis using Random walks and spectral graph theory for derivation of graph property with impact on mobility.
- Correlation of fitted simulation data with analytical data.

Hybrid Routing System

This thesis explored the integration of infrastructure-less Delay Tolerant Networks with infrastructure-based networks. Based upon state of the art in overlay-based and opportunistic routing, the Hybrid Routing System has been developed that integrates both types of networks seamlessly and transparently. The Hybrid Routing System is used in this thesis to implement two exemplary use cases: When infrastructure access is sparse, the Hybrid Routing System enables communication for otherwise partitioned Delay Tolerant Networks in disconnected areas. If infrastructure access is widely available, the Hybrid Routing System can offload traffic from infrastructure-based networks by preferably routing messages in Delay Tolerant Networks.

Heterogeneous infrastructure access of mobile devices is supported through autonomous management of infrastructure awareness by mechanisms of the integrated Delay Tolerant Network protocol. Awareness for infrastructure access is used for initial routing of messages towards infrastructure through a mixed routing metric. This routing metric takes awareness for the destination device itself, and awareness for infrastructure access into account for routing messages either towards the destination device directly, or towards the infrastructure that can provide a geographic shortcut with short delay to overcome long distance.

Infrastructure-capable devices build up a distributed overlay network to collaboratively manage routing information. Two schemes for distributed overlays have been developed that can be used to implement a distributed announcement system. Routing information from Delay Tolerant Network protocols is used for registering proxies in the announcement system, e. g. based upon probability of future device encounters. The announcement system provides lookup functionality to decide which infrastructure-capable devices are best applicable for routing messages into the Delay Tolerant Network. This enables routing decisions *without* requiring knowledge of device locations, nor information about infrastructure access, or device capabilities. Rather, messages are routed purely based on stable flat identifiers, both in the Delay Tolerant Network and in the overlay network. New infrastructure access possibilities and infrastructure-capabilities of devices are propagated autonomously by devices, without manual configuration. Furthermore, no dedicated systems are required, but the Hybrid Routing System set up spontaneous and self-organizing through mobile devices themselves.

A novel categorization for Delay Tolerant Network routing protocol allows to integrate existing protocols into the Hybrid Routing System. This enables deployment of the Delay Tolerant Network routing protocol that works best in a given scenario.

The contributions are summarized as follows:

- The Hybrid Routing System that integrates infrastructure-less Delay Tolerant Networks and infrastructure-based overlay networks.
- Two distributed overlay schemes, applicable for different times scales of contact stability.
- Implementation and evaluation of two use cases with the Hybrid Routing System to provide communication, and offload infrastructure.
- A novel categorization that allows integration of existing Delay Tolerant Network routing protocols.

Framework for Overlay-based Services

In this thesis a framework for overlay-based services was developed that provides an underlay abstraction to simplify development and deployment of distributed services. It abstracts from the underlay, looking homogeneous and stable to the developer, while today's underlays actually are heterogeneous and dynamic. This supports developers to handle the increasing complexity of today's network which requires tremendous efforts to cope with.

The framework is split into two main parts: In the lower layer the Base-Communication abstracts from heterogeneity in protocols, and provides end-to-end communication between participants. In the upper layer the Base-Overlay provides a distributed per-service context through a scalable overlay protocol. While the BaseCommunication abstracts from underlay-specific addressing through flat virtual link identifiers, the BaseOverlay provides the abstraction of identifier-based addressing of nodes. Two interfaces have been developed for use of the framework: The developer interface provides an API for developing novel services, while the legacy interface allows deployment of existing services transparently upon the framework.

Fundamental security—in terms of link confidentiality, integrity, and node authenticity—is provided transparently through the use of crypto-based identifiers. The framework rungs on multiple platforms (Linux, Android, Open-Wrt, Maemo, iOS), and is released as Open Source for research and industry.

The contributions are summarized as follows:

- A framework for overlay-based services that provides seamless development and deployment of distributed services.
- Support for novel services through a developer interface, and support for existing services through a legacy interface.
- Analysis of providing fundamental security transparently through crypto-based identifiers.
- Open Source implementation of the framework with support for several important platforms.

6.2 Perspectives

This thesis analyzed the impact of graph structures on mobility which is important for development and deployment for Delay Tolerant Network routing protocols that heavily rely on mobility. It was shown in this thesis that especially random mobility models are strongly influenced by the underlying graph. It is an interesting question whether, given inter-contact time distributions from real-world traces, graphs can be generated so that mobility on those graphs results in the same inter-contact time distribution. Such an approach could, e. g., be used for simulative evaluation of DTN protocols. In contrast to replaying traces that describe just a single seed, simulation using such generated graphs would allow for statistical confidence and usage of simple mobility models like Random walk upon the graph. Furthermore, the presented mobility modeling approach can be extended, e. g. to take popularity of geographic areas into account, and model the volume of mobile devices according to time of day.

The Hybrid Routing System has been developed around a novel categorization, based upon structure and use of routing information. For unicast communication, destination-aware protocols have been identified best suited and three such protocols integrated. It is interesting to analyze the applicability of the remaining two protocol categories for other communication paradigms. For example the self-aware category allows for routing towards devices with high self-awareness, e. g. devices that are very central in the social graph, or very active devices. Such devices can preferably be used for message dissemination in hybrid routing. For such use cases other requirements on the overlay network result.

The message model used for evaluation is based on uniformly distributed message destinations. Using social relations for messaging is interesting. Furthermore, the impact of different message lifetime and generation processes is interesting. Finally, analytical models are important that describe behavior of hybrid routing, e. g. based on the number of social geographic clusters and different fraction of infrastructure-capabilities inside each cluster.

A. Simulation Environment

In this appendix the simulation environment used for the evaluation of mobility modeling in Chapter 3, and the Hybrid Routing System in Chapter 4 is described. Initially, insight is provided into the decision for a simulator-based evaluation in Section A.1, which is in contrast to a trace-driven evaluation. For better understanding of the extensions that are required for the simulative evaluations performed in this thesis, the ONE simulator is introduced in Section A.2 as simulation basis. Extensions that have been made to this simulator are described in Section A.3 from an architectural perspective. The most important components of this extension are then described in Sections A.4–A.8. The mobility model and work on the underlying street maps—used in Chapter 3 and Chapter 4—are presented in Section A.9, and Section A.10. Finally, an overview of reporting enhancements is described in Section A.11 as basis for the performance metrics presented in Section 4.9.2.

A.1 Simulative vs. Trace-Driven Evaluation

Several real-world experiments have been performed, mainly on university campuses or in conference settings. Well-known contact trace files resulting from these experiments are e. g. DieselNet [35], INFOCOM'06 [43], or MIT Reality Mining [70]. A larger number of DTN protocols have been evaluated on the basis of such contact traces [15, 35, 120, 257]. However, the simulative evaluation based upon realistic mobility models provides more flexibility, and statistical confidence. While contact traces are of high necessity [257] as they provide great insight into human behavior and have been analyzed thoroughly [42, 43, 136], they suffer from the fact that for actual protocol evaluation they only provide "one seed", i. e. the contact trace is replayed and the DTN protocol evaluated based upon the mobility or contact information in the trace. No flexibility is given, e. g. in the configuration of scenarios, or scaling of number of devices. Furthermore one may optimize its protocol unknowingly to the specific conditions that created a specific contact trace. Rather, the approach used in this thesis is based upon higher-level properties—like statistical distribution of inter-contact times—that have been extracted from traces [42, 43, 136] and uses a mobility model that reflects this behavior. Therewith, the realism benefits that mobility traces inherently provide is regained, but flexibility achieved, e. g. for simulation seeding.

Figure A.1 gives an overview on the interrelation of contact traces and mobility models. The left part of Figure A.1 shows the use of contact traces for simulation, while the right part of Figure A.1 shows the use of contact traces for developing mobility models which are then used for simulation. Originally, contact logging from pairs of devices are obtained in real-world experiments. In such experiments, humans are given devices that are capable of logging proximity with other such devices, e. g. through Bluetooth, that represent potential communication opportunities. Logging facilities store start timestamp and end timestamp, as well as addresses of encountered devices. The combination of multiple such contact logs is combined to an assembled contact trace that can be directly used for replay and evaluation. Additionally, spatial information in form of GPS traces might be available that describes movement of individual devices. On the other hand, the higher-order properties of the contact trace can be analyzed and inherent properties of human behavior extracted in formal models. Together with—if available—spatial information, mobility models for use in simulations can be developed that reflect the contact behavior of real-world experiments. In combination with real-world maps that restrict possible movement between destination locations generated by the mobility model, walking paths are calculated per device, and movement as well as resulting device contacts simulated.

A.2   ONE Simulator

The simulation environment used in this thesis is based upon the *Opportunistic Network Environment* (ONE) [138, 139]. ONE is used for evaluation of DTN protocols and is actively developed at the Department of Communications and Networking at the Aalto University. ONE is written in Java and follows a strict object-oriented approach with focus on easy extensibility to allow for development of, e. g., new DTN protocols, or mobility models. A set of well-known DTN protocols and mobility models are shipped with ONE.

An important characteristic of simulations is their definition of *time*. To define time and especially a *point in time*—which is represented through a *timestamp*—a discretization of time must be achieved. Generally, time-discrete models can be differentiated as *event-driven*, and *time-stepped* [81, p. 30]. While

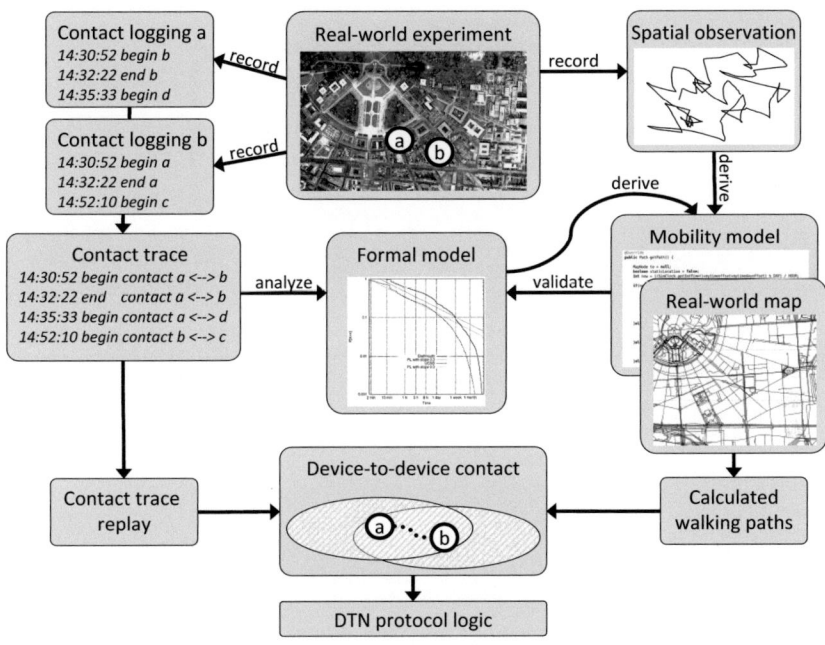

Figure A.1 Interrelation of trace-driven and simulative evaluation.

in event-driven simulations the simulation time is enhanced to an arbitrary timestamp defined through an event, a time-stepped simulation advances the simulation time based on a configuration-specific clock-step. Therewith, in an event-driven model only the exact timestamps of events do actually exist, while in a time-stepped model all timestamps exist that are a multiude of the configuration-specific clock-step. I. e. in an event-driven simulation the simulation time advances with arbitrary and non uniform steps, while in a time-stepped simulation the simulation time advances as a sequence of equally sized steps.

ONE follows a time-stepped approach. This is in contrast to simulators like OMNeT++[245] that follow an event-driven approach. ONE continuously enhances the simulation time by a configuration-defined clock-step and calls respective `update()`-functions on all registered modules that can decide to execute protocol specific functionality. Changes in the system state can therefore only be performed at discrete points in time which are a multiude of the clock-step. The clock-step has therefore important impact on the simulation granularity and precision. Modules in ONE can still schedule events, but those are only processed at *clock-step specific times* and not arbitrary times like in an event-driven approach. In contrast, in event-driven simulators such

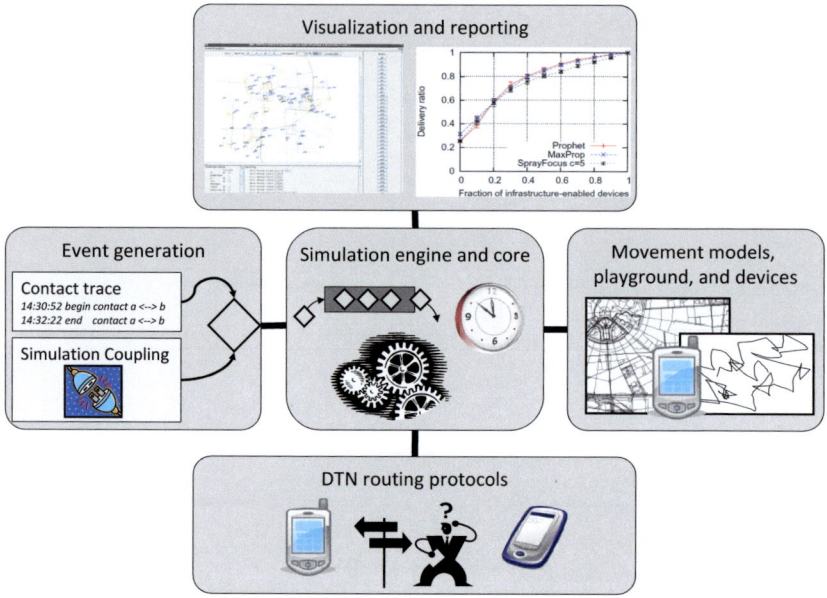

Figure A.2 Architectural view of the main components of the ONE simulator.

events are queued and processed at the *exact* time defined in the event for processing and, notably, only by the target module. I. e. an event-driven simulator orders events by their future time of processing. It can then "jump" to the simulation time where the next event needs to be processed. Therewith, a time-stepped simulator is not as efficient, due to the clock-step based calling of protocol update functionality on *all* modules, even if no protocol work is to be performed. While an event-driven approach provides better simulation performance, the time-stepped approach in ONE simplifies development.

From an architectural perspective, ONE can be divided into five major components, as shown in Figure A.2:

Simulation Engine and Core The Simulation Engine implements the time-stepped simulation processing and contains e. g. the simulation clock, and event queue. Furthermore, the Core is responsible to coordinate all simulation mechanisms such as the network area, reporting, and setup/teardown of the simulation and its objects.

Movement models, network area, and devices An important part of mobile device simulation is the network area where devices move. ONE supports a plain network area of configurable size, but further allows to use street maps as basis for movement restrictions of devices. Maps must be given in a subset of the *Well-Known Text* (WKT) [105] format defined by the Open Geospatial Consortium. WKT is a textual format that defines a set of landmarks, which together make up a street. Coordinates are in meters with the upper left corner of the network area being defined as the coordinate system origin $(0,0)$. Multiple maps can be used—e. g. street maps, tram lines, or points-of-interest—which can be assigned to different groups of mobile devices. Similar to the DTN routing protocols, ONE provides the basic functionality for movement models and several well-known movement models built upon this, e. g. *RandomWaypoint* [3], or *Working-Day Movement Model* [73] (cf. Section A.9). When movement is configured to be based on street maps, the length-shortest path through the street map is calculated and used for reaching the next destination, instead of walking there in a straight line in case of a plain network area (cf. Section A.10). Detecting when two devices are within communication range is based on the *unit-disc model* introduced in [97, p. 1510]. ONE employs a grid-based algorithm that does not require connectivity checks between all devices in $\mathcal{O}(n^2)$, n being the number of mobile devices. Rather, each device remembers its current field in a grid which is overlayed onto the network area; with grid size depending on the device communication range. Only devices in the same and neighboring fields of the grid are checked for connectivity, therewith lowering computational requirements[1].

DTN routing protocols For actual DTN evaluation, ONE contains a set of base functionality required for simulation of mobile devices and device-to-device communication. Furthermore, trivial routing protocols like Epidemic [244] or DirectDelivery [138] are provided as upper and lower bounds for performance measurements. Several state of the art protocols are shipped with ONE such as MaxProp [35], Spray&Wait [228], or Prophet [154]. The DTN protocol base classes provide common protocol functionality so that implementation of a new DTN protocol can be achieved with comparable small effort.

Event generation Despite the time-stepped simulation processing, ONE still allows to schedule events. These are, however, only processed during a time-step after the main simulation is updated, e. g. after all devices have moved and executed their routing functionality. Such events can be either generated internally—e. g. message generation for DTN payload traffic—or generated externally such as reading traces for mo-

---

[1]Segmenting the network area into k fields results in an average of n/k mobile devices per field. For every of the k fields, every device within the field must be checked for connectivity with the other $n/k - 1$ devices in its own field, and with all devices of the 8 neighboring fields. This results in an overall complexity of $\mathcal{O}(k \cdot ((n/k) \cdot (9 \cdot (n/k)))) = \mathcal{O}(n^2/k)$. The possible value for k depends directly on the wireless communication range and the size of the network area, so that only communication with devices in the own field, and neighboring fields is possible.

bility, or for synchronization in case of simulator coupling (cf. Section A.5), or hardware-in-the-loop real-world integration.

Visualization and Reporting For evaluation of simulation scenarios and protocols ONE has a set of reporting functionality that can be extended to gather performance metrics. Reports are either time-based in that they describe performance metrics discrete over time, or summary-based in that they are written at the end of the simulation and provide overall statistical values. Besides textual reporting, ONE has a graphical visualization that is mainly used for demonstration purpose. The visualization shows the network area—with underlying street map—and movement of devices. Symbols indicate communication, as well as device queue size.

A.3   Overview of Simulator Extensions

In the following, an overview of simulator extensions and mechanisms is given that have been developed in this thesis to allow for evaluation of the hybrid routing scheme presented in Chapter 4. Parts of the work described in the following are used in Chapter 3 for mobility modeling.

- **Infrastructure**, Section A.4: Major extensions have been developed to incorporate mobile infrastructure access through persistent and temporary mechanisms for mobile devices. This is in contrast to the pure ad hoc communication originally available in ONE.

- **Overlay**, Section A.5: Mechanisms for overlay handling in terms of types and data structures have been developed that are necessary to evaluate the hybrid routing scheme. On the one hand, for handling overlay protocols on the device side, and on the other hand, for managing different overlays. A simulator coupling with OverSim [24] has been developed that allows to evaluate the hybrid routing scheme with a large number of overlay protocols.

- **Hybrid Routing**, Section A.6: The implementation of the hybrid routing approach has been integrated through interfaces that allow to develop new overlay-based hybrid routing protocols easily.

- **DTN Integration**, Section A.7: DTN protocols have been adapted through interfaces that allow to integrate new DTN protocols and allow the hybrid scheme to work based upon a large set of existing DTN protocols through the categorization presented in Section 4.3.2.

- **Copy-mode**, Section A.8: Copy-modes have been implemented generically for all DTN protocols to allow for using different degrees of replication in the hybrid approach. Every DTN protocol can therewith be run as single-copy and multi-copy variant to evaluate the performance gains at additional cost. Furthermore, combination of single-copy and multi-copy in the hybrid routing is possible, depending on the four protocol steps presented in Section 4.4.

- **Mobility model**, Section A.9: For evaluation, a mobility model has been implemented that requires only minor configuration and is based upon human working day behavior.

- **Street maps**, Section A.10: For running simulations upon realistic street maps, the osm2wkt tool has been developed to convert freely available map data from OpenStreetMap into a format usable in ONE. The map data is further used in Chapter 3 for analyzing the impact of different underlying street graphs on mobility.

- **Reporting**, Section A.11: Additional reporting functionality has been implemented to allow for in-depth evaluation of the hybrid routing approach over a wide range of scenarios and configurations.

A.4 Mobile Infrastructure Access

ONE has been developed to simulate mobile DTN networks that can perform communication *without* the help of infrastructure. In this thesis, however, the integration of infrastructure-capable devices into a hybrid scenario is of interest. To evaluate the Hybrid Routing System developed in Chapter 4 for such hybrid networks, two types of mobile infrastructure access are required: *persistent* infrastructure access, and *temporary* infrastructure access. Persistent infrastructure access presents e. g. flat-rate data plan of mobile devices which continuously access the infrastructure through cellular networks like UMTS or LTE. The actual cellular network technology is abstracted to reduce complexity, rather an error-free and continuous connectivity to the infrastructure is assumed. On the other hand, temporary infrastructure access is implemented through WiFi access points which are placed on the network area where devices move. Again, the WiFi access technology is modeled through a simplistic unit-disc model and provides infrastructure access. See Section 4.9.1 for simplifications made in the evaluations to reduce complexity.

For infrastructure access the `OverlayNode` class is implemented that provides infrastructure access for each `DTNHost` in the simulated network. In each call of `DTNHost.update()` (cf. Section A.2 for the time-stepped simulation model in ONE) the `DTNHost` updates its member object `OverlayNode` which checks whether a new infrastructure-state has been reached through the following functions:

- `stateShouldJoin()`: Infrastructure access has been achieved since the last `update()` call. Internally the `DTNHost` is now connected to the infrastructure and may access the overlay through its `OverlayNode`.

- `stateIsJoined()`: The `DTNHost` still has access to the infrastructure in comparison to the last `update()` call. It can update its state through its `OverlayNode` object.

- `stateShouldLeave()`: Since the last `update()` call the state of infrastructure access has changed and access will be lost in the next `update()` call. The host can now e. g. sign-off from the overlay and move distributed state to other nodes. Note, that churn is modeled as graceful behavior.

Each device has a configuration-specific parameter that assigns it an infrastructure-class `InfrastructureAccess`, which can be any of `persistent`, `wifi`, or `none`. Assignment is defined in the configuration file based on percentage values $\in [0,1]$ per class. With each device creation at simulation startup a random number is drawn from $[0,1]$ and assigned based on the percentage values assigned by configuration-specific `InfrastructureAccess`. In case of a `persistent` value, `stateShouldJoin()` returns `true` on first call and therewith allows the device infrastructure access on creation. Devices set to `none` are never allowed infrastructure access through `stateShouldJoin()`, therewith always returning `false`. In case of an `InfrastructureAccess` value `wifi`, geographical device-to-infrastructure checks are performed: For implementing device infrastructure communication checks, the same approach as the device-to-device communication checks are used, based on a grid structure for segmenting the network area.

A.5 Overlay Simulation

The infrastructure described in the previous Section A.4 allows generic access to a communication infrastructure system, based on temporary or persistent access. Three different infrastructure systems have been implemented, based on overlay networks:

- `NoneCommunication` described in Section A.5.1 does not provide infrastructure access and is mainly used for easy switching in simulation settings.
- `CentralCommunication` in Section A.5.2 centrally emulates a KBR overlay with low simulation time overhead.
- `OverSimCommunication` in Section A.5.3 provides a simulator coupling with OverSim for fine-grained overlay simulation.

Each infrastructure system is based upon four interfaces that have to be implemented:

- `ChurnInterface`: For joining and removing nodes from the overlay this interfaces provides respective functionality and keeps track of joined overlay nodes.
- `CommunicationInterface`: This interface manages to send data to a node in the overlay, based on identifier-based addressing.

- `CommunicationServerInterface`: Receiving of messages from the overlay needs to be implemented in this interface, using identifier-based addressing. The two interfaces for sending and receiving are separated, as they can require asynchronous implementation, e. g. in case of the OverSim coupling in Section A.5.3.
- `SchedulerInterface`: In case of simulator coupling, this interface allows to control the coupled simulator's simulation time. This is explained in detail for the OverSim coupling in Section A.5.3.

A.5.1   None Overlay

The `NoneOverlay` provides a convenient way to switch off all infrastructure communication without exhaustive re-configuration of the simulation, and therewith fall back to pure DTN routing. It is mainly an empty implementation of the aforementioned classes that does allow devices to access the infrastructure, but mimics that the device is the only device in the infrastructure at any times. It therewith prevents all communication through the infrastructure and falls back to DTN routing.

A.5.2   Centralized Overlay

For evaluation of the Hybrid Routing System a reliable overlay is required to analyze the *inherent* performance opportunities, without influence of a specific overlay protocol that introduces message loss factors. Therefore, the `CentralizedOverlay` has been implemented that manages the set of joined nodes centrally, computes KBR paths, and performs message delivery. Despite a centralized implementation and management of nodes, the `CentralizedOverlay` emulates a distributed overlay in terms of routing, maintenance, and overhead. While `SchedulerInterface` and `CommunicationServerInterface` interfaces are not required in this implementation, details are given in the following on the `ChurnInterface`, and `CommunicationInterface`.

`ChurnInterface` is implemented in the centralized version as `CentralChurn`. It manages the set of joined nodes, and works based upon a symmetric KBR overlay, comparable to a modified symmetric Chord [238] (cf. Section 2.5.4.1). For each node a logarithmic finger-table based upon a 160 bit identifier-space is maintained that is used in the KBR part of the protocol for routing messages. Furthermore, for each node its predecessor and successor are maintained. Joins and leaves are handled in an atomic way so that they are calculated completely before the simulation is continued. This way, the central overlay is stabilized after every join and leave, therewith being consistent at every point in simulation time. The goal of this consistent overlay is to analyze the general performance gains that can be achieved with the hybrid routing approach, and in a next step analyze the impact of different distributed overlay protocols separately using the OverSim integration described in the next Section A.5.3. For sending and receiving messages, the `Central-izedOverlay` implements the `CommunicationInterface` which uses the centralized managed set of overlay nodes and their finger-tables for calculating KBR paths for actual delivery of messages. Therewith, forwarding nodes are calculated as well as the actual receiving node, based on the closest-match behavior of KBR protocols. Routing is implemented in *recursive-mode* (see e. g. [23] for an exhaustive overview of routing modes): nodes receiving messages autonomously select the best next-hop node and forward the message directly.

A.5.3 OverSim Overlay

For evaluation with focus on the overlay protocol a simulator coupling between ONE and the OverSim overlay simulator has been implemented that provides a large set of state of the art overlay protocols [24]. Both ONE and OverSim implement a time-discrete simulation. But while ONE implements a time-stepped approach where events are generated and processed every defined clock-step (cf. Section A.2), OverSim is event-driven and only protocol modules generate events on demand. For coupling both simulators, ONE has been chosen as the main instance that dictates simulation time and progress to OverSim, i. e. ONE controls the actual simulation as *master* while OverSim is used as *slave* simulator. This decision is built upon the fact that the main simulation goal is the DTN, and the overlay is an enabling protocol. The requirement from the HRS perspective on the overlay protocol is KBR functionality. As OverSim provides a clean separation of functionality according to the Common API design [54], a KBR interface allows to employ a large number of overlay protocols in OverSim as control structure for HRS.

The simulator coupling is implemented through several XML-RPC-based services [255] that each of the simulators provides to the other. Selection of XML-RPC was chosen due to its simplicity, availability of libraries in both languages (ONE is developed in Java, OverSim is developed in C++), support for complex data types, and its ability to perform synchronous and asynchronous remote procedure calls.

For coupling of the two simulators, extensions on both sides are required. An overall of four communication client/server pairs are required for coupling. Furthermore, several custom components are required for processing the communication calls correctly on both the ONE and OverSim side. The architectural view of coupling ONE and OverSim is shown in Figure A.3:

- To control simulation time of the coupled simulators, ONE runs a client that dictates a server instance in OverSim the simulation time. To implement this simulation time dictation, OverSim requires a new scheduler module.

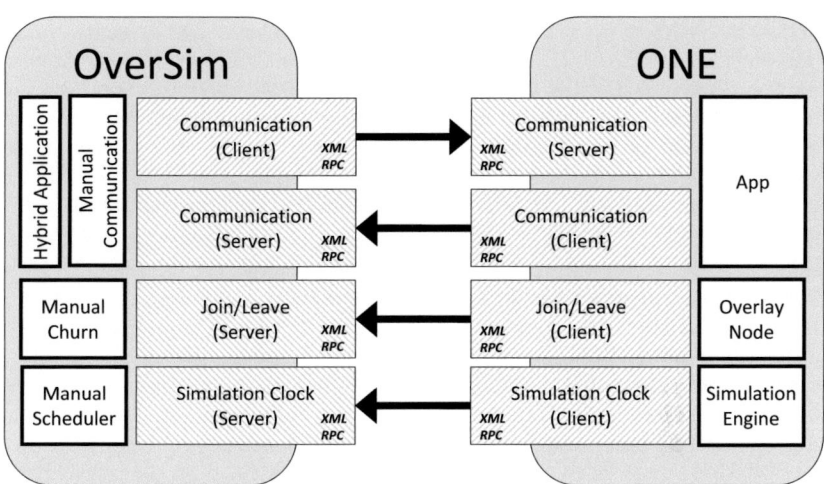

Figure A.3 Architectural view of the simulator coupling for ONE and Over-
Sim based upon XML-RPC for parallel simulation of the DTN in
ONE, and simulation of the HRS overlay in OverSim.

- For joining and leaving nodes from the overlay, ONE runs a client to execute the join/leave commands on an OverSim server instance. To implement the join/leave operations, OverSim requires a new churn module.

- For sending and receiving message through the KBR overlay in Over-
  Sim, both ONE and OverSim require a combination of client/server pair
  for sending and receiving, respectively. Additionally, new application
  modules are required on both sides to support the injection of messages
  from the other simulator.

Simulation Clock Synchronization

As described above, ONE has a master role in the simulator coupling, while
OverSim has a slave role. Therefore, the simulation control resides in ONE
which dictates the clock cycle for the coupled simulation. Due to the different
simulation paradigms—time-stepped in ONE, and event-driven in OverSim—
a jointly used paradigm has to be selected. A time-stepped approach has been
selected for coupling as, first, extending OverSim to perform a time-stepped-
compatible simulation can be implemented through the given event-based
design, while extension of ONE for an event-driven processing would require
a complete redesign of the simulator core. Second, as ONE has a master role
in the coupling, therefore the simulation paradigm of ONE should be employed in the coupled simulation. The configuration-specific clock interval of
ONE—set to 1 s for all simulations—is used for triggering the processing of

events in OverSim up to ONE's current simulation time. I. e. in each simulation step XML-RPC functionality is used to dictate OverSim the current simulation time, and instruct that all events up to the given simulation time are to be processed. This enables a synchronous parallel coupled simulation of both simulators within time shifts bounded to a worst-case of 1 s. This worst-case time shift is within error bounds that are acceptable for DTNs simulation where comparably slow device mobility relaxes strong time requirements.

Besides the XML-RPC client with respective communication format definition, the extensions on the side of ONE are comparably low. In contrast, OverSim requires a new scheduler module, called `ManualScheduler`, that implements the externally generated simulation clocking. The `ManualScheduler` extends the OMNeT++-specific `cScheduler` class and implements respective functions. Most notably, the `getNextEvent()` function returns the next event from the OMNeT++-managed event queue. Each event in this queue has been scheduled with a future timestamp. The purpose of `getNextEvent()` is to decide when the next event can be processed from this queue. The `ManualScheduler` therewith implements a locking scheme through several mutexes and conditions that allows the `getNextEvent()` function to block in the OMNeT++ main thread loop until ONE triggers the processing of events up to a simulation timestamp communicated through XML-RPC. The `getNextEvent()` function then processes all events in the queue which have timestamps that are smaller or equal to the simulation timestamp communicated by ONE. Enabling the scheduler is configuration specific using the `scheduler-class` attribute in the `[General]` section of the `omnetpp.ini` configuration file.

Joining and Leaving Overlay Nodes

Similar to the simulation time synchronization, joining and leaving nodes from the OverSim overlay requires a new module `ManualChurn` that implements the `ChurnGenerator` interface provided by OverSim. Communication for joining and leaving nodes is performed based on NodeIDs. As changes to the simulation state are only possible through explicitly executed events in OMNeT++, the joining and leaving of nodes has to be triggered through an event. Therefore, communication with ONE is performed through XML-RPC, but in an asynchronous manner, i. e. XML-RPC calls return immediately and schedule an event in OMNeT++ for next possible execution. This event then performs the actual joining or leaving of nodes in the overlay by creating or deleting a node through OverSim's `UnderlayConfigurator`. While nodes in OverSim normally chose random NodeIDs, the new churn module explicitly dictates the NodeID which is given to OverSim through the XML-RPC call. NodeIDs are initially generated in ONE and require a node with the same NodeID in OverSim.

Through this mechanism both real, as well as virtual nodes are created to implement both HRS schemes (cf. Chapter 4). From OverSim's perspective, nodes are all equal and no differentiation for the HRS schemes necessary. Only OverSim's KBR functionality is used for implementing HRS.

Application communication

Communication between OverSim and ONE is required for implementing KBR functionality. I. e. an `OverlayNode` in ONE can send a message through KBR towards a destination NodeID. This message, as well as source and destination NodeIDs, have to be transferred to OverSim and there injected into a stub application of the overlay source node. This source node then performs a KBR routing request with the given message and destination NodeID. Upon receipt of the message at a node with its NodeID closest to the destination NodeID—with respect to an overlay-specific distance metric—the message is forwarded to ONE, and delivered in the DTN simulation to the DTN device whose `OverlayNode` has the respective NodeID.

Similar to the churn functionality described above, a message sent by ONE to OverSim can only be injected through a manually scheduled event. Therefore, messages arriving from ONE through the KBR communication at the `ManualCommunication` module in OverSim are initially queued. A periodic timer event in OverSim checks the queue for new messages. If a new message has arrived from ONE, it must first be checked whether the sending node has joined the overlay up to a state that allows messages to be sent out. If this is not yet the case, the message is inserted to a second queue which is regularly checked at a faster interval. In case a message could not be sent from a node as this node has not joined the overlay successfully after a configuration-specific timeout, the message is discarded. If the sending node is connected in the overlay, the message is injected into a per-node stub application—called `HybridDtnApp`—of this node that can perform KBR functionality in terms of sending, receiving, and forwarding messages. Similarly, receipt of KBR messages through the `HybridDtnApp` are delivered to the `ManualCommunication` module and there sent out to ONE directly. On side of ONE, similarly, queues are employed to first store any messages that are received from OverSim and process them in the time-stepped simulator loop `update()` calls. Therefore, the respective `DTNHost` has to be found who owns an `OverlayNode` object that is addressed with the correct NodeID the message is destined for. Processing is then performed in the next `update()` call of the `DTNHost`.

A.6   Hybrid Routing Variants

The `OverlayNode` class introduced in Section A.4 provides mechanisms for implementing special behavior on how to register nodes in the infrastructure-based overlay for cooperative hybrid routing. For this cooperative approach two protocols have been implemented: `HrsOverlayNode` implements the HRS scheme based on virtual nodes, while `HrsIndirectionOverlayN-ode` implements the HRS scheme based on indirection. Both classes need to implement the interface shown in Listing A.1 that is required by the `Over-layNode` class. All functions are called on one specific overlay node object that is bound to one `DTNHost` device; the algorithms therewith work in a distributed way. The `onJoin()` and `onLeave()` functions are called right after the overlay node has joined the overlay, and right before the overlay node is about to leave the overlay, respectively. Request to register itself as proxy for a set of DTN devices is performed using the `joinVirtual()` function, respectively the `leaveVirtual()` function requests to remove all registrations from the overlay. Similar, adaptation of registrations can be performed periodically on every `correctVirtual()` call. For sending and receiving messages to and from the overlay, the `sendMessages()` function requests the node to send all pending messages through the overlay. Finally, the callback `receiveMessage()` is used to inject a message that was received in the overlay by this node, i. e. messages where this node's NodeID is equal or currently closest to the message destination's NodeID.

Listing A.1 Simplified interface functions of the `OverlayNode` that need to be implementation by HRS schemes.

```
void onJoin ();
void onLeave ();
void joinVirtual ();
void correctVirtual ();
void sendMessages ();
void leaveVirtual ();
boolean receiveMessage ( OverlayIdentifier source ,
        OverlayIdentifier dest , OverlayIdentifier
        receiver , DTNHost dtnsource , DTNHost dtndest ,
        DTNHost dtnreceiver , String data );
```

A.7   DTN Protocol Interface

The integration of DTN protocols has been extended through a generic interface to run hybrid routing schemes over *applicable* DTN protocols. Protocols need to exhibit information on the quality of a local device for routing towards a given destination device. Section 4.3.2 presented a classification and concluded that *Destination-aware* protocols are best suited for hybrid routing. Respectively, an interface called `DestinationAwareRouter` has been extracted for generic integration of DTN protocols. The simplified version of this interface is shown in Listing A.2.

Listing A.2 Simplified interface of the `DestinationAwareRouter` for generic integration of Destination-aware DTN protocols.

```
public interface DestinationAwareRouter {
  public Map<DTNHost, Double> getDestAwareness ();
  public Double getDestAwareness (DTNHost host)
  public double ageAwareness (double val,
    double timestamp );
}
```

Each DTN protocol that implements this interface can be used with any of the infrastructure access mechanisms described in Section A.4, in combination with both hybrid overlay schemes described in Section A.6. Accessing the `DestinationAwareRouter` interface is performed from the HRS-specific `OverlayNode` class that decides which contacts to register in the overlay—either through virtual nodes or through indirection.

A.8   Copy-Modes

With respect to replication, DTN protocols can be classified as either *single-copy*, or *multi-copy*—sometimes also called forwarding-based, or replication-based. Protocols that work as single-copy perform routing through a single copy of a message, i. e. messages are never replicated but rather the message is forwarded to another device and deleted locally. Respectively, multi-copy protocols perform replication of messages when they are given to another device, i. e. the message is not deleted locally. As described in Chapter 4.4 the decision to perform single-copy or multi-copy occurs much more often in the hybrid approach than in pure DTN protocols, and notably in different states of the protocol. While a normal DTN protocol has only one such state and performs either single- or multi-copy in it, hybrid routing have multiple protocol-states and the copy strategy can be differentiated on each of them:

- State 1: Routing in the source DTN.
- State 2: Moving the message into the overlay from the source DTN.
- State 3: Moving the message from the overlay into the destination DTN.
- State 4: Routing in the destination DTN.

Protocol states 2 and 3 are simple to detect as the device performing the action explicitly is aware of the routing between DTN and overlay. For differentiation of routing states 1 and 4, *marking* of the message is performed through a single bit when moving the message from DTN to overlay in routing state 2. Therewith, differentiation of routing states 1 and 4 is possible as in state 1 the message is not marked, but marked in state 4.

To perform an in-depth evaluation of the impact of different combinations of copy-modes, copying logic has been moved away from higher-layer DTN protocols into the simulator core where more generic influence can be taken on copying decisions. This required changes in the simulator core of ONE, and smaller changes to DTN protocols. Furthermore, the above described differentiation between protocol states has been implemented by message marking and respective decisions on message replication in the simulator core. Every protocol state can be individually configured—irrespective of the DTN protocol or overlay scheme—in the configuration file through the notation

```
Group.copyStyle = [copymode-copymode-copymode-copymode]
```

with ordered protocol states 1 to 4. Each of the `copymode` items is replaced by either `single`, or `multi` to reflect application of single-copy, or multi-copy in the respective protocol state.

A.9   Mobility Model

Most evaluation in this thesis uses the SWIM [142, 166] mobility model described in Section 2.3.3, as it is well-studied and easy to apply to different underlying graphs. SWIM, however, has no per-day behavior but rather a continuous behavior that does not reflect the day/night cycle of humans. For evaluation of awareness behavior and for evaluation of long-term stability, the mobility model described here is used. This model can be seen as simplified version of [73] in that it builds up periodicity of human behavior and a day-model that humans follow, i. e. they get up in the morning, to work, go to lunch, etc. This results in the observed periodicity and characteristic behavior of the inter-contact times between pairs of humans.

Initial Setup Initially a number of so-called *hotspots* is defined that represent positions on the network area of special interest. Hotspots are divided into working-specific hotspots through HOTSPOTS_WORK, and leisure-specific hotspots through HOTSPOTS_LEISURE. Depending on the size of the network area employed for simulation, adaptation of these parameters is required. E. g. these values are set to HOTSPOTS_WORK=10, and HOTSPOTS_LEISURE=30 for a 2x2 km square network area based on a real-world map (cf. Section A.10). The number of leisure places a device selects is defined as DEVICE_LEISURE=6. Furthermore, a maximal distance where devices use walking speed through is defined. Moving to a next-point on the map further away results in higher movement speed to emulate car driving.

Per-Device Setup A mobile device-specific working day schedule is defined that simulates human behavior. The mobile device is exposed to the mobility behavior of a human owner. At simulation startup, each device selects a general device-specific time-shift between $[-3,3]$ hours. The regular daily schedule is further shifted on a per-device basis in the night for the next day within $[-0.5, 0.5]$ hours. Each device selects its home individually on the network area, and one work location from the prior defined set of work places. Half of `DEVICE_LEISURE` leisure places are selected from the predefined common set, and half selected individually from the complete map. When selecting a new leisure place, one of the two sets individual-set and common-set is randomly selected, and the leisure place randomly selected in the selected set.

Runtime Behavior The main schedule—with respective per-device and further per-day shifts—is defined as follows: 0 am to 7 am home, 7 am to 12 am work, 12 am to 1 pm lunch, 1 pm to 5 pm work, 5 pm to 8 pm leisure1 or home, 8 pm to 10 pm leisure2 or home. For the time 5 am to 8 am, and 8 pm to 10 pm a device selects randomly either a new place for free time, or its home as next destination. When selecting a leisure place it is randomly taken from the set of individual and common leisure places, as defined in the per-device setup above. For the time a device stays at one place, it moves within a predefined range but always returns to the main landmark that defines the hotspot.

A.10 Real-World Street Maps

For evaluation of the protocols presented in this thesis, mobility is of high importance. Mobility models like *Random Direction*, or *Random Walk* do not reflect human behavior [43]. Furthermore, DTN protocols that built up routing state based on periodicity of devices are not able to stabilize their state in random mobility models. As described in Section A.9, a mobility model based on human day-to-day behavior has been implemented. Often, mobility models are run on plain network area, resulting in unrealistic paths being taken. The ONE simulator provides support for map-based movement, based on street graphs that are given in WKT format, as described in Section A.2. However, the manual creation of such maps is time-consuming and error-prone, on the other hand, purchase of high-quality map data very costly.

The OpenStreetMap [96] project is a community-driven effort to create street maps of all around the world for free use. It is based on a similar idea such as the well-known Wikipedia project: contributions from users. Users willing to participate can upload GPS traces which are assembled on the OpenStreetMap servers, resulting in complete maps editable and annotatable through a browser-interface. Finally, OpenStreetMap allows export of street data from the browser-interface in *OpenStreetMap XML* (OSM) [184] format, based upon the *Extensible Markup Language* (XML) [33].

For running simulations on a large variety of different street maps the *osm2wkt* [161] program has been implemented and released to the community as Open Source. osm2wkt can convert OSM data into WKT for running simulations with ONE based on street map data. In the following the steps necessary for conversion will be described that are implemented by osm2wkt. While the two formats OSM and WKT are not described in detail, focus is given on different data organization and conversion.

The OSM format is based on the concept of landmarks, called `<node>` in the XML structure. Each `<node>` has a unique numerical identifier and GPS coordinates in the form of latitude and longitude. Further information available about the user that contributed the landmark as well as timestamps are ignored in the following. A street is defined as `<way>`, again having a unique numerical identifier. Inside a `<way>` definition, an ordered set of `<node>` items are placed through references to their identifier. A street is therewith defined as a `<way>` that is made up of multiple `<node>` landmarks in a specific ordering. Furthermore, a `<way>` can have meta information—such as the street name, or type of street—that are ignored in the following. Further tags are defined in OSM that are not of interest for the conversion described in this section. The conversion requires the following steps:

1. All `<node>` and `<way>` items are parsed from XML and stored in two data structures for landmarks, and for streets, respectively. Latitude/-longitude pairs are stored with the landmarks for later processing.

2. Next, the bounds of the map are determined by searching for the outer most landmarks. From this information the geographic dimensions are calculated in meters.

3. All landmarks are translated based on a (0,0) coordinate system in the upper left corner. Therefore, the distance in meters between two pairs of latitude/longitude is calculated through the Haversine formula [251] that provides conversion while taking earth sphere curvature into account. After this step all landmarks have (x,y) coordinates in meters with respect to a coordinate system with upper left corner defined as (0,0). The map is herewith projected onto a flat network area with distance between landmarks in meters.

4. ONE requires explicit landmarks at street crossings to allow devices to turn left/right. Therefore, the data is in the next step analyzed for crossings with missing landmarks, and complemented if necessary. This is implemented by calculating crossing points between every two street parts and checking whether a landmark is defined for this crossing within predefined accuracy.

5. Next, the graph is checked for partitions. As ONE initially distributes the devices randomly on the map, therewith placement of a device in a partitioned map part results falsified results as this device can not communicate with all other devices. Often, OpenStreetMap data contains circles around buildings that are not connected to the remaining streets, therewith forming graph partitions. All partitions but the largest are removed in this process. In all analyzed cases this achieved that only the main graph remained while all detected partitions were of small size.

6. As final cleanup step bogus street parts are searched that are smaller than 1 m. Such street parts are removed and the main street reconnected.

After processing and cleanup the street graph is written in WKT format. For each street one `LINESTRING` definition is used. E. g. a `LINESTRING(l1, l2, l3 ...)` defines one edge made up of multiple vertices `l1, l2, l3 ...`. Landmarks are written as coordinates in meters with origin in the upper left corner defined as (0,0). Figure A.4 shows exemplary street maps that have been converted from OpenStreetMap data with osm2wkt for use in the ONE simulator.

Finally, osm2wkt allows to assemble multiple maps. This enables to generate a larger map of multiple city maps, but with no connections between the cities. Through this assembled network area multiple cities can be simulated in parallel, whereas HRS provides for communication between the partitions. Such scenarios constitute extremes of geographic scale where pure DTNs can no longer work.

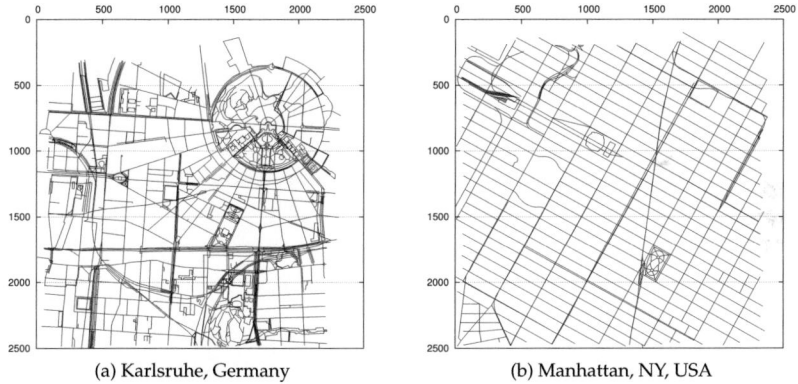

(a) Karlsruhe, Germany   (b) Manhattan, NY, USA

Figure A.4 Exemplary city street maps converted from OpenStreetMap data.

A.11 Reporting

As described in Section A.2 ONE provides a rich set of reporting functionality that can be easily extended. Reporting is separated in event interfaces—so-called *listeners*—and actual reports. Listeners are loosely coupled with reports and are registered at simulation startup with a large number of components in the simulator that provide information of interest. For example, ONE has a `ConnectionListener` that is called whenever a connection between two devices goes up, or down. Listeners can be implemented by any class that wants to get notified of such events. Report classes heavily built upon these listeners to generate either time-dependent reports, or summary reports.

For the hybrid approach ONE has been extended with listeners and reports to gather statistics on e. g. overlay load, and extended reporting to gather additional performance metrics that allow for conclusions on the impact of hybrid routing. The following new reports have been implemented, reports that have been extended are not listed:

- `DestinationAwareRoutingTableReport`: Allows to store the routing tables of destination-aware protocols through the interface described in Section A.7.

- `MapPartitionStatsReport`: In Section A.10 it has been described how osm2wkt can assemble different cities towards an unconnected large map for simulation of extreme cases of geographic partitioning. This report allows to gather statistics on the partitioning situation and the number of devices in each partition.

- `MessageRedundancyReport`: For measuring load in the network the number of replicas of a message is important. This report allows to get periodic snapshots of the redundancy degree of all messages that are currently in the network. In combination with different copy-mode combinations that are presented in Section A.8, this allows for performance vs. cost evaluation.

- `OverlayEventReport`: This report is event-based and logs all activity performed in the overlay, e. g. joins and leaves, or sending of messages.

- `OverlayNodeReport`: A cost-based report is generated that allows to analyze the per-node load in terms of messages sent, received, and forwarded, for both data and control messages.

- `OverlayReport`: In contrast to the prior report, this report provides a view on the complete overlay in terms of e. g. number of nodes.

- `OverlayStabilityReport`: This report stores information on joins and leaves of real and virtual nodes to allow for analysis of node stability. Such information is important for the choice of the overlay protocol as different protocols provide different performance under churn.

Bibliography

[1] 6bone Consortium. 6bone Legacy IPv6 Testbed. http://www.go6.net/ipv6-6bone/, 2006.

[2] ABC30. AT&T to Charge iPhone Wireless Data Hogs. http://abclocal.go.com/kfsn/story?section=news/technology&id=7162748, December 2009.

[3] Muhammad Abdulla and Robert Simon. Characteristics of Common Mobility Models for Opportunistic Networks. In *Proceedings of International Workshop on Modeling Analysis and Simulation of Wireless and Mobile Systems (PM2HW2N)*, pages 105–109, Chanai, Crete Island, Greece, October 2007.

[4] Muhammad Abdulla and Robert Simon. A Simulation Study of Common Mobility Models for Opportunistic Networks. In *Proceedings of Spring Simulation Multi-Conference (SpringSim)*, pages 43–50, Ottawa, Canada, April 2008.

[5] Adobe Systems Incorporated. Cirrus. http://labs.adobe.com/technologies/cirrus, May 2011.

[6] Ashish Agarwal and P. R. Kumar. Capacity Bounds for Ad hoc and Hybrid Wireless Networks. *ACM SIGCOMM Computer Communication Review*, 34(3):71–81, July 2004.

[7] Jó Ágila Bitsch Link, Nicolai Viol, André Goliath, and Klaus Wehrle. SimBetAge: Utilizing Temporal Changes in Social Networks for Pocket Switched Networks. In *Proceedings of ACM Workshop on User-provided Networking: Challenges and Opportunities (U-NET)*, pages 13–18, Rome, Italy, December 2009.

[8] Bengt Ahlgren, Jari Arkko, Lars Eggert, and Jarno Rajahalme. A Node Identity Internetworking Architecture. In *Proceedings of IEEE INFO-*

COM Global Internet Workshop (GI), pages 1–6, Barcelona, Spain, April 2006.

[9] Jari Arkko, James Kempf, Brian Zill, and Pekka Nikander. SEcure Neighbor Discovery (SEND). RFC 3971 (Proposed Standard), March 2005.

[10] AT&T. AT&T Strengthens 3G Wireless Coverage in New York and New Jersey Areas. http://www.att.com/gen/press-room?pid=4800&cdvn=news&newsarticleid=27069, September 2009.

[11] AT&T. AT&T to Make Faster 3G Technology Available in Six Major Cities This Year. http://www.att.com/gen/press-room?pid=4800&cdvn=news&newsarticleid=27068, September 2009. Press release.

[12] Tuomas Aura. Cryptographically Generated Addresses (CGA). In *Proceedings of International Conference on Information Security (ISC)*, volume 2851 of *Lecture Notes in Computer Science*, pages 29–43, Bristol, UK, October 2003.

[13] Tuomas Aura. Cryptographically Generated Addresses (CGA). RFC 3972 (Proposed Standard), March 2005. Updated by RFCs 4581, 4982.

[14] Aruna Balasubramanian, Brian Levine, and Arun Venkataramani. DTN Routing as a Resource Allocation Problem. *ACM SIGCOMM Computer Communication Review*, 37(4):373–384, October 2007.

[15] Aruna Balasubramanian, Brian Neil Levine, and Arun Venkataramani. Replication Routing in DTNs: A Resource Allocation Approach. *IEEE/ACM Transactions on Networking*, 18(2):596–609, April 2010.

[16] Aruna Balasubramanian, Ratul Mahajan, and Arun Venkataramani. Augmenting Mobile 3G Using WiFi. In *Proceedings of International Conference on Mobile Systems, Applications and Services (MobiSys)*, pages 209–222, San Francisco, CA, USA, June 2010.

[17] Nilanjan Banerjee, Mark D. Corner, and Brian Neil Levine. An Energy-Efficient Architecture for DTN Throwboxes. In *Proceedings of IEEE International Conference on Computer Communications (INFOCOM)*, pages 776–784, Anchorage, AK, USA, May 2007.

[18] Nilanjan Banerjee, Mark D. Corner, Don Towsley, and Brian N. Levine. Relays, Base Stations, and Meshes: Enhancing Mobile Networks with Infrastructure. In *Proceedings of International Conference on Mobile Computing and Networking (MobiCom)*, pages 81–91, San Francisco, CA, USA, September 2008.

[19] Nilanjan Banerjee, Jacob Sorber, Mark D. Corner, Sami Rollins, and Deepak Ganesan. Triage: A Power-Aware Software Architecture for Tiered Microservers. Technical Report 05-22, University of Massachusetts-Amherst, Amherst, MA, USA, April 2005.

[20] Suman Banerjee, Bobby Bhattacharjee, and Christopher Kommareddy. Scalable Application Layer Multicast. *ACM SIGCOMM Computer Communication Review*, 32(4):205–217, October 2002.

[21] Stefano Basagni, Marco Conti, Silvia Giordano, and Ivan Stojmenovic, editors. *Mobile Ad Hoc Networking*. Wiley-IEEE Press, 1st edition, August 2004.

[22] Salman Abdul Baset and Henning Schulzrinne. An Analysis of the Skype Peer-to-Peer Internet Telephony Protocol. In *Proceedings of IEEE International Conference on Computer Communications (INFOCOM)*, pages 1–11, Barcelona, Spain, April 2006.

[23] Ingmar Baumgart. *Verteilter Namensdienst für dezentrale IP-Telefonie*. Dissertation, Karlsruhe Institute of Technology (KIT), Karlsruhe, Germany, February 2010.

[24] Ingmar Baumgart, Bernhard Heep, and Stephan Krause. OverSim: A Flexible Overlay Network Simulation Framework. In *Proceedings of IEEE INFOCOM Global Internet Workshop (GI)*, pages 79–84, Anchorage, AK, USA, May 2007.

[25] Christian Becker and Gregor Schiele. New Mechanisms for Routing in Ad Hoc Networks through World Models. In *Proceedings of Plenary Cabernet Workshop*, Pisa, Italy, October 2001.

[26] Christian Bettstetter and Christian Wagner. The Spatial Node Distribution of the Random Waypoint Mobility Model. In *Proceedings of Mobile Ad-Hoc Netzwerke (WMAN)*, pages 41–58, Ulm, Germany, March 2002.

[27] Philippe Blanchard and Dimitri Volchenkov. *Mathematical Analysis of Urban Spatial Networks*. Springer, Berlin, Germany, 1st edition, December 2009.

[28] Roland Bless, Christian Hübsch, Christoph P. Mayer, and Oliver P. Waldhorst. *Future Internet Services and Service Architectures*, chapter SpoVNet: An Architecture for Easy Creation and Deployment of Service Overlays, pages 23–47. River Publishers Series in Communications. River Publishers, Aalborg, Denmark, 1st edition, June 2011.

[29] Roland Bless, Oliver P. Waldhorst, and Christoph P. Mayer. The Spontaneous Virtual Networks Architecture for Supporting Future Internet

Services and Applications. Presentation at 1st GI/ITG KuVS Meeting on Future Internet, Heidelberg, Germany, June 2008. extended abstract.

[30] Uri Blumenthal and Purushottam Goel. Pre-Shared Key (PSK) Cipher-suites with NULL Encryption for Transport Layer Security (TLS). RFC 4785 (Proposed Standard), January 2007.

[31] Dan Boneh and Matt Franklin. Identity Based Encryption from the Weil Pairing. *SIAM Journal of Computing*, 32(3):586–615, March 2003.

[32] Dan Boneh and Matthew K. Franklin. Identity-Based Encryption from the Weil Pairing. In *Proceedings of Annual International Cryptology Confer-ence on Advances in Cryptology (CRYPTO)*, pages 213–229, Santa Barbara, CA, USA, August 2001.

[33] Tim Bray, Jean Paoli, C. M. Sperberg-McQueen, Eve Maler, and François Yergeau. Extensible Markup Language (XML) 1.0 (Fifth Edition). http://www.w3.org/TR/REC-xml/, November 2008.

[34] Thomas Brinkhoff. Mobile Cellular Telephones of the World. http://world.bymap.org/MobilePhones.html, October 2010.

[35] John Burgess, Brian Gallagher, David Jensen, and Brian Neil Levine. MaxProp: Routing for Vehicle-Based Disruption-Tolerant Networks. In *Proceedings of IEEE International Conference on Computer Communications (INFOCOM)*, pages 1–11, Barcelona, Spain, April 2006.

[36] Brendan Burns, Oliver Brock, and Brian Neil Levine. MV Routing and Capacity Building in Disruption Tolerant Networks. In *Proceedings of IEEE International Conference on Computer Communications (INFOCOM)*, pages 398–408, Miami, FL, USA, March 2005.

[37] Matthew Caesar, Miguel Castro, Edmund B. Nightingale, Greg O'Shea, and Antony Rowstron. Virtual Ring Routing: Network Routing In-spired by DHTs. *ACM SIGCOMM Computer Communication Review*, 36(4):351–362, October 2006.

[38] Han Cai and Do Young Eun. Crossing Over the Bounded Domain: From Exponential to Power-law Inter-meeting Time in MANET. In *Pro-ceedings of International Conference on Mobile Computing and Networking (MobiCom)*, pages 159–170, Montreal, QC, Canada, September 2007.

[39] Han Cai and Do Young Eun. Toward Stochastic Anatomy of Inter-meeting Time Distribution under General Mobility Models. In *Proceed-ings of ACM Symposium on Mobile Ad hoc Networking and Computing (Mo-biHoc)*, pages 273–282, Hong Kong, SAR, China, May 2008.

[40] Tracy Camp, Jeff Boleng, and Vanessa Davies. A Survey of Mobility Models for Ad Hoc Network Research. *Wireless Communication and Mobile Computing (WCMC)*, 2(5):483–502, August 2002.

[41] Vinton G. Cerf, Scott C. Burleigh, Adrian J. Hooke, Leigh Torgerson, Robert C. Durst, Keith L. Scott, Kevin Fall, and Howard S. Weiss. Delay-Tolerant Networking Architecture. RFC 4838 (Informational), April 2007.

[42] Augustin Chaintreau, Pan Hui, Jon Crowcroft, Christophe Diot, Richard Gass, and James Scott. Pocket Switched Networks: Real-world Mobility and its Consequences for Opportunistic Forwarding. Technical Report UCAM-CL-TR-617, Computer Laboratory, University of Cambridge, February 2005.

[43] Augustin Chaintreau, Pan Hui, Christophe Diot, Richard Gass, James Scott, and Jon Crowcroft. Impact of Human Mobility on Opportunistic Forwarding Algorithms. *IEEE Transactions on Mobile Computing*, 6(6):606–620, June 2007.

[44] Subrahmanyan Chandrasekhar. Stochastic Problems in Physics and Astronomy. *Review of Modern Physics*, 15(1):1–89, January 1943.

[45] Bin Bin Chen and Mun Choon Chan. MobiCent: a Credit-Based Incentive System for Disruption Tolerant Network. In *Proceedings of IEEE International Conference on Computer Communications (INFOCOM)*, pages 1–9, San Diego, CA, USA, March 2010.

[46] Yang Chen, Wenrui Zhao, Mostafa Ammar, and Ellen Zegura. Hybrid Routing in Clustered DTNs with Message Ferrying. In *Proceedings of ACM MobiSys Workshop on Mobile Opportunistic Networking (MobiOpp)*, pages 75–82, San Juan, Puerto Rico, USA, June 2007.

[47] Cisco Systems Inc. Cisco Visual Networking Index: Global Mobile Data Traffic Forecast Update, 2010-2015. `http://newsroom.cisco.com/dlls/ekits/Cisco_VNI_Global_Mobile_Data_Traffic_Forecast_2010_2015.pdf`, February 2011.

[48] David Dana Clark. Toward the Design of a Future Internet. `http://groups.csail.mit.edu/ana/People/DDC/FutureInternet7-0.pdf`, October 2009. version 7.0.

[49] Ian Clarke, Oskar Sandberg, Brandon Wiley, and Theodore W. Hong. Freenet: A Distributed Anonymous Information Storage and Retrieval System. In *Proceedings of International Workshop on Designing Privacy Enhancing Technologies: Design Issues in Anonymity and Unobservability*, pages 46–66, Berkeley, CA, United States, July 2001.

[50] Aaron Clauset, Cosma Rohilla Shalizi, and Mark Newman. Power-law Distributions in Empirical Data. *SIAM Review*, 51(4):661–703, November 2009.

[51] Marco Conti and Mohan Kumar. Opportunities in Opportunistic Computing. *IEEE Computer*, 43(1):42–50, January 2010.

[52] Jim Cowie. Egypt Leaves The Internet. Presentation at North American Network Operators Group Meeting (NANOG), `http://www.renesys.com/tech/presentations/pdf/` `nanog-51-Egypt-Gone.pdf`, February 2011.

[53] Jon Crowcroft. Cold Topics in Networking. *ACM SIGCOMM Computer Communication Review*, 38(1):45–47, January 2008.

[54] Frank Dabek, Ben Zhao, Peter Druschel, John Kubiatowicz, and Ion Stoica. Towards a Common API for Structured Peer-to-Peer Overlays. In *Proceedings of International Workshop on Peer-to-Peer Systems (IPTPS)*, pages 33–44, Berkeley, CA, USA, February 2003.

[55] Elizabeth M. Daly and Mads Haahr. Social Network Analysis for Routing in Disconnected Delay-tolerant MANETs. In *Proceedings of ACM Symposium on Mobile Ad hoc Networking and Computing (MobiHoc)*, pages 32–40, Montreal, QC, Canada, September 2007.

[56] Elizabeth M. Daly and Mads Haahr. Social Network Analysis for Information Flow in Disconnected Delay-Tolerant MANETs. *IEEE Transactions on Mobile Computing*, 8(5):606–621, May 2009.

[57] Quynh Dang. Recommendation for Applications Using Approved Hash Algorithms. NIST Special Publication 800-107, February 2009.

[58] James A. Davis, Andrew H. Fagg, and Brian N. Levine. Wearable Computers as Packet Transport Mechanisms in Highly-Partitioned Ad-Hoc Networks. In *Proceedings of IEEE International Symposium on Wearable Computers (ISWC)*, pages 141–148, Zurich, Switzerland, October 2001.

[59] Etienne C. R. de Oliveira and Célio V. N. de Albuquerque. NECTAR: A DTN Routing Protocol Based on Neighborhood Contact History. In *Proceedings of ACM Symposium on Applied Computing (SAC)*, pages 40–46, Honolulu, Hawaii, March 2009.

[60] Giuseppe DeCandia, Deniz Hastorun, Madan Jampani, Gunavardhan Kakulapati, Avinash Lakshman, Alex Pilchin, Swaminathan Sivasubramanian, Peter Vosshall, and Werner Vogels. Dynamo: Amazon's Highly Available Key-value Store. In *Proceedings of ACM SIGOPS Symposium on Operating Systems Principles (SOSP)*, pages 205–220, Stevenson, WA, USA, October 2007.

[61] Stephen E. Deering. Host extensions for IP multicasting. RFC 1112 (Standard), August 1989. Updated by RFC 2236.

[62] Stephen E. Deering and Robert M. Hinden. Internet Protocol, Version 6 (IPv6) Specification. RFC 2460 (Draft Standard), December 1998. Updated by RFCs 5095, 5722.

[63] Wim Diepstraten and Greg Ennis. DFWMAC - Distributed Foundation Wireless Medium Access Control. IEEE P802.11-93/190, available at http://www.ieee802.org/11/Documents/DocumentArchives/1993_docs/1193190.doc, November 1993.

[64] Tim Dierks and Eric Rescorla. The Transport Layer Security (TLS) Protocol Version 1.2. RFC 5246 (Proposed Standard), August 2008. Updated by RFC 5746.

[65] Christophe Diot, Brian Neil Levine, Bryan Lyles, Hassan Kassem, and Doug Balensiefen. Deployment Issues for the IP Multicast Service and Architecture. *IEEE Network Magazine Special Issue on Multicasting*, 14(1):78–88, February 2000.

[66] Michael Doering, Wolf-Bastian Pöttner, Tobias Pögel, and Lars Wolf. Impact of Radio Range on Contact Characteristics in Bus-based Delay Tolerant Networks. In *Proceedings of International Conference on Wireless On-Demand Network Systems and Services (WONS)*, pages 195–202, Bardonecchia, Italy, January 2011.

[67] Merlin Dorfman and Richard H. Thayer, editors. *Standards, Guidelines, and Examples on System and Software Requirements Engineering*. IEEE Computer Society Press Tutorial, August 1994.

[68] Avri Doria, Maria Uden, and Durga Prasad Pandey. Providing Connectivity to the Saami Nomadic Community. In *Proceedings of International Conference on Open Collaborative Design for Sustainable Innovation*, Bangalore, India, December 2002.

[69] Henri Dubois-Ferriere, Matthias Grossglauser, and Martin Vetterli. Age Matters: Effcient Route Discovery in Mobile Ad Hoc Networks Using Encounter Ages. In *Proceedings of ACM Symposium on Mobile Ad hoc Networking and Computing (MobiHoc)*, pages 257–266, Annapolis, MD, USA, June 2003.

[70] Nathan Eagle and Alex Pentland. Reality Mining: Sensing Complex Social Systems. *Personal and Ubiquitous Computing*, 10(4):255–268, May 2006.

[71] Donald E. Eastlake and Paul E. Jones. US Secure Hash Algorithm 1 (SHA1). RFC 3174 (Informational), September 2001. Updated by RFC 4634.

[72] Kjeld B. Egevang and Paul Francis. The IP Network Address Translator (NAT). RFC 1631 (Informational), May 1994. Obsoleted by RFC 3022.

[73] Frans Ekman, Ari Keränen, Jouni Karvo, and Jörg Ott. Working Day Movement Model. In *Proceedings of MobilityModels*, pages 33–40, Hong Kong, China, May 2008.

[74] Vijay Erramilli, Mark Crovella, Augustin Chaintreau, and Christophe Diot. Delegation Forwarding. In *Proceedings of ACM Symposium on Mobile Ad hoc Networking and Computing (MobiHoc)*, pages 251–260, Hong Kong, China, May 2008.

[75] Robert Faris and Jonathan Zittrain. Web Tactics. *Index on Censorship*, 38(4):90–96, November 2009.

[76] Stephen Farrell and Russell Housley. An Internet Attribute Certificate Profile for Authorization. RFC 3281 (Proposed Standard), April 2002. Obsoleted by RFC 5755.

[77] Stephen Farrell, Alex McMahon, Eoin Meehan, Stefan Weber, and Kerry Hartnett. Report on an Arctic Summer DTN Trial. *Wireless Networks*, 17(5):1127–1156, May 2011.

[78] Federal Highway Administration. Manual on Uniform Traffic Control Devices. http://mutcd.fhwa.dot.gov, December 2009.

[79] Erina Ferro and Francesco Potorti. Bluetooth and Wi-Fi Wireless Protocols: A Survey and a Comparison. *IEEE Wireless Communications*, 12(1):12–26, February 2005.

[80] Bryan Alexander Ford. *UIA: A Global Connectivity Architecture for Mobile Personal Devices*. PhD Thesis, Massachusetts Institute of Technology, Cambridge, MA, USA, September 2008.

[81] Richard M. Fujimoto. *Parallel and Distributed Simulation Systems*. Wiley Series on Parallel and Distributed Computing. John Wiley & Sons, 1st edition, January 2000.

[82] Wojciech Galuba, Karl Aberer, Zoran Despotovic, and Wolfgang Kellerer. ProtoPeer: A P2P Toolkit Bridging the Gap Between Simulation and Live Deployement. In *Proceedings of International Conference on Simulation Tools and Techniques (SIMUTools)*, pages 60:1–60:9, Rome, Italy, March 2009.

[83] Abbas El Gamal, James Mammen, Balaji Prabhakar, and Devavrat Shah. Throughput-delay Trade-off in Wireless Networks. In *Proceedings of IEEE International Conference on Computer Communications (INFOCOM)*, pages 464–475, Hong Kong, SAR, China, March 2004.

[84] Michele Garetto, Paolo Giaccone, and Emilio Leonardi. Capacity Scaling in Delay Tolerant Networks with Heterogeneous Mobile Nodes. In *Proceedings of ACM Symposium on Mobile Ad hoc Networking and Computing (MobiHoc)*, pages 41–50, Montreal, QC, Canada, September 2007.

[85] James Glanz and John Markof. U.S. Underwrites Internet Detour Around Censors. https://www.nytimes.com/2011/06/12/world/12internet.html, June 2011.

[86] Marta C. González, César A. Hidalgo, and Albert-László Barabási. Understanding Individual Human Mobility Patterns. *Nature*, 453(7196):779–782, June 2008.

[87] Charles Miller Grinstead and James Laurie Snell. *Introduction to Probability*. American Mathematical Society, 2nd edition, July 1997.

[88] Robin Groenevelt, Philippe Nain, and Ger Koole. The Message Delay in Mobile Ad Hoc Networks. *Performance Evaluation*, 62(1–4):210–228, October 2005.

[89] Matthias Grossglauser and David N. C. Tse. Mobility Increases the Capacity of Ad Hoc Wireless Networks. *IEEE/ACM Transactions on Networking*, 10(4):477–486, August 2002.

[90] Matthias Grossglauser and Martin Vetterli. Locating Nodes with EASE: Last Encounter Routing in Ad Hoc networks through Mobility Diffusion. *IEEE/ACM Transactions on Networking*, 14(3):457–469, June 2006.

[91] Shimin Guo, Mohammad Derakhshani, Hossein Falaki, Usman Ismail, Rowena Luk, Earl Oliver, Sumair Ur Rahman, Aaditeshwar Seth, Matei Zaharia, and Srinivasan Keshav. Design and Implementation of the KioskNet System. *Computer Networks*, 55(1):264–281, January 2011.

[92] Shimin Guo, Hossein Falaki, Earl Oliver, Sumair Ur Rahman, Aaditeshwar Seth, Matei Zaharia, Usman Ismail, and Srinivasan Keshav. Design and Implementation of the KioskNet System. In *Proceedings of IEEE/ACM International Conference on Information and Communication Technologies and Development (ICTD)*, pages 1–10, Bangalore, India, December 2007.

[93] Piyush Gupta and P. R. Kumar. Critical Power for Asymptotic Connectivity. In *Proceedings of IEEE Conference on Decision and Control (CDC)*, pages 1106–1110, Tampa, FL , USA, December 1998.

[94] Piyush Gupta and P. R. Kumar. The Capacity of Wireless Networks. *IEEE Transactions on Information Theory*, 46(2):388–404, March 2000.

[95] Andrei Gurtov. *Host Identity Protocol (HIP): Towards the Secure Mobile Internet*. Wiley, Chichester, United Kingdom, 1st edition, June 2008.

[96] Mordechai Haklay and Patrick Weber. OpenStreetMap: User-Generated Street Maps. *IEEE Pervasive Computing*, 7(4):12–18, October 2008.

[97] William K. Hale. Frequency Assignment: Theory and Applications. *Proceedings of the IEEE*, 68(12):1497–1514, December 1980.

[98] Bo Han, Pan Hui, Madhav V. Marathe, Guanhong Pei, Aravind Srinivasan, and Anil Vullikanti. Cellular Traffic Offloading Through Opportunistic Communications: A Case Study. In *Proceedings of International Workshop on Challenged Networks (CHANTS)*, pages 31–38, Chicago, IL, USA, September 2010.

[99] Bo Han, Pan Hui, and Aravind Srinivasan. Mobile Data Offloading in Metropolitan Area Networks. *ACM SIGMOBILE Mobile Computing and Communications Review*, 14(4):28–30, October 2010.

[100] Mark Handley. Why the Internet Only Just Works. *BT Technology Journal*, 24(3):119–129, July 2006.

[101] Mark Handley, Henning Schulzrinne, Eve Schooler, and Jonathan Rosenberg. SIP: Session Initiation Protocol. RFC 2543 (Proposed Standard), March 1999. Obsoleted by RFCs 3261, 3262, 3263, 3264, 3265.

[102] Radu Handorean, Christopher Gill, and Gruia-Catalin Roman. Accommodating Transient Connectivity in Ad Hoc and Mobile Settings. In *Proceedings of Pervasive*, pages 305–322, Vienna, Austria, April 2004.

[103] Guanghui He, Jennifer Hou, Wei-Peng Chen, and Takeo Hamada. One Size Does Not Fit All: A Detailed Analysis and Modeling of P2P Traffic. In *Proceedings of IEEE Global Telecommunications Conference (GLOBECOM)*, pages 393–398, Washington, DC, USA, November 2007.

[104] Bernhard Heep. dCBR: A Global View on Network Coordinates for More Efficient Peer-to-Peer Systems. In *Proceedings of International Conference on Ubiquitous and Future Networks (ICUFN)*, pages 372–377, Jeju Island, South Korea, June 2010.

[105] John R. Herring. OpenGIS Implementation Standard for Geographic Information - Simple Feature Access - Part 1: Common Architecture. OpenGIS Implementation Standard OGC 06-103r4, Open Geospatial Consortium Inc., Wayland, MA, USA, August 2010.

[106] Ralph Holz, Christoph P. Mayer, Sebastian Mies, Heiko Nieder-mayer, and Muhammad Adnan Tariq. SpoVNet Security Task Force Report. Telematics Technical Report TM-2009-3, Institute of Telematics, University of Karlsruhe (TH), Germany, December 2009. http://doc.tm.uka.de/tr, ISSN 1613-849X.

[107] Adrian Hooke. The Interplanetary Internet. *Communications of the ACM,* 44(9):38–40, September 2001.

[108] Jeff Hoye. FreePastry Website. http://www.freepastry.org, March 2009.

[109] Christian Hübsch, Christoph P. Mayer, Sebastian Mies, Roland Bless, Oliver P. Waldhorst, and Martina Zitterbart. Reconnecting the Internet with ariba: Self-Organizing Provisioning of End-to-End Connectivity in Heterogeneous Networks. In *Proceedings of ACM Conference on Applications, Technologies, Architectures, and Protocols for Computer Communications (SIGCOMM),* pages 131–132, Barcelona, Spain, August 2009. Demo.

[110] Christian Hübsch, Christoph P. Mayer, Sebastian Mies, Roland Bless, Oliver P. Waldhorst, and Martina Zitterbart. Reconnecting the Internet with ariba: Self-Organizing Provisioning of End-to-End Connectivity in Heterogeneous Networks. *ACM SIGCOMM Computer Communication Review,* 40(1):131–132, January 2010. (an earlier version appeared in Proceedings of ACM SIGCOMM 2009, Barcelona, Spain).

[111] Christian Hübsch, Christoph P. Mayer, Sebastian Mies, Roland Bless, Oliver P. Waldhorst, and Martina Zitterbart. Using Legacy Applications in Future Heterogeneous Networks with ariba. In *Proceedings of IEEE International Conference on Computer Communications (INFOCOM),* San Diego, CA, USA, March 2010. Demo.

[112] Christian Hübsch, Christoph P. Mayer, Sebastian Mies, Roland Bless, Oliver P. Waldhorst, and Martina Zitterbart. ariba: Rahmenwerk für Overlay-basierte Dienste. *Praxis der Informationsverarbeitung und Kommunikation (PIK),* 34(3):151–155, 2011.

[113] Christian Hübsch, Christoph P. Mayer, Sebastian Mies, Roland Bless, Oliver P. Waldhorst, and Martina Zitterbart. ariba: Rahmenwerk für Overlay-basierte Dienste. In *Proceedings of Kommunikation in Verteilten Systemen (KiVS),* Kiel, Germany, March 2011. Demo.

[114] Christian Hübsch, Christoph P. Mayer, and Oliver P. Waldhorst. Ariba: A Framework for Developing Decentralized Services. Presentation at GI/ITG KuVS NGN Service Delivery Platforms & Service Overlay Networks, Berlin, Germany, December 2009. extended abstract.

[115] Christian Hübsch, Christoph P. Mayer, and Oliver P. Waldhorst. The Ariba Framework for Application Development using Service Overlays. *Praxis der Informationsverarbeitung und Kommunikation (PIK)*, 33(1):7–11, March 2010.

[116] Christian Hübsch, Christoph P. Mayer, and Oliver P. Waldhorst. User-perceived Performance of the NICE Application Layer Multicast Protocol in Large and Highly Dynamic Groups. In *Proceedings of International GI/ITG Conference on "Measurement, Modelling and Evaluation of Computing Systems" and "Dependability and Fault Tolerance" (MMB & DFT)*, pages 62–77, Essen, Germany, March 2010.

[117] Pan Hui, Augustin Chaintreau, Richard Gass, James Scott, Jon Crowcroft, and Christophe Diot. Pocket Switched Networking: Challenges, Feasibility, and Implementation Issues. In *Proceedings of Workshop on Autonomic Communications (WAC)*, pages 1–12, Athens, Greece, October 2005.

[118] Pan Hui and Jon Crowcroft. How Small Labels Create Big Improvements. In *Proceedings of ACM Conference on Emerging Networking Experiments and Technologies (CoNEXT) PhD Workshop*, pages 34:1–34:2, Lisboa, Portugal, December 2006. Poster.

[119] Pan Hui and Jon Crowcroft. How Small Labels Create Big Improvements. In *Proceedings of IEEE International Workshop on Intermittently Connected Mobile Ad hoc Networks (ICMAN)*, pages 65–70, New York, NY, USA, March 2007.

[120] Pan Hui, Jon Crowcroft, and Eiko Yoneki. Bubble Rap: Social-based Forwarding in Delay Tolerant Networks. In *Proceedings of ACM Symposium on Mobile Ad hoc Networking and Computing (MobiHoc)*, pages 241–250, Hong Kong, China, May 2008.

[121] Pan Hui, Jon Crowcroft, and Eiko Yoneki. BUBBLE Rap: Social-Based Forwarding in Delay Tolerant Networks. *IEEE Transactions on Mobile Computing*, 10(11):1576–1589, November 2011.

[122] Pan Hui and Anders F. Lindgren. Phase Transitions of Opportunistic Communications. In *Proceedings of ACM MobiCom Workshop on Challenged Networks (CHANTS)*, San Francisco, CA, USA, September 2008. digital.

[123] Pan Hui, Anders F. Lindgren, and Jon Crowcroft. Empirical Evaluation of Hybrid Opportunistic Networks. In *Proceedings of International Conference on COMmunication Systems and NETworkS (COMSNETS)*, pages 1–10, Bangalore, India, January 2009.

[124] Pan Hui, Eiko Yoneki, Shu-Yan Chan, and Jon Crowcroft. Distributed Community Detection in Delay Tolerant Networks. In *Proceedings of ACM SIGCOMM Workshop on Mobility in the Evolving Internet Architecture (MobiArch)*, pages 7:1–7:8, Kyoto, Japan, August 2007.

[125] Mark L. Huson and Arunabha Sen. Broadcast Scheduling Algorithms for Radio Networks. In *Proceedings of IEEE Military Communications Conference (MILCOM)*, pages 647–651, San Diego, CA , USA, November 1995.

[126] International Telecommunication Union. Public-Key and Attribute Certificate Frameworks. ITU-T Recommendation X.509, November 2008.

[127] International Telecommunication Union. The World in 2010: Facts and Figures. http://www.itu.int/ITU-D/ict/material/ FactsFigures2010.pdf, October 2010.

[128] Van Jacobson, Bob Braden, and Dave Borman. TCP Extensions for High Performance. RFC 1323 (Proposed Standard), May 1992.

[129] Sushant Jain, Michael Demmer, Rabin Patra, and Kevin Fall. Using Redundancy to Cope with Failures in a Delay Tolerant Network. In *Proceedings of ACM Conference on Applications, Technologies, Architectures, and Protocols for Computer Communications (SIGCOMM)*, pages 109–120, Philadelphia, PA, USA, August 2005.

[130] Sushant Jain, Kevin Fall, and Rabin Patra. Routing in a Delay Tolerant Network. In *Proceedings of ACM Conference on Applications, Technologies, Architectures, and Protocols for Computer Communications (SIGCOMM)*, pages 145–158, Portland, OR, USA, August 2004.

[131] Inwhee Joe and Sang-Bo Kim. A Message Priority Routing Protocol for Delay Tolerant Networks (DTN) in Disaster Areas. In *Proceedings of Future Generation Information Technology (FGIT)*, volume 6485 of *Lecture Notes in Computer Science*, pages 727–737, Jeju Island, Korea, December 2010.

[132] David B. Johnson. Routing in Ad Hoc Networks of Mobile Hosts. In *Proceedings of Workshop on Mobile Computing Systems and Applications (HotMobile)*, pages 158–163, Santa Cruz, CA, USA, December 1994.

[133] Evan P.C. Jones and Paul A.S. Ward. Routing Strategies for Delay-Tolerant Networks. http://ccng.uwaterloo.ca/~pasward/ publications.shtml (unpublished), May 2007.

[134] Dilip Joseph, Jayanthkumar Kannan, Ayumu Kubota, Karthik Lakshminarayanan, Ion Stoica, and Klaus Wehrle. OCALA: An Architecture

for Supporting Legacy Applications over Overlays. In *Proceedings of USENIX/ACM Symposium on Networked Systems Design and Implementation (NSDI)*, pages 267–280, San Jose, CA, USA, May 2006.

[135] John Jubin and Janet D. Tornow. The DARPA Packet Radio Network Protocols. *Proceedings of the IEEE*, 75(1):21–32, January 1987.

[136] Thomas Karagiannis, Jean-Yves Le Boudec, and Milan Vojnović. Power Law and Exponential Decay of Inter Contact Times between Mobile Devices. In *Proceedings of International Conference on Mobile Computing and Networking (MobiCom)*, pages 183–194, Montréal, QC, Canada, September 2007.

[137] Jouni Karvo and Jörg Ott. Time Scales and Delay-tolerant Routing Protocols. In *Proceedings of ACM Workshop on Challenged Networks (CHANTS)*, pages 33–40, San Francisco, CA, USA, September 2008.

[138] Ari Keränen, Teemu Kärkkäinen, and Jörg Ott. Simulating Mobility and DTNs with the ONE. *Journal of Communications*, 5(2):92–105, February 2010.

[139] Ari Keränen, Jörg Ott, and Teemu Kärkkäinen. The ONE Simulator for DTN Protocol Evaluation. In *Proceedings of International Conference on Simulation Tools and Techniques (SIMUTools)*, pages 55–65, Rome, Italy, May 2009.

[140] Torsten Kleinz. Netzprobleme: Smartphone-Boom überfordert O2. http://www.spiegel.de/netzwelt/web/0,1518,798550,00.html, November 2011.

[141] Chris Kohlhoff. Asio C++ Library . http://think-async.com/Asio/, March 2011.

[142] Sokol Kosta, Alessandro Mei, and Julinda Stefa. Small World in Motion (SWIM): Modeling Communities in Ad-Hoc Mobile Networking. In *Proceedings of IEEE Communications Society Conference on Sensor, Mesh and Ad Hoc Communications and Networks (SECON)*, pages 1–9, Boston, MA, USA, June 2010.

[143] Spiro Kostof. The Design of Cities. *Places*, 5(4):85–88, Spring 1989.

[144] Ulaş C. Kozat and Leandros Tassiulas. Throughput Capacity of Random Ad Hoc Networks with Infrastructure Support. In *Proceedings of International Conference on Mobile Computing and Networking (MobiCom)*, pages 55–65, San Diego, CA, USA, September 2003.

[145] Hugo Krawczyk, Mihir Bellare, and Ran Canetti. HMAC: Keyed-Hashing for Message Authentication. RFC 2104 (Informational), February 1997.

[146] Kyunghan Lee, Seongik Hong, and Seong Joon Kim. SLAW: A New Mobility Model for Human Walks. In *Proceedings of IEEE International Conference on Computer Communications (INFOCOM)*, pages 855–863, Rio de Janeiro, Brazil, April 2009.

[147] Kyunghan Lee, Injong Rhee, Joohyun Lee, Song Chong, and Yung Yi. Mobile Data Offloading: How Much Can WiFi Deliver? In *Proceedings of ACM Conference on Emerging Networking EXperiments and Technologies (CoNEXT)*, pages 26:1–26:12, Philadelphia, PA, USA, December 2010.

[148] Uichin Lee, Soon Y. Oh, Kang-Won Lee, and Mario Gerla. Scaling Properties of Delay Tolerant Networks with Correlated Motion Patterns. In *Proceedings of ACM Workshop on Challenged Networks (CHANTS)*, pages 19–26, Beijing, China, September 2009.

[149] Jérémie Leguay. *Heterogeneity and Routing in Delay Tolerant Networks*. PhD Thesis, University Pierre and Marie Curie Paris VI, UPMC, Paris, France, July 2007.

[150] Jérémie Leguay, Timur Friedman, and Vania Conan. DTN Routing in a Mobility Pattern Space. In *Proceedings of ACM SIGCOMM Workshop on Delay Tolerant Networking (WDTN)*, pages 276–283, Philadelphia, PA, USA, August 2005.

[151] Jörg Liebeherr, Jianping Wang, and Guimin Zhang. Programming Overlay Networks with Overlay Sockets. In *Proceedings of Workshop on Networked Group Communications (NGC)*, number 2816 in Lecture Notes in Computer Science, pages 242–253, Munich, Germany, September 2003.

[152] Anders F. Lindgren, Avri Doria, Elwyn Davies, and Samo Grasic. Probabilistic Routing Protocol for Intermittently Connected Networks. http://tools.ietf.org/html/ /draft-irtf-dtnrg-prophet-09, April 2011. Internet-Draft (experimental).

[153] Anders F. Lindgren, Avri Doria, Jan Lindblom, and Mattias Ek. Networking in the Land of Northern Lights - Two Years of Experiences from DTN System Deployments. In *Proceedings of ACM Workshop on Wireless Networks and Systems for Developing Regions (WiNS-DR)*, pages 1–8, San Francisco, CA, USA, September 2008.

[154] Anders F. Lindgren, Avri Doria, and Olov Schelén. Probabilistic Routing in Intermittently Connected Networks. *ACM SIGMOBILE Mobile Computing and Communications Review*, 7(3):19–20, July 2003.

[155] Anders F. Lindgren, Avri Doria, and Olov Schelén. Probabilistic Routing in Intermittently Connected Networks. In *Proceedings of Service Assurance with Partial and Intermittent Resources (SAPIR)*, volume 3126 of *Lecture Notes in Computer Science*, pages 239–254, Fortaleza, Brazil, August 2004.

[156] Andres F. Lindgren, Christophe Diot, and James Scott. Impact of Communication Infrastructure on Forwarding in Pocket Switched Networks. In *Proceedings of ACM SIGCOMM Workshop on Challenged Networks (CHANTS)*, pages 261–268, Pisa, Italy, September 2006.

[157] Benyuan Liu, Zhen Liu, and Don Towsley. On the Capacity of Hybrid Wireless Networks. In *Proceedings of IEEE International Conference on Computer Communications (INFOCOM)*, pages 1543–1552, San Francisco, CA, USA, March 2003.

[158] László Lovász. Random Walks on Graphs: A Survey. *Combinatorics, Paul Erdős is Eighty*, 2(1):1–46, January 1993.

[159] Eng Keong Lua, Jon Crowcroft, Marcelo Pias, Ravi Sharma, and Steven Lim. A Survey and Comparison of Peer-to-Peer Overlay Network Schemes. *IEEE Communications Surveys & Tutorials*, 7(2):72–93, March 2004.

[160] Naoki Masuda and Norio Konno. Return Times of Random Walk on Generalized Random Graphs. *Physical Review E*, 69(6):066113–1–066113–7, June 2004.

[161] Christoph P. Mayer. osm2wkt - OpenStreetMap to WKT Conversion. http://www.tm.kit.edu/ mayer/osm2wkt, April 2010.

[162] Christoph P. Mayer and Oliver P. Waldhorst. Offloading Infrastructure using Delay Tolerant Networks and Assurance of Delivery. In *Proceedings of IFIP Wireless Days (WD)*, pages 1–7, Niagara Falls, ON, Canada, October 2011.

[163] Christoph P. Mayer and Oliver P. Waldhorst. On the Impact of Graph Structure on Mobility in Opportunistic Mobile Networks. In *Proceedings of INFOCOM Workshop on Network Science for Communication Networks (NetSciCom, INFOCOM WKSHPS)*, pages 899–904, Shanghai, China, April 2011.

[164] Petar Maymounkov and David Mazières. Kademlia: A Peer-to-peer Information System Based on the XOR Metric. In *Proceedings of International workshop on Peer-To-Peer Systems (IPTPS)*, pages 53–65, Cambridge, MA, USA, March 2002.

[165] Alex McMahon and Stephen Farrell. Delay- and Disruption-Tolerant Networking. *IEEE Internet Computing*, 13(6):82–87, November 2009.

[166] Alessandro Mei and Julinda Stefa. SWIM: A Simple Model to Generate Small Mobile Worlds. In *Proceedings of IEEE International Conference on Computer Communications (INFOCOM)*, pages 2106–2113, Rio de Janeiro, Brazil, April 2009.

[167] Shashidhar Merugu, Mostafa H. Ammar, and Ellen W. Zegura. Routing in Space and Time in Networks with Predictable Mobility. CC Technical Report GIT-CC-04-07, Georgia Institute of Technology, Atlanta, GA, USA, March 2004.

[168] David Meyer, Lixia Zhang, and Kevin Fall. Report from the IAB Workshop on Routing and Addressing. RFC 4984 (Informational), September 2007.

[169] Microsoft. MSDN Library: Network Communication, Peer-to-Peer. http://msdn.microsoft.com/en-us/library/aa371704%28v=VS.85%29.aspx, July 2010.

[170] Sebastian Mies and Oliver P. Waldhorst. Autonomous Detection of Connectivity. In *Proceedings of IEEE International Conference on Peer-to-Peer Computing (P2P)*, pages 44–53, Kyoto, Japan, August 2011.

[171] Sebastian Mies, Oliver P. Waldhorst, and Hans Wippel. Towards End-to-End Connectivity for Overlays Across Heterogeneous Network. In *Proceedings of IEEE International Conference on Communications (ICC) Workshops*, pages 1–6, Dresden, Germany, June 2009.

[172] Paul Mockapetris. Domain names - implementation and specification. RFC 1035 (Standard), November 1987. Updated by RFCs 1101, 1183, 1348, 1876, 1982, 1995, 1996, 2065, 2136, 2181, 2137, 2308, 2535, 2845, 3425, 3658, 4033, 4034, 4035, 4343.

[173] Gabriel Montenegro and Claude Castelluccia. Statistically Unique and Cryptographically Verifiable (SUCV) Identifiers and Addresses. In *Proceedings of Network and Distributed System Security Symposium (NDSS)*, pages 1–13, San Diego, CA, USA, February 2002.

[174] Gabriel Montenegro and Claude Castelluccia. Crypto-based Identifiers (CBIDs): Concepts and Applications. *ACM Transactions on Information and System Security (TISSEC)*, 7(1):97–127, February 2004.

[175] Abderrahmen Mtibaa, Augustin Chaintreau, Jason LeBrun, Earl Oliver, Anna-Kaisa Pietilainen, and Christophe Diot. Are you Moved by your Social Network Application? In *Proceedings of Workshop on Online Social Networks (WOSN)*, pages 67–72, Seattle, WA, USA, August 2008.

[176] Abderrahmen Mtibaa, Martin May, Christophe Diot, and Mostafa Ammar. PeopleRank: Combining Social and Contact Information for Opportunistic Forwarding. In *Proceedings of IEEE International Conference on Computer Communications (INFOCOM) Mini Conference*, pages 1–5, San Diego, CA, USA, March 2010.

[177] Peter Murray. Vint Cerf on the Origins of 32-bit IP Addressing. http://dltj.org/article/vint-cerf-ip-addressing/, March 2008.

[178] Mirco Musolesi, Stephen Hailes, and Cecilia Mascolo. Adaptive Routing for Intermittently Connected Mobile Ad Hoc Networks. In *Proceedings of IEEE International Symposium on a World of Wireless Mobile and Multimedia Networks (WoWMoM)*, pages 183–189, Taormina, Italy, June 2005.

[179] Samuel Nelson, Mehedi Bakht, and Robin Kravets. Encounter-Based Routing in DTNs. In *Proceedings of IEEE International Conference on Computer Communications (INFOCOM)*, pages 846–854, Rio de Janeiro, Brazil, April 2009.

[180] New York Times. iPhones Overload AT&T's Network, Angering customer. http://www.nytimes.com/2009/09/03/technology/companies/03att.htmls, May 2009.

[181] Mark Newman. Power laws, Pareto distributions and Zipf's law. *Contemporary Physics*, 46(5):323–351, September 2005.

[182] Erik Nordmark and Marcelo Bagnulo. Multihoming L3 Shim Approach. draft-ietf-multi6-l3shim-00.txt, January 2005. Internet-Draft.

[183] Scott Oaks, Bernard Travaset, and Li Gong. *Jxta in a Nutshell*. In a Nutshell. O'Reilly Media, October 2002.

[184] OpenStreetMap Project. OpenStreetMap Data Primitives. http://wiki.openstreetmap.org/wiki/Data_Primitives, August 2010.

[185] Greg O'Shea and Michael Roe. Child-proof authentication for MIPv6 (CAM). *ACM SIGCOMM Computer Communication Review*, 31(2):4–8, April 2001.

[186] Jörg Ott, Dirk Kutscher, and Christoph Dwertmann. Integrating DTN and MANET Routing. In *Proceedings of ACM SIGCOMM Workshop on Challenged Networks (CHANTS)*, pages 221–228, Pisa, Italy, September 2006.

[187] Mathew D. Penrose. The Longest Edge of the Random Minimal Spanning Tree. *Annals of Applied Probability*, 7(2):340–361, May 1997.

[188] Alex Pentland, Richard Fletcher, and Amir Hasson. DakNet: Rethinking Connectivity in Developing Nations. *IEEE Computer*, 37(1):78–83, January 2004.

[189] Charles E. Perkins. IP Mobility Support for IPv4. RFC 3344 (Proposed Standard), August 2002. Updated by RFC 4721.

[190] Charles E. Perkins, Elizabeth M. Belding-Royer, and Samir R. Das. Ad hoc On-Demand Distance Vector (AODV) Routing. RFC 3561 (Experimental), July 2003.

[191] Charles E. Perkins and Pravin Bhagwat. Highly Dynamic Destination-Sequenced Distance-Vector Routing (DSDV) for Mobile Computers. *ACM SIGCOMM Computer Communication Review*, 24(4):234–244, October 1994.

[192] Mikko Pitkänen, Teemu Kärkkäinen, and Jörg Ott. Opportunistic Web Access via WLAN Hotspots. In *Proceedings of IEEE International Conference on Pervasive Computing and Communications (PerCom)*, pages 20–30, Mannheim, Germany, April 2010.

[193] Mikko Pitkänen, Ari Keränen, and Jörg Ott. Message Fragmentation in Opportunistic DTNs. In *Proceedings of WoWMoM Workshop on Autonomic and Opportunistic Communications (AOC)*, pages 1–7, Newport Beach, CA, USA, June 2008.

[194] Jon Postel. User Datagram Protocol. RFC 768 (Standard), August 1980.

[195] Jon Postel. Internet Protocol. RFC 791 (Standard), September 1981. Updated by RFC 1349.

[196] Jon Postel. Transmission Control Protocol. RFC 793 (Standard), September 1981. Updated by RFCs 1122, 3168.

[197] Jane Radatz. IEEE Standard Glossary of Software Engineering Terminology, September 1990.

[198] Rao Naveed Bin Rais. *Communication Mechanisms for Message Delivery in Heterogeneous Networks Prone to Episodic Connectivity*. PhD Thesis, INRIA, Sophia Antipolis, France, February 2011.

[199] Rao Naveed Bin Rais, Marc Mendonca, Thierry Turletti, and Katia Obraczka. Towards Truly Heterogeneous Internets: Bridging Infrastructure-based and Infrastructure-less Networks. In *Proceedings of International Conference on COMmunication Systems and NETworkS (COMSNETS)*, pages 1–10, Bangalore, India, January 2011.

[200] Rao Naveed Bin Rais, Thierry Turletti, and Katia Obraczka. MeDeHa - Efficient Message Delivery in Heterogeneous Networks with Intermittent Connectivity. INRIA Research Report 7227, Institut National de Recherche en Informatique et en Automatique (INRIA), Sophia Antipolis, France, March 2010.

[201] Manikantan Ramadas, Scott C. Burleigh, and Stephen Farrell. Licklider Transmission Protocol - Specification. RFC 5326 (Experimental), September 2008.

[202] Ram Ramanathan and Jason Redi. A Brief Overview of Ad Hoc Networks: Challenges and Directions. *IEEE Communications Magazine*, 40(5):20–22, May 2002.

[203] Joshua Reich and Augustin Chaintreau. The Age of Impatience: Optimal Replication Schemes for Opportunistic Networks. In *Proceedings of ACM Conference on Emerging Networking Experiments and Technologies (CoNEXT)*, pages 85–96, Rome, Italy, December 2009.

[204] Yakov Rekhter and Tony Li. An Architecture for IP Address Allocation with CIDR. RFC 1518 (Historic), September 1993.

[205] Yakov Rekhter, Robert G Moskowitz, Daniel Karrenberg, Geert Jan de Groot, and Eliot Lear. Address Allocation for Private Internets. RFC 1918 (Best Current Practice), February 1996.

[206] Eric Rescorla. *SSL and TLS: Designing and Building Secure Systems*. Addison-Wesley Professional, Indianapolis, IN, USA, 1st edition, August 2001.

[207] Injong Rhee, Minsu Shin, Seongik Hong, Kyunghan Lee, and Song Chong. Human Mobility Patterns and Their Impact on Routing in Human-Driven Mobile Networks. In *Proceedings of ACM Hot Topics in Networks (HotNets)*, Atlanta, GA, USA, November 2007. digital.

[208] Injong Rhee, Minsu Shin, Seongik Hong, Kyunghan Lee, and Song Chong. On the Levy-Walk Nature of Human Mobility. In *Proceedings of IEEE International Conference on Computer Communications (INFOCOM)*, pages 924–932, Phoenix, AZ, USA, April 2008.

[209] Adolfo Rodriguez, Charles Killian, Sooraj Bhat, Dejan Kostić, and Amin Vahdat. MACEDON: Methodology for Automatically Creating, Evaluating, and Designing Overlay Networks. In *Proceedings of USENIX Symposium on Networked Systems Design and Implementation (NSDI)*, pages 20–20, San Francisco, CA, USA, March 2004.

[210] Jonathan Rosenberg, Joel Weinberger, Christian Huitema, and Rohan Mahy. STUN - Simple Traversal of User Datagram Protocol (UDP) Through Network Address Translators (NATs). RFC 3489 (Proposed Standard), March 2003. Obsoleted by RFC 5389.

[211] Ant Rowstron and Peter Druschel. Pastry: Scalable, Decentralized Object Location and Routing for Large-scale Peer-to-Peer Systems. In *Proceedings of IFIP/ACM International Conference on Distributed Systems Platforms (Middleware)*, volume 2218 of *Lecture Notes in Computer Science*, pages 329–350, Heidelberg, Germany, November 2001.

[212] Kevin Savetz, Neil Randall, and Yves Lepage. *MBONE: Multicasting Tomorrow's Internet*. Hungry Minds Inc, U.S., March 1996.

[213] Bruce Schneier. *Applied Cryptography*. John Wiley & Sons, New York, NY, USA, 2nd edition, October 1996.

[214] James Scott, Richard Gass, Jon Crowcroft, Pan Hui, Christophe Diot, and Augustin Chaintreau. CRAWDAD trace cambridge/haggle/imote/cambridge (v. 2006-01-31). Downloaded from http://crawdad.cs.dartmouth.edu/cambridge/haggle/imote/cambridge, January 2006.

[215] James Scott, Richard Gass, Jon Crowcroft, Pan Hui, Christophe Diot, and Augustin Chaintreau. CRAWDAD trace cambridge/haggle/imote/infocom (v. 2006-01-31). Downloaded from http://crawdad.cs.dartmouth.edu/cambridge/haggle/imote/infocom, January 2006.

[216] James Scott, Richard Gass, Jon Crowcroft, Pan Hui, Christophe Diot, and Augustin Chaintreau. CRAWDAD trace cambridge/haggle/imote/intel (v. 2006-01-31). Downloaded from http://crawdad.cs.dartmouth.edu/cambridge/haggle/imote/intel, January 2006.

[217] James Scott, Richard Gass, Jon Crowcroft, Pan Hui, Christophe Diot, and Augustin Chaintreau. CRAWDAD trace cambridge/haggle/imote/infocom2006 (v. 2009-05-29). Downloaded from http://crawdad.cs.dartmouth.edu/cambridge/haggle/imote/infocom2006, May 2009.

[218] James Scott, Pan Hui, Jon Crowcroft, and Christophe Diot. Haggle: a Networking Architecture Designed Around Mobile Users. In *Proceedings of Conference on Wireless On-demand Network Systems and Services (WONS)*, pages 78–86, Les Ménuires, France, January 2006.

[219] Keith L. Scott and Scott Burleigh. Bundle Protocol Specification. RFC 5050 (Experimental), November 2007.

[220] Aaditeshwar Seth and Srinivasan Keshav. Practical Security for Disconnected Nodes. In *Proceedings of IEEE ICNP Workshop on Secure Network Protocols (NPSec)*, pages 31–36, Boston, MA, USA, November 2005.

[221] Aaditeshwar Seth, Darcy Kroeker, Matei Zaharia, Shimin Guo, and Srinivasan Keshav. Low-cost Communication for Rural Internet Kiosks Using Mechanical Backhaul. In *Proceedings of International Conference on Mobile Computing and Networking (MobiCom)*, pages 334–345, Los Angeles, CA, USA, September 2006.

[222] Tallat M. Shafaat, Ali Ghodsi, and Seif Haridi. A Practical Approach to Network Size Estimation for Structured Overlays. In *Proceedings of International Workshop on Self-Organizing Systems (IWSOS)*, pages 71–83, Vienna, Austria, December 2008.

[223] Rahul C. Shah, Sumit Roy, Sushant Jain, and Waylon Brunette. Data MULEs: Modeling a Three-tier Architecture for Sparse Sensor Networks. In *Proceedings of IEEE International Workshop on Sensor Network Protocols and Applications*, pages 30–41, Anchorage, AK, USA, May 2003.

[224] Adi Shamir. Identity-Based Cryptosystems and Signature Schemes. In *Proceedings of Advances in Cryptology (CRYPTO)*, pages 47–53, Santa Barbara, CA, USA, August 1984.

[225] Upendra Shevade, Han Hee, Song Lili Qiu, and Yin Zhang. Incentive-aware Routing in DTNs . In *Proceedings of IEEE International Conference on Network Protocols (ICNP)*, pages 238–247, Orlando, FL, USA, October 2008.

[226] Kazuyuki Shudo, Yoshio Tanaka, and Satoshi Sekiguchi. Overlay Weaver: An Overlay Construction Toolkit. *Computer Communications*, 31(2):402– 412, February 2008.

[227] Hamed Soroush, Nilanjan Banerjee, Mark D. Corner, Brian Neil Levine, and Brian Lynn. DOME: A Diverse Outdoor Mobile Testbed. In *Proceedings of ACM Workshop on Hot Topics of Planet-Scale Mobility Measurements (HotPlanet)*, pages 2:1–2:6, Kraków, Poland, June 2009.

[228] Thrasyvoulos Spyropoulos, Konstantinos Psounis, and Cauligi S. Raghavendra. Spray and Wait: An Efficient Routing Scheme for Intermittently Connected Mobile Networks. In *Proceedings of ACM SIGCOMM Workshop on Delay Tolerant Networking (WDTN)*, pages 252–259, Philadelphia, PA, USA, August 2005.

[229] Thrasyvoulos Spyropoulos, Konstantinos Psounis, and Cauligi S. Raghavendra. Spray and Focus: Efficient Mobility-Assisted Routing for

Heterogeneous and Correlated Mobility. In *Proceedings of IEEE International Conference on Pervasive Computing and Communications Workshops (PerComW)*, pages 79–85, White Plains, NY, USA, March 2007.

[230] Thrasyvoulos Spyropoulos, Konstantinos Psounis, and Cauligi S. Raghavendra. Efficient Routing in Intermittently Connected Mobile Networks: The Single-Copy Case. *IEEE/ACM Transactions on Networking*, 16(1):63–76, February 2008.

[231] Moritz Steiner, Taoufik En-Najjary, and Ernst W. Biersack. A Global View of KAD. In *Proceedings of Internet Measurement Conference (IMC)*, pages 117–122, San Diego, CA, USA, October 2007.

[232] Moritz Steiner, Taoufik En-Najjary, and Ernst W. Biersack. Long Term Study of Peer Behavior in the KAD DHT. *IEEE/ACM Transactions on Networking*, 17(5):1371–1384, October 2009.

[233] Ralf Steinmetz and Klaus Wehrle, editors. *Peer-to-Peer Systems and Applications*, volume 3485 of *Lecture Notes on Computer Science*. Springer Publishing, 1st edition, September 2005.

[234] W. Richard Stevens, Bill Fenner, and Andrew M. Rudoff. *UNIX Network Programming: The Sockets Networking API*, volume 1. Addison-Wesley Professional, 3rd edition, November 2003.

[235] Randall R. Stewart, Qiaobing Xie, Ken Morneault, Chip Sharp, Hanns Juergen Schwarzbauer, Tom Taylor, Ian Rytina, Malleswar Kalla, Lixia Zhang, and Vern Paxson. Stream Control Transmission Protocol. RFC 2960 (Proposed Standard), October 2000. Obsoleted by RFC 4960, updated by RFC 3309.

[236] Martin Stiemerling. System Design of SATO and ASI. Deliverable D12-F.1, Ambient Networks Project, 2006.

[237] Ion Stoica, Daniel Adkins, Shelley Zhuang, Scott Shenker, and Sonesh Surana. Internet Indirection Infrastructure. *IEEE/ACM Transactions on Networking*, 12(2):205–218, April 2004.

[238] Ion Stoica, Robert Morris, David Karger, M. Frans Kaashoek, and Hari Balakrishnan. Chord: A Scalable Peer-to-peer Lookup Service for Internet Applications. In *Proceedings of ACM Conference on Applications, Technologies, Architectures, and Protocols for Computer Communications (SIGCOMM)*, pages 149–160, San Diego, CA, USA, August 2001.

[239] Ion Stoica, Robert Morris, David Karger, M. Frans Kaashoek, and Hari Balakrishnan. Chord: A Scalable Peer-to-peer Lookup Service for Internet Applications. *ACM SIGCOMM Computer Communication Review*, 31(4):149–160, August 2001.

[240] Kun Tan, Qian Zhang, and Wenwu Zhu. Shortest Path Routing in Partially Connected Ad Hoc Networks. In *Proceedings of IEEE Global Telecommunications Conference (GLOBECOM)*, volume 2, pages 1038–1042, San Francisco, CA, USA, December 2003.

[241] Fabrice Tchakountio and Ram Ramanathan. Tracking Highly Mobile Endpoints. In *Proceedings of IEEE International Symposium on a World of Wireless Mobile and Multimedia Networks (WoWMoM)*, pages 83–94, Rome, Italy, July 2001.

[242] Jing Tian, Joerg Haehner, Christian Becker, Illya Stepanov, and Kurt Rothermel. Graph-Based Mobility Model for Mobile Ad Hoc Network Simulation. In *Proceedings of Annual Simulation Symposium (SS)*, pages 337–345, San Diego, CA, USA, April 2002.

[243] Joe Touch. The X-Bone. In *Proceedings of Workshop on Research Directions for the Next-Generation Internet*, Vienna, VA, May 1997.

[244] Amin Vahdat and David Becker. Epidemic Routing for Partially-Connected Ad Hoc Networks. Technical Report CS-200006, Department of Computer Science, Duke University, Durham, NC, USA, April 2000.

[245] András Varga and Rudolf Hornig. An Overview of the OMNeT++ Simulation Environment. In *Proceedings of International Conference on Simulation Tools and Techniques for Communications, Networks and Systems (SIMUTools)*, pages 60:1–60:10, Marseille, France, March 2008.

[246] Dimitry Volchenkov and Philippe Blanchard. Random Walks along the Streets and Canals in Compact Cities: Spectral Analysis, Dynamical Modularity, Information, and Statistical Mechanics. *Physical Review E*, 75(2):026104-1–026104-14, February 2007.

[247] Oliver P. Waldhorst, Christian Blankenhorn, Dirk Haage, Ralph Holz, Gerald Koch, Boris Koldehofe, Fleming Lampi, Christoph P. Mayer, and Sebastian Mies. Spontaneous Virtual Networks: On the Road towards the Internet's Next Generation. *it – Information Technology Special Issue on Next Generation Internet*, 50(6):367–375, December 2008.

[248] Oliver P. Waldhorst and Jochen Dinger. Decentralized Bootstrapping of P2P Systems: A Practical View. In *Proceedings of IFIP TC6 International Conference on Networking (NETWORKING)*, pages 703–715, Aachen, Germany, May 2009.

[249] Wall Street Journal. iPad Struggles at Some Colleges. `http://online.wsj.com/article/SB10001424052748703594404575192330930646778.html`, May 2010.

[250] Peng Wang, James Tyra, Eric Chan-Tin, Tyson Malchow, Denis Foo Kune, Nicholas Hopper, and Yongdae Kim. Attacking the Kad Network. In *Proceedings of International Conference on Security and Privacy in Communication Networks (SecureComm)*, page 23, Istanbul, Turkey, September 2008. digital.

[251] Eric W. Weisstein. Haversine. From MathWorld – A Wolfram Web Resource. http://mathworld.wolfram.com/Haversine.html, October 2010.

[252] John Whitbeck and Vania Conan. HYMAD: Hybrid DTN-MANET Routing for Dense and Highly Dynamic Wireless Networks. In *Proceedings of IEEE Workshop on Autonomic and Opportunistic Communications (AOC)*, pages 1–7, Kos, Greece, June 2009. digital.

[253] John Whitbeck, Yoann Lopez, Jeremie Leguay, Vania Conan, and Marcelo Dias de Amorim. Relieving the Wireless Infrastructure: When Opportunistic Networks Meet Guaranteed Delays. In *Proceedings of IEEE International Symposium on a World of Wireless Mobile and Multimedia Networks (WoWMoM)*, Lucca, Italy, June 2011.

[254] Jörg Widmer and Jean-Yves Le Boudec. Network Coding for Efficient Communication in Extreme Networks. In *Proceedings of ACM SIGCOMM Workshop on Delay Tolerant Networking (WDTN)*, pages 284–291, Philadelphia, PA, USA, August 2005.

[255] Dave Winer. XML-RPC Specification. http://www.xmlrpc.com/spec, June 1999.

[256] Wolfgang Woess. *Random Walks on Infinite Graphs and Groups.* Cambridge University Press, 1st edition, February 2000.

[257] Eiko Yoneki. The Importance of Data Collection for Modelling Contact Networks. In *Proceedings of International Workshop on Social Computing with Mobile Phones and Sensors: Modeling, Sensing and Sharing (SCMPS)*, pages 940–943, Vancouver, Canada, August 2009.

[258] Quan Yuan, Ionut Cardei, and Jie Wu. Predict and Relay: An Efficient Routing in Disruption-Tolerant Networks. In *Proceedings of ACM Symposium on Mobile Ad Hoc Networking and Computing (MobiHoc)*, pages 95–104, New Orleans, LA, USA, May 2009.

[259] Zhensheng Zhang. Routing in Intermittently Connected Mobile Ad Hoc Networks and Delay Tolerant Networks: Overview and Challenges. *IEEE Communications Surveys & Tutorials*, 8(1):24–37, 1st quarter 2006.

[260] Wenrui Zhao, Mostafa Ammar, and Ellen Zegura. A Message Ferrying Approach for Data Delivery in Sparse Mobile Ad Hoc Networks. In *Proceedings of ACM Symposium on Mobile Ad hoc Networking and Computing (MobiHoc)*, pages 187–198, Roppongi Hills, Tokyo, Japan, May 2004.

[261] Wenrui Zhao, Yang Chen, Mostafa Ammar, Mark Corner, Brian Levine, and Ellen Zegura. Capacity Enhancement using Throwboxes in DTNs. In *Proceedings of IEEE International Conference on Mobile Adhoc and Sensor Systems (MASS)*, pages 31–40, Vancouver, Canada, October 2006.

[262] Hai Zhuge, Xue Chen, Xiaoping Sun, and Erlin Yao. HRing: A Structured P2P Overlay Based on Harmonic Series. *IEEE Transactions on Parallel and Distributed Systems*, 19(2):145–158, February 2008.

[263] Xuejun Zhuo, Wei Gao, Guohong Cao, and Yiqi Dai. Win-Coupon: An Incentive Framework for 3G Traffic Offloading. In *Proceedings of IEEE International Conference on Network Protocols (ICNP)*, Vancouver, BC, Canada, October 2011.